CONTENTS

The Dynamic Cell (Vol. 1)

prepared for the Course Team by
Mark Hirst, David Male and Robert Saunders

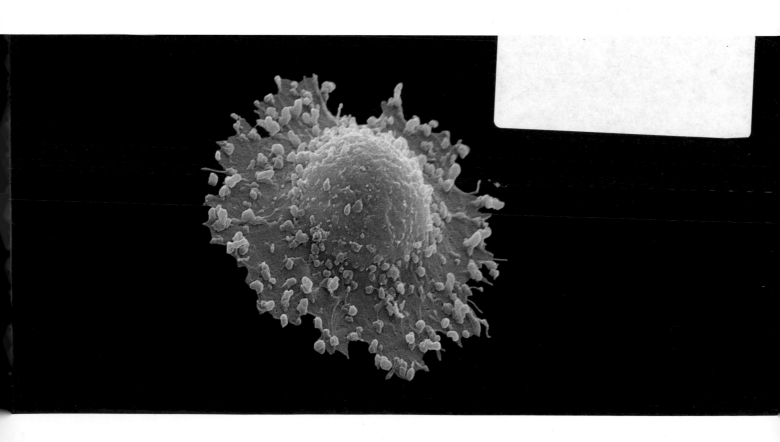

The S377 Course Team

Course Team Chair
David Male

Course Managers
Viki Burnage
Colin Walker

Course Team Assistants
Rebecca Efthimiou
Lara Knight

Course Team authors
Mark Hirst
Jane Loughlin
David Male
Radmila Mileusnic
Sotiris Missailidis
Ignacio Romero
Jill Saffrey
Robert Saunders

Consultant author
Sally Cowley

Editors
Gerry Bearman
Ian Nuttall
Dick Sharp
Margaret Swithenby

Academic Reader
Christine Gorman

External Course Assessor
Iain Campbell

OU Graphic Design
Roger Courthold
Sara Hack
Jenny Nockles

Video production
Wilf Eynon
Michael Francis

CD-ROM production
Greg Black
Eleanor Crabb
Hilary MacQueen

Rights Executive
Chris Brady

Picture Research
Lydia Eaton

Indexer
Jane Henley

Course website
Patrina Law
Louise Olney

The Open University, Walton Hall, Milton Keynes, MK7 6AA, United Kingdom

First published 2004. Third edition 2008.

Edited, designed and typeset by The Open University.

Printed and bound in the United Kingdom by the University Press, Cambridge.

ISBN 978 0 7492 26749

This publication forms part of an Open University course S377 *Molecular and cell biology*. Details of this and other Open University courses can be obtained from the Course Information and Advice Centre, PO Box 724, The Open University, Milton Keynes MK7 6ZS, United Kingdom: tel. +44 (0)1908 653231, e-mail general-enquiries@open.ac.uk

Alternatively, you may visit the Open University website at http://www.open.ac.uk where you can learn more about the wide range of courses and packs offered at all levels by The Open University.

To purchase a selection of Open University course materials visit the webshop at www.ouw.co.uk, or contact Open University Worldwide, Michael Young Building, Walton Hall, Milton Keynes MK7 6AA, United Kingdom for a brochure. tel. +44 (0)1908 858785; fax +44 (0)1908 858787; email ouwenq@open.ac.uk

S377 Book 2 i3.1

7 INTRODUCING THE DYNAMIC CELL

In Book 1, we looked at the building blocks of life, the main groups of biological molecules and macromolecules, and suggested that life most likely arose from collections of prebiotic organic molecules. We also noted that living processes accord with the laws of physics and chemistry even though living systems are very much more complex than simple chemical systems. In Books 2 and 3, you will be looking at the increasingly complex subcellular structures and functions of cells, which have arisen over time, and which have allowed the development of multicellular organisms.

7.1 Cell structures and functions

The evolutionary divergence between eukaryotes and prokaryotes and the development of multicellularity are both associated with many interrelated changes at the cellular level. Such changes include cell diversification and specialization, the development of complex control and coordination mechanisms, an increase in the size of genomes and increased efficiencies of certain biochemical reactions and cellular processes. A multicellular organism is clearly a highly dynamic and responsive system. In this book and the one that follows, we consider the life and death of cells and explore a number of important aspects of their function and activities which are introduced briefly in this chapter.

7.1.1 Cell diversity

Examining the fundamental processes of life, it is remarkable to see how similar, at the molecular level, these processes are in different organisms. As discussed in Chapter 1, this uniformity leads us to conclude that all living organisms have most likely evolved from a common ancestor. Since all cells must conform to the laws of thermodynamics, we can see how 'cells' (meaning open thermodynamic systems; see Figure 4.1) can become increasingly complex by their metabolism, which increases disorder elsewhere in the Universe. We might think, therefore, that the uniformity of cells is due, in the most part, to fundamental constraints that follow from the laws of physics and chemistry, and this is partly true. Nevertheless, what is striking about living systems is their extraordinary diversity. As biologists, we seek to understand how this great diversity arises in cells that all obey these same basic principles.

◯ At the molecular level, what distinguishes cell types and determines their different characteristics?

◼ It is principally the proteins present, their locations and activities, that determine the form and function of a cell. Of particular importance are the structural roles of proteins, both intracellular and extracellular, which determine the morphology of a cell and of a whole multicellular organism.

Ultimately, how a cell's genome is expressed determines which proteins are made within that cell and hence its properties. However, many alterations in cellular activity are determined by changes in the activity and localization of proteins, and are independent of expression. We shall return to this point later, when we consider the different levels at which cellular activity is controlled.

○ How can enzymes contribute towards cellular diversity, when the reactions that they catalyse are constrained by the laws of thermodynamics, which apply equally to all cells. (Think back to Chapter 4.)

● Enzymes determine only the *rates* of reactions, not which reactions are possible and which impossible. This means that enzymes can be used to regulate how reactants are channelled through different pathways, and this may differ between cell types.

7.1.2 The control and coordination of cellular processes

The regulation of cellular processes lies at the very heart of cell biology. Not only do enzymes accelerate reactions and control the relative rates of reactions within the cell, but they may also respond to changing conditions, such as an increase or decrease in substrate concentration. Changes in protein activities, location and expression allow cells to respond to changes in their environment (Table 7.1).

○ Fill in the empty spaces in the last column yourself, using either specific examples or a generic category of protein modification given in Chapter 3.

Table 7.1   Adaptations that affect protein activity, location and expression within the cell.

Adaptation	How effected	Timescale	Examples
(1) Protein activity	conformational change	<1 second	
(2) Protein activity	structural change	<10 seconds	
(3) Protein localization	structural modification	<30 seconds	
(4) Protein localization	movement between compartments	<5 minutes	removal of receptors from the plasma membrane in clathrin-coated pits (Chapter 12)
		<30 minutes	mRNA localization and translation (Chapter 11)
(5) Protein expression	increased transcription and translation	>1 hour	transcription of genes induced by cytokines and growth factors (Chapter 13)
(6) Protein expression	increased degradation	<1 hour	ubiquitin tagging of proteins and proteolysis in proteasomes (Chapter 11)

■ (1) Allosteric regulation of enzyme activity occurs via conformational change and can be mediated by other proteins, or by upstream and downstream intermediates in biochemical pathways. (2) Phosphorylation of proteins (e.g. Src) can stabilize the enzyme in an active or inactive conformation. (3) Palmitoylation and prenylation of proteins causes them to localize to the plasma membrane.

We have already looked at how allosteric or structural modifications can affect enzyme activity. In this part of the course, we shall be looking at how cells control their activity by altering gene expression, a process that can be controlled at many levels between genome and protein (Figure 7.1). For example, as discussed in Chapter 5, chromatin structure, and modifications to it, play key roles in transcriptional control. This is explored further in Chapter 10, where we look at the control of gene expression in more detail. The activity of proteins can also be changed by directing them to different cellular compartments as they are synthesized, by redistributing them between compartments, or by degrading them – processes that are discussed in Chapters 11 and 12.

Coordination of cellular activity is also seen during cell division. Not only must cells divide at the appropriate time, but all aspects of the cell division process have to be orchestrated so that the cell components (chromosomes, mitochondria, etc.) are distributed appropriately to the daughter cells, processes that are described in Chapter 8. In eukaryotes, dissolution and reformation of the nuclear membrane and cell fission are also closely linked to these processes and coordinated with nuclear division.

The complexity and maintenance of the genome

In general, the size of the genome, as measured by the number of DNA base pairs, is larger in what we might consider to be more complex organisms.

◯ To the nearest order of magnitude, how big are the haploid genomes of *E. coli*, *C. elegans* and *H. sapiens*?

■ *E. coli*, 10^6 bp; *C. elegans*, 10^8 bp; *H. sapiens*, 10^9 bp. (The actual values are given in Table 5.1.)

Genome size measured in this way is, however, a fairly crude measure of potential complexity, because it does not accurately reflect the numbers of mRNAs that are expressed or the numbers of proteins they encode. For example, the number of genes encoding proteins in the human genome (~30 000) is only twice that in *C. elegans* (~15 000), even though the human genome is roughly 40 times larger than that of *C. elegans*. This distinction between a genome size and the number of expressed proteins also creates some interesting anomalies. For example, the puffer fish has a genome about one-tenth the size of the human genome, but with a similar number of expressed genes. This is because puffer fish genes are more closely packed, with considerably less non-protein-coding DNA. A further consideration in eukaryotes is that the RNA transcribed from a single gene may be spliced in a number of ways to produce mRNAs for effectively different proteins. We can see, therefore, that the size of a genome is only roughly correlated with the number of proteins that it encodes.

Organisms must maintain the integrity of their genome, both in germ cells and in somatic stem cells, at least until they have reproduced. The problem of maintaining the genome is made more acute by the longer reproductive periods seen in many complex multicellular organisms. The pathways by which DNA damage arises were discussed in Chapter 5, and in this book we discuss how the genome repairs this damage and ensures that each of the new daughter cells receives a full complement of intact DNA. It is important that individual cells can produce correct copies of each protein, and this too depends on DNA integrity. DNA damage may lead to cell death, as explained in Chapters 14 and 18, or in some cases may result in tumour development (Chapter 19).

Intracellular processes

Two further important features of eukaryotic cells that distinguish them from prokaryotes are their larger size and the presence of distinctive subcellular compartments. Although enzymes increase reaction rates, metabolic steps are still potentially limited by the diffusion rates of substrates. This limitation has been partially overcome by the grouping of sets of enzymes into compartments and/ or in complexes, which allows successive intermediates to be passed directly from one enzyme to the next. In eukaryotic cells, compartmentalization allows different regions of the cell to become specialized for different functions, but it does produce a new problem: the increase in size of eukaryotic cells and their compartmentalization lead to a requirement for intracellular transport systems which are dependent on the cytoskeleton and motor proteins. These compartments and the transport systems that operate between them are described in Chapter 12.

A major theme of this course is the dynamic processes occurring within cells. We have known for a long time that cells and their contents are highly active. A simple observation of protoctists from pondwater under a microscope shows that many of them are highly mobile, as they move towards food and migrate in response to environmental stimuli such as light or dissolved chemicals. Only more recently have techniques been developed that allow us to look at the dynamic processes occurring *inside* cells. The use of fluorescent markers and improvements in microscopy and imaging have allowed the production of pictures of live cells that are instructive and often also quite beautiful.

Movie gallery

Go to the Study Skills file: *Introduction to the* Movie gallery. To introduce the concept of the 'dynamic cell', we have assembled a collection of video clips ('movies') that show different aspects of cellular function and activity and illustrate the high level of cell activity and movement seen both at the cellular and subcellular levels. Each of the movies shows a particular aspect of cell division, movement, signalling or intracellular traffic that will be discussed or examined in a later chapter. Work through the introduction to familiarize yourself with the gallery, viewing the movies as directed. You will be directed to relevant movies in later chapters.

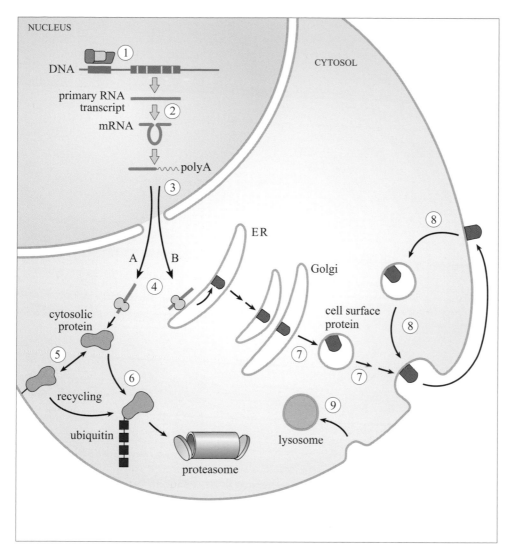

Figure 7.1   Levels at which protein expression may be controlled. (1) Transcription of a gene is controlled by transcription factors that bind to promoters and enhancers and through modulations of local chromatin structure. (2) The primary RNA transcript may be spliced in a number of different ways, to produce mRNAs with different sets of exons. (3) Export of the mRNA from the nucleus is controlled by modifications such as polyadenylation. (4) In the cytosol, the mRNA is translated on ribosomes (route A), which may be directed to the endoplasmic reticulum membrane (route B) if the protein is destined for the cell surface or secretion. (5) The localization of cytosolic proteins, and consequently their activity, may be modified by prenylation or fatty acylation, which directs the protein to another region of the cell (e.g. the inner leaflet of the plasma membrane as shown here). (6) The degradation of misfolded and recycled proteins is controlled by the addition of ubiquitin, which directs the molecule to proteasomes for proteolysis. (7) Cell surface expression of proteins is determined by how they are directed through the different intracellular compartments. (8) A protein expressed at the cell surface may be re-internalized and re-used. (9) Cell surface proteins are degraded by being internalized and directed to lysosomes. Notice how processes 1–4 are related to protein production; 5, 7 and 8 are related to protein localization; and 6 and 9 are related to degradation. In addition to the processes shown here, protein activity is continuously modulated by structural and conformational changes.

8 THE CELL CYCLE

8.1 Introduction

The division of a cell to yield two identical daughter cells is of fundamental importance to every organism. Each cell must receive the appropriate amount of DNA and numbers of the various organelles if it is to survive and flourish, whether it be as part of a multicellular organism or as a free-living cell. The consequences of failure to divide without errors can be severe: cell death, or in the case of multicellular organisms, genetic changes that could lead to the formation of tumours. In this chapter, we will be concerned with the process of mitotic cell division, and how each stage of this highly complex but essential cellular activity is regulated. We will also cover meiosis, the reductional cell division that gives rise to gametes. Prokaryotes face the same regulatory challenges as eukaryotes, but as we shall see, the means by which division is achieved in prokaryotes, a process called binary fission, is rather different from eukaryotic cell division.

A recurring theme in this course is that many, if not all, biological processes are evolutionarily conserved, both in terms of their mechanism and in the structural similarity of components of the relevant pathways. This is particularly true of mitosis, a cellular activity that is universal among eukaryotes. Many of the findings we will discuss in this chapter are derived from the study of simple unicellular eukaryotes, such as yeasts, but as we shall see, the conservation of these processes through evolution means that discoveries made in yeast systems have effectively illuminated the homologous processes in higher eukaryotes such as humans. Where appropriate, differences (mostly in terms of additional complexity) between higher eukaryotes and the simple model systems will be highlighted. A similar approach is valid for the study of meiosis.

8.1.1 Overview of structural events in mitosis

Mitosis is a complex process, and a detailed picture of the sequence of events that make up this this process has only emerged from many years of ultrastructural, genetic and biochemical analyses. The mitotic cycle, the sequence of events through which a dividing cell proceeds, is summarized in Figure 8.1. This cycle contains four distinct phases: G1, or first gap phase; S, in which DNA synthesis takes place; G2, or second gap phase; and M, mitosis itself, in which the chromosomes are partitioned between the two daughter cells. G1, S and G2 are indistinguishable by microscopic analysis and are referred to collectively as **interphase**; however, these phases are biologically distinct. The time spent in each phase varies widely in different cells. Typically, embryonic cell cycles are very rapid, with little time spent in G1 or G2.

G1 phase

During G1, the first gap phase, the cell prepares for the synthetic activities of S phase – principally the synthesis of DNA. As part of this preparation, the cell performs a series of checks to verify that growth conditions are appropriate and that DNA damage has not occurred. These are known as **checkpoints**, and if they

Figure 8.1
The typical eukaryotic cell cycle.
Eukaryotic cells cycle through four
distinct phases: two gap phases, G1
and G2; the S phase, in which DNA
is replicated; and mitosis itself, or M
phase. A third gap phase, G0, may
be entered and this may reflect an
extended period of quiescence, or
lead to terminal differentiation. The
relative duration of each phase can vary
greatly between different cell types.
G1, S and G2 are collectively known as
interphase.

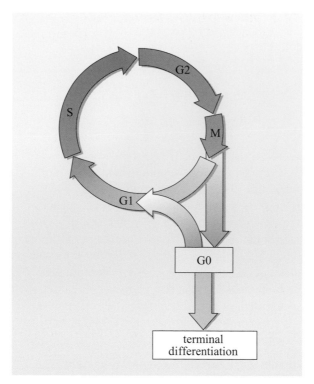

are not satisfied, the cell will be inhibited from further progression through the cell
cycle. There are further checkpoints in subsequent phases of the cell cycle, which
are discussed in detail later in this chapter. In some experimental systems, namely
those in which embryonic cell cycles are studied, the G1 phase may be brief, or even
absent (as in the case of *Drosophila* embryos).

Cells can exit from the mitotic cycle during G1, to enter a quiescent state known
as G0 (pronounced 'G zero'). Cells in G0 can either re-enter the mitotic cycle or
can terminally differentiate; that is, they can attain a differentiated state from which
they are unable to return to the cycle. During G1, the chromosomes are present in
a decondensed form and are diffuse within an intact nuclear envelope, although
occupying discrete areas of the nucleus (Section 5.8.2, Figure 5.42a).

○ Can you recall what level of DNA compaction is present in human interphase
   chromatin?

■ Interphase chromatin exists in variable degrees of compaction: as 10 nm fibres
   (nucleosomes), as 30 nm fibres (variably compacted nucleosomes), and as tightly
   packed chromonema fibres (Section 5.8, particularly Figure 5.43).

S phase

It is in S phase that the cell's DNA is replicated in preparation for partition
between the two daughter cells during mitosis. A typical mammalian cell contains
approximately 6 billion base pairs of DNA, so the accurate copying of all this
genetic material is a major undertaking for the cell. Of course, errors do occur –
they are the source of genetic variation – but it is imperative that the cell does not
proceed into mitosis with an incompletely replicated genome. Similarly, breaks in

the DNA must not persist into mitosis as this could lead to loss of genetic information. A detailed description of the biochemistry of DNA replication and repair will be presented in Chapter 9.

G2 phase

This second gap phase can be lengthy, as it is the period during which the cell carries out several checks to ensure that DNA synthesis has been completed, that the chromosomes are intact, and that the growth conditions are appropriate for proceeding with mitosis.

M phase

M phase is when mitosis itself occurs. As the cell enters mitosis, a great many changes take place. Several of these changes are quite dramatic, notably chromatin condensation and the breakdown of the nuclear envelope.

⬭ What changes to the structure of interphase chromatin are responsible for its condensation to form the mitotic chromosomes?

⬛ While the structural changes associated with chromatin condensation are not clearly understood, they are thought to involve coiling together of scaffolds into higher-order structures (Figure 5.43). Phosphorylation of histone H1 proteins appears to facilitate further compaction.

As we look more deeply into the physical changes and events in the cell cycle, we can detail five distinct stages, based upon the position or status of the chromosomes, as shown schematically in Figure 8.2.

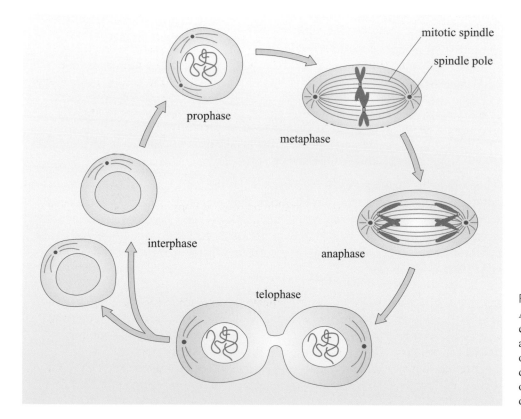

Figure 8.2
A schematic illustration of the eukaryotic cell cycle, which involves a series of complex reorganizations of cellular structures. The phases are described in the text. For simplicity, only a single pair of chromosomes is depicted.

During **prophase**, the newly replicated chromosomes begin to condense within the intact nuclear envelope. They look like thin threads, and continue to condense until they are clearly visible as paired chromatids. At this stage, the nuclear envelope is still intact. A dynamic structure composed of microtubules, the **mitotic spindle**, forms and each chromosome attaches to it through a structure called a **kinetochore**, a plate/disc-shaped structure attached to the centromere. The spindle is formed by the initiation of microtubules at specific organelles, the centrosomes, located at the spindle poles (Section 8.2.3).

By **metaphase**, the nuclear envelope has broken down, and the condensed chromosomes are aligned at the equator of the mitotic spindle. The process by which chromosomes associate with the spindle microtubules and are moved to the spindle equator is known as **congression**. During **anaphase**, the chromatids separate abruptly and migrate towards the poles of the spindle, reaching the poles during **telophase**. During this stage, the chromosomes begin to decondense, and the nuclear envelope begins to re-form. Finally, during **cytokinesis**, the cell membrane contracts in a cleavage furrow, and the two daughter cells separate. It is important to remember that these phases of mitosis constitute a dynamic series of events, and cells normally proceed through them in a smooth and seamless progression.

8.1.2 Biological systems for studying mitosis

It is very difficult to study the cell cycle in great detail biochemically within the cells of a multicellular organism. Historically, studies of mitosis have therefore focused on more easily manipulable systems. These include two very different yeast species, the insect *Drosophila melanogaster*, the early zygotic divisions of amphibian embryos (notably those of the African clawed toad, *Xenopus laevis*) and cultured mammalian cells. Each of these systems has one or more experimental advantages, but none of them is perfect for all studies.

> A brief description of these and other major model organisms can be found in the Glossary.

Microscopic investigations are frequently used, particularly in combination with immunofluorescence (Box 8.1), to study the localization of proteins in dividing cells or to examine the dynamics of the division process.

One problem in studying a cyclic process such as the cell cycle is that in an *in vitro* culture, cells are present at all stages; that is, they are asynchronous. Techniques for manipulating cells both physically and biochemically have been developed in order to synchronize the culture so that all the cells are at the same stage of the cell cycle. Synchronization of cultures permits the isolation of large numbers of cells at the same stage of the cycle.

Box 8.1 Immunofluorescence

In *Experimental investigation 1*, you saw how antibodies can be used to identify proteins separated by SDS–PAGE (the technique of Western blotting). Antibodies may also be used to determine the distribution of proteins *within* tissues or cells.

The primary antibody (i.e. the antibody that recognizes the protein of interest) is added to cell or tissue sections of fixed and permeabilized material and incubated to allow the antibody molecules to bind to proteins carrying suitable epitopes. Excess, unbound, primary antibody is removed before the sample is incubated with the secondary antibody. This second antibody will recognize and bind only the primary antibody and not to any cellular component. Typically, the secondary antibody is tagged with a molecule that enables it to be visualized. For immunofluorescence, the tag is a fluorescent chemical, such as fluorescein or Texas red, which fluoresce green or red respectively when excited by

a beam of ultraviolet light. The relationship between the antigen and the primary and secondary antibodies is shown in Figure 8.3.

○ Why is excess, unbound, primary antibody washed from the preparation before application of the secondary antibody?

■ If the preparation has large amounts of unbound primary antibody remaining when the secondary antibody is added, the secondary antibody will bind to it, resulting in a high level of non-specific or 'background' staining.

As an example, antibodies to a microtubule protein called β-tubulin, a major component of the mitotic spindle, will bind specifically to β-tubulin molecules in the cell. To make the bound anti-β-tubulin antibody visible microscopically, we use a second antibody, this time directed against the anti-β-tubulin antibody.

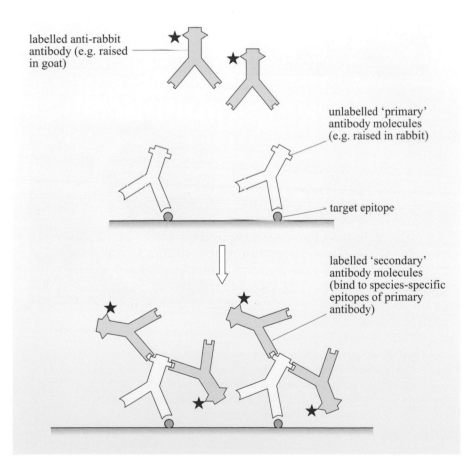

labelled anti-rabbit antibody (e.g. raised in goat)

unlabelled 'primary' antibody molecules (e.g. raised in rabbit)

target epitope

labelled 'secondary' antibody molecules (bind to species-specific epitopes of primary antibody)

Figure 8.3
A schematic outline of the stages of immunofluorescence detection. An epitope of a human cellular protein (represented by the blue circle) is recognized by an antibody raised in rabbit. This primary antibody is recognized by the secondary antibody raised against rabbit immunoglobulin in goat. The secondary antibody is tagged with Texas red, a chemical that emits red light when excited by UV light (depicted as a red star).

This secondary antibody is directed towards the primary antibody protein itself. For example, an anti-β-tubulin antibody raised in a rabbit might have as a suitable secondary antibody, an anti-rabbit antibody raised in a goat. After the secondary antibody has been purified, the fluorescent tag is attached covalently to it.

Because different fluorescent tags may have emissions of different colours, several cellular proteins may be studied in a single preparation simultaneously. In this case, each primary antibody is raised in a different species, such as mouse, rat, or rabbit, and suitable anti-mouse, anti-rat, or anti-rabbit secondary antibodies raised in a different species, such as sheep or goat. Each secondary antibody would have a different fluorescent molecule covalently attached, each having a characteristic emission wavelength.

An example of this technique is shown in Figure 8.4, where the nuclei in *Drosophila* embryos are visualized using antibodies directed towards β-tubulin (a) and a protein present in cellular bodies called centrosomes located at the spindle poles (b). In addition, fluorescent dyes that bind to DNA are used to identify DNA and therefore chromosomes (c).

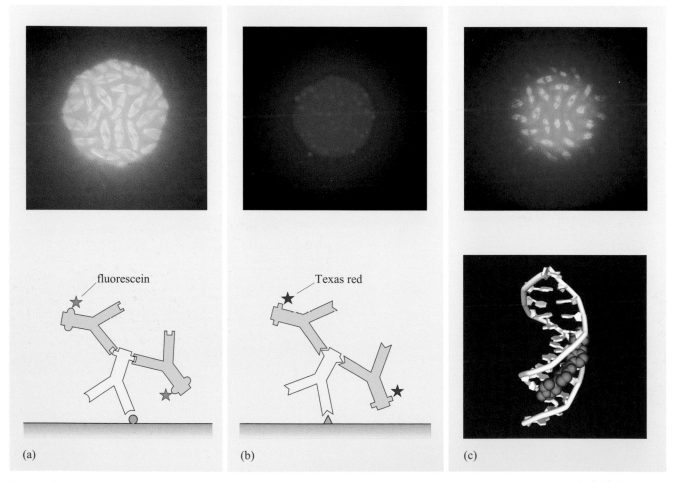

Figure 8.4   Immunofluorescence analysis of a *Drosophila* embryo. (a) Fluorescein-labelled antibodies (green) to anti-β-tubulin antibodies reveal the mitotic spindles. (b) Texas red-labelled antibodies to anti-centrosomal protein antibodies show the location of centrosomes at the spindle poles. (c) Hoechst 33258 staining (blue) reveals the location of chromosomal DNA. Both the labelled antibodies and the Hoechst 33258 stain fluoresce when illuminated by UV light. Also shown are schematic diagrams of the fluorescently labelled antibodies and a molecular model of Hoechst 33258-stained DNA.

The yeasts

Two species of yeast have dominated cell cycle research for several decades: the budding yeast, *Saccharomyces cerevisiae*, and the fission yeast, *Schizosaccharomyces pombe*. Despite both organisms being referred to as 'yeasts', they differ from each other in a variety of ways. In the context of cell cycle research, however, the principal difference lies in the details of cell division. *S. pombe* divides by fission, as you might expect from its common name. In other words, a mother cell splits to give rise to two equal-sized daughter cells. In contrast, *Saccharomyces cerevisiae*, again as implied by its common name, divides by budding. In this case, the daughter cell is distinct in terms of size from the mother cell, i.e. it is much smaller. Both yeasts can be readily synchronized and grow rapidly.

One of the limitations of working with these yeasts is the small size of the cells, which makes detailed microscopic analyses difficult, although not impossible, as the immunofluorescence microscopy images in Figure 8.5 illustrate. In this case, both the mitotic spindles and the centrosomes can be seen clearly, despite the small size of these cells.

The importance of these two yeast species lies in the power of the genetics that has been developed in them. Many of the genes that encode proteins vital for regulating progression through the cell cycle were originally identified by genetic analyses in the yeasts, and it is an indication of the evolutionary conservation of biological processes that homologues of these genes have been found in all organisms studied. It is interesting to note that because of the asymmetry in division of *S. cerevisiae*, budding yeast, in contrast to other unicellular organisms, can be said to age: a mother cell can bud many times, but it will eventually die. The age of these cells, in terms of numbers of cell divisions the cell has undergone, can be estimated by counting the numbers of 'scars' left by the detached daughter cells.

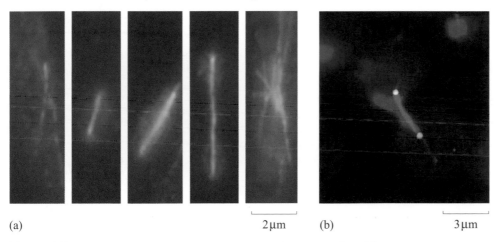

(a)   2 µm   (b)   3 µm

Figure 8.5   The cell cycle observed in two yeast species. (a) A series of fluorescence micrographs of the fission yeast (*Schizosaccharomyces pombe*) in which centrosomes are stained in red, chromosomes in blue, and the mitotic spindles in green. Several successive stages of mitosis are shown. (Courtesy H. Ohkura, University of Edinburgh) (b) The mitotic spindle of the budding yeast (*Saccharomyces cerevisiae*). The spindle is stained red, and the chromosomes in blue. The location of the spindle pole bodies (see Section 8.2.3) is revealed by the staining (green) of a protein that co-localizes to these structures. (Courtesy Dr Rong Li, Harvard University)

The significance of these experiments was underlined by the award of the 2001 Nobel Prize for Medicine to Paul Nurse and Lee Hartwell, for their work on the cell cycle in fission yeast and budding yeast respectively. (The third recipient, Tim Hunt, discovered one of the components of cell cycle regulation, cyclins, in sea-urchin eggs.)

Drosophila *and* Xenopus *embryos*

Of all the stages in the life cycles of multicellular organisms, the early embryonic divisions are of particular utility in studying the cell cycle. Amphibian eggs are relatively large. For example, the eggs of the African clawed toad (*Xenopus laevis*) and those of the common frog, as found in ponds in the UK, are several millimetres in diameter. The early cell cycles of the developing embryo are rapid and, at least in the initial stages, fairly synchronous. They are fuelled exclusively by maternally provided components and are therefore largely independent of gene transcription.

○ What features do the two yeasts and *Xenopus* eggs have in common that make them useful in laboratory experiments investigating the cell cycle?

● You might have thought of: (1) easy to obtain significant quantities, (2) rapid cell divisions, and (3) easy to obtain synchronized cells.

Many clues to the biochemistry of cell cycle regulation have been discovered by the use of biochemical extracts made from *Xenopus* oocytes, making this system attractive for analysis. The major disadvantage of amphibian systems, however, is that genetic analysis is lacking.

In contrast to vertebrate embryonic systems, the fruit-fly *Drosophila* is highly suited to genetic analysis. There are well defined procedures for generating and analysing mutations, and for creating transgenic animals. The *Drosophila* embryo is also suited to microscopic studies of the cell cycle. Early *Drosophila* embryos are **syncytial**; they consist of a single large cell that contains many nuclei. These nuclei divide very rapidly and synchronously in a layer just under the cell surface, making this system ideal for analysing some aspects of cell cycle progression. The nuclei within the syncytium divide synchronously every 10 minutes. These are abbreviated cell cycles, in which G1 and G2 are virtually absent, and DNA replication is extremely fast. Some mitotic stages in such syncytial nuclear divisions are shown in Figure 8.6.

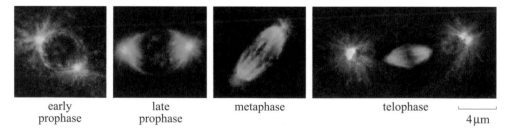

| early prophase | late prophase | metaphase | telophase | 4 μm |

Figure 8.6   Mitosis in *Drosophila*. A sequence of mitotic stages seen in syncytial nuclear divisions in a *Drosophila* embryo. Chromosomes are visualized in red, microtubules in green and centrosomes in blue.

Mammalian cells

Laboratory cultured mammalian cells more closely reflect the biology of humans and therefore yield information more directly relevant to medicine, especially to the study of cancer. Mammalian cells are easily examined using microscopy (Figure 8.7), but it is more difficult to apply the genetic manipulations that are so powerful in other systems to these cells. Studies on cultured cells have, however, revealed that the number and complexity of the controls used to regulate mammalian cell division are greater than in yeast cell division.

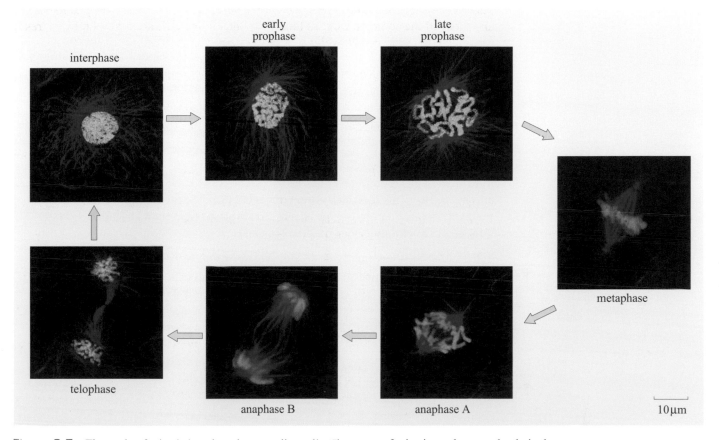

Figure 8.7   The study of mitosis in cultured mammalian cells. The stages of mitosis can be seen clearly in these immunofluorescence micrographs. Microtubules are shown in red, and chromosomes in blue. The location of the spindle poles may be inferred from the spindle structure in metaphase and anaphase. Anaphase A and anaphase B are characteristically separate parts of anaphase and will be discussed later in this chapter. (Courtesy A. Merdes, University of Edinburgh)

Summary of Section 8.1

1   The cell cycle comprises four distinct phases; G1, S, G2 and M. Cells can exit the cycle and enter a further stage, G0.

2   Large-scale cellular changes during the cell cycle can be visualized microscopically.

3   Mitosis is a dynamic process that is highly conserved between evolutionarily distant species.

4   Several different model experimental systems permit the biochemical study of microscopically invisible events of the cell cycle.

8.2 Mitosis

Before we discuss the means by which eukaryotic cells regulate progression through the mitotic cell cycle, we will review in greater detail the individual cellular components of the mitotic apparatus, and the dynamic nature of the changes required to facilitate cell division. The various structural elements of the cell undergo dramatic and complex alterations during cell division, and an understanding of these changes is essential for understanding cell cycle regulation at the molecular level.

8.2.1 Chromosome condensation

The appearance of chromosomes as discrete entities is perhaps one of the most microscopically visible events in mitosis. A considerable degree of compaction results in a change in chromosome morphology from diffuse interphase chromatin to dense mitotic chromosomes. Compaction is mediated by proteins known as **condensins**, which assemble on the newly replicated DNA and which facilitate its progressive condensation. The activation of condensins at the appropriate point in the cell cycle is brought about by their phosphorylation.

There are several issues to be considered in relation to the condensation of chromatin to form metaphase chromosomes. Firstly, there is the issue of compaction itself: what are the mechanisms by which chromatin condenses? Secondly, how does the newly replicated pair of chromosomes (**sister chromatids**) stay bound together? Finally, why don't the chromosomes become tangled?

Sister chromatids are tightly bound together by protein complexes known as **cohesins**, which are distributed along their length. This binding is important, as the sister chromatids must remain paired until anaphase to ensure their accurate segregation to daughter cells. If chromosomes aligned at the equator were unpaired, they could randomly segregate to the poles, leading to **aneuploid** daughter cells, i.e. cells that have either fewer or more than the normal number of chromosomes.

The proteins that form the cohesin complex are evolutionarily highly conserved. At the core of the complex is a dimer of Smc1 and Smc3 proteins. The Smc1/Smc3 dimers form long, rod-like structures connecting two chromatin-binding domains to a central 'hinge' region. (Figure 8.8a). Two additional proteins, Scc1 and Scc3, bind to this hinge region. The relationship between the cohesin complexes and chromosome cohesion is shown schematically in Figure 8.8b. The cohesin complexes on each sister chromatid associate via their hinge regions through interactions between the Scc proteins, ensuring that the sister chromatids are held together.

The models shown in Figure 8.8 are based upon the mitotic cohesion complex, but it is known that a similar system functions in meiosis (Section 8.4), and that there are related proteins specific for meiotic division.

8.2.2 Nuclear envelope breakdown

The **nuclear envelope** (**NE**), which is continuous with membranes of the endoplasmic reticulum, is a highly complex structure consisting of a double membrane and a protein scaffold, or **nuclear lamina** (Figure 8.9a). This lamina consists of a network of structural proteins including the **nuclear lamins**, which

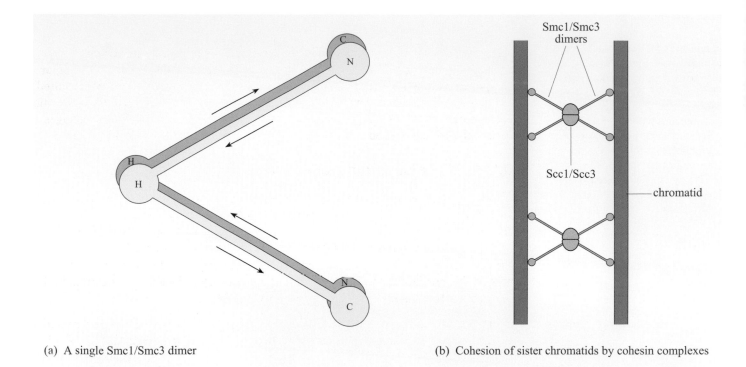

(a) A single Smc1/Smc3 dimer

(b) Cohesion of sister chromatids by cohesin complexes

are members of the intermediate filament family of proteins. The NE functions to regulate the entry and exit of macromolecules to or from the nucleoplasm, including transcription factors, RNA molecules such as mRNA and tRNA, chromatin proteins and components of the DNA replication, repair and transcription machinery. The transport of these molecules occurs via complex structures known as **nuclear pore complexes** (**NPCs**). The chromosomes themselves are also anchored to inner nuclear membrane at their telomeres and this attachment helps determine their distribution within the interphase nucleus (Chapter 5).

In most systems, the nuclear envelope breaks down in mitosis, allowing components such as the mitotic spindle access to the chromosomes to effect their segregation. This process is known as **nuclear envelope breakdown** (**NEBD**). The nuclear envelope then re-forms during telophase (Figure 8.9b). The process by which the nuclear envelope breaks down and reassembles in the cell cycle is poorly understood. Microscopically, it appears to initially break down into large cisternae that progressively become broken into smaller vesicles and membrane fragments. Many of the inner-membrane proteins become dissociated during this process.

The nuclear lamina is also disassembled during NEBD, as a result of phosphorylation of its component lamins by kinases that function specifically in mitosis. As NEBD progresses, the lamins disperse throughout the cell. The two types of nuclear lamin, A and B, behave differently during NEBD. These differences are most likely to be due to their post-translational modification: B type lamins are modified by the addition of a farnesyl group, whilst the A type lamins are not.

⬤ How does farnesyl modification affect protein localization?

⬤ Farnesylation influences a protein's interaction with lipid membranes, such as the nuclear envelope (Section 3.3.3, Figure 3.25).

Figure 8.8
Schematic representation of the cohesin complex structure. (a) The Smc1/Smc3 dimer lies at the core of the cohesin complex. It has two globular chromatin-binding domains, N-terminal (N) and C-terminal (C), linked by coiled-coil chains to a 'hinge' region (H). Arrows indicate the polarity of the coiled-coil domains of each protein. (b) Cohesion between chromatids is brought about by the association of chromatin-bound cohesins via the assembly of Scc1/Scc3 subunits to their hinge regions.

Figure 8.9
The nuclear envelope and changes in mitosis. (a) The nuclear envelope comprises two lipid bilayer membranes, with an underlying nuclear lamina, composed of proteins called lamins. The nuclear envelope is continuous with the endoplasmic reticulum, and is pierced by nuclear pore complexes (NPC) which permit entry and exit of macromolecules. (b) The cycle of nuclear envelope breakdown and re-formation in the cell cycle.

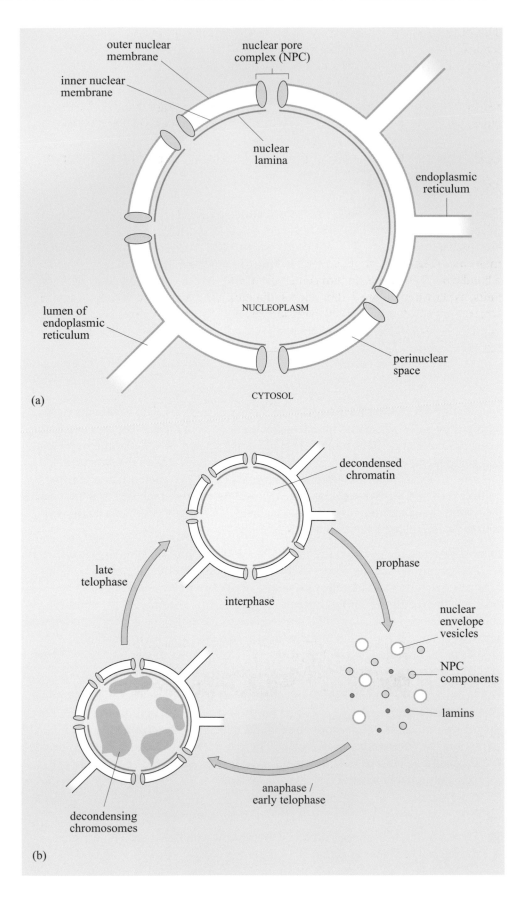

This difference in post-translational modification means that during NEBD, the A type lamins become soluble cytosolic proteins as they are released from the nuclear lamina, whereas the B type lamins remain associated with the membrane components.

As the nuclear envelope breaks down, so do the nuclear pore complexes, which become reduced into soluble subcomplexes. It is probable that the disassembly of the nuclear envelope and the nuclear pore complexes is also brought about by phosphorylation.

8.2.3 Microtubules and the microtubule organizing centre

Microtubule structure

The spindle to which chromosomes attach during mitosis (Figure 8.2) is composed of microtubules. Microtubules are a major cytoskeletal component of the cell. They are composed of tubulin subunits, each of which is a heterodimer of α- and β-tubulin molecules (Figure 8.10a). Each microtubule has a cylindrical structure, composed of a bundle of 13 filaments, in turn composed of a linear arrangement of tubulin dimer units, as shown in Figure 8.10b. The tubulin dimers assemble in a specific orientation, which means that each filament, and therefore also the entire microtubule, has a defined polarity. One end of a microtubule has α-tubulin exposed and is called the minus end, the other has α-tubulin exposed and is called the plus end.

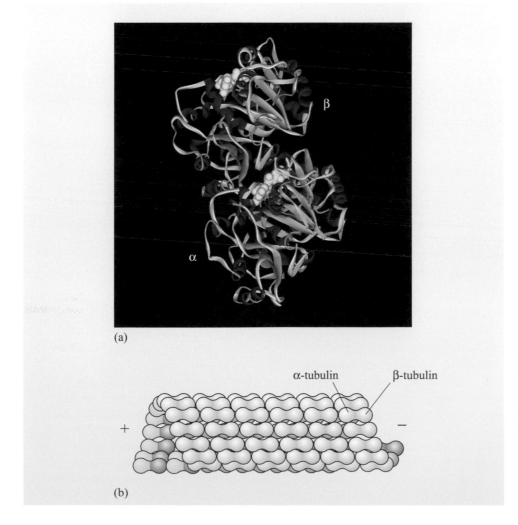

(a)

(b)

α-tubulin   β-tubulin

+   −

Figure 8.10
(a) A molecular model of the αβ-tubulin heterodimer. The α chain (lower) and β chain (upper) are structurally very similar and both bind GTP (shown in yellow). Regions of α helix are shown in red, β sheet in cyan and regions lacking any secondary structure in white. (b) Monomers of the tubulin heterodimer assemble end to end, with α-tubulin at the plus end. Thirteen filaments of tubulin assemble to form a microtubule.

The microtubule organizing centre

Microtubules are nucleated (i.e. initiated) by a specialist organelle called the **microtubule organizing centre** (**MTOC**). In fungi, such as the yeasts, the MTOC is a disc-like structure known as the spindle pole body (SPB) (Figure 8.5). Molecular genetic analyses of SPBs in yeast (especially in *S. cerevisiae*) have revealed some of their protein components, but the precise nature of the functions of and interactions between the known SPB components are in many cases unknown or uncertain. In plant cells, microtubules appear to be organized by structures located within the nuclear envelope. In animal cells, the MTOC is called the **centrosome**. Figure 8.11 shows a pictorial representation of the relationship between the centrosome and other cellular components in a non-dividing animal cell.

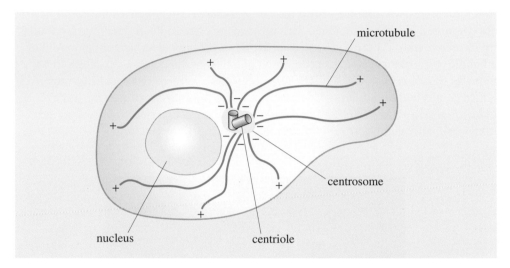

Figure 8.11   Microtubule distribution in the non-dividing animal cell. Microtubules originate in the centrosome, which stabilizes their minus ends.

The centrosome is a complex, though ill-defined, organelle. A diagrammatic representation of the typical components of a centrosome are shown in Figure 8.12. At its core is a pair of **centrioles**, small cylindrical structures composed of tubulin, oriented orthogonally with respect to each other (i.e. at right angles). The two centrioles are not functionally equivalent to each other: only one functions to nucleate microtubules. Surrounding the centrioles is a cloud of diffuse material, known as the **centrosome matrix**. It is within this matrix that the microtubules of the spindle appear to nucleate.

Central to the microtubule nucleating function of the centrosome are smaller structures called **γ-tubulin ring complexes** (**γ-TuRCs**). These are composed of several proteins, including γ-tubulin which, although related to α- and β-tubulin protein subunits, is distinct from them. There are approximately 50 γ-TuRCs in each centrosome, distributed within the surrounding matrix. The γ-TuRCs act by nucleating microtubules within the centrosome, serving as an anchor for their minus ends. Microtubules emanating from the centrosome undergo highly dynamic changes in their length as a result of assembly/disassembly at the plus end through the addition or removal of αβ-tubulin heterodimers. Microtubules can become more stable if their ends are capped through a protein or ligand interaction. The details of this process will be described in more detail in Chapter 12 when we discuss the cytoskeleton.

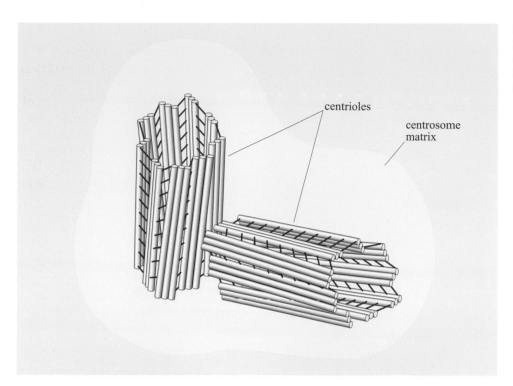

Figure 8.12
Diagrammatic representation of a centrosome. The centrosome consists of two orthogonally oriented centrioles surrounded by centrosome matrix.

centrioles

centrosome matrix

Each time a cell undergoes mitosis, the centrosomes are separated into the two daughter cells, so this organelle must also be duplicated. Centrosome duplication occurs as the cell divides. The centrosome, with its pair of centrioles, duplicates after cytokinesis, through G1 and S, in readiness for the formation of the mitotic spindle in the next mitosis (Figure 8.13). Each mother centriole duplicates and a daughter is synthesized. In the subsequent mitosis, only the mother centriole will nucleate microtubules. It is interesting to note that in some systems, the centrosomal duplication cycle can be decoupled from the nuclear division cycle. For example, the nuclei of syncytial *Drosophila* embryos that have been injected with the DNA synthesis inhibitor aphidicolin do not divide, but the centrosomes continue to duplicate, organize spindles and disperse to the cortex (the region of the cytoplasm adjacent to the plasma membrane) as normal. The precise details of how centrosome duplication is regulated are unknown.

8.2.4 The structure and function of the mitotic spindle

The three classes of microtubules in the mitotic spindle

Microtubules that form the mitotic spindle can be classified by the direction of their growth from the MTOC and the cellular structures that they contact. They fall into three classes, the positions of which are shown diagrammatically in Figure 8.14 for an animal cell at the metaphase stage of mitosis.

As prophase proceeds, the centrosomes, with their attached microtubules, migrate to opposite sides of the nucleus, each bearing a cluster of microtubules. These **astral microtubules** radiate outwards to the cell cortex and play an important role in orienting the spindle within the cell and influencing the plane of division along which the two daughter cells will eventually separate after mitosis is complete. Extending from the centrosomes to the kinetochore of each chromosome are the **kinetochore microtubules**.

Figure 8.13
Centrosomes through the cell cycle.
Centrosomes, each composed of a pair
of centrioles surrounded by a diffuse
cloud of centrosome matrix (indicated
here in yellow) duplicate during G1/S,
yielding a mother (dark green) and
daughter (pale green) centriole pair.
By M phase, the centrosomes have
migrated to opposite sides of the
nucleus. After cell division, mother
and daughter centrioles separate and
each then begins a new round of
centriole duplication.

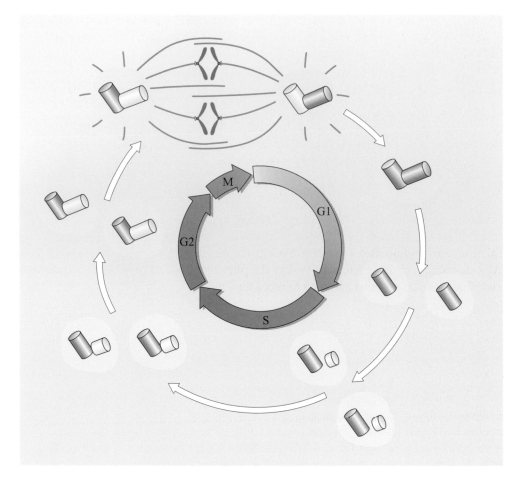

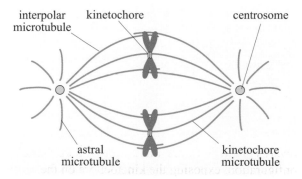

Figure 8.14   A diagrammatic representation of the
mitotic spindle of a dividing animal cell, showing the
three classes of microtubules, which are defined by their
orientation with respect to the kinetochores and cell.
Astral microtubules radiate outwards from the centrosome.
Kinetochore microtubules extend from the centrosome to
a kinetochore (or terminate without reaching the opposite
centrosome). Interpolar microtubules extend from one
centrosome to the centre of the spindle and overlap
with similar microtubules originating from the opposite
centrosome.

Finally, **interpolar** microtubules extend from each MTOC inwards towards the equator of the cell, overlapping with microtubules originating at the opposite MTOC.

○ Why are interpolar microtubules not connected to both MTOCs, forming an unbroken microtubule?

● Each MTOC interacts only with minus ends of microtubules, and as the ends of microtubules from the opposite pole will be plus ends, no interaction occurs. Therefore, interpolar microtubules overlap, but do not join.

Motor proteins and movement of the mitotic spindle

Motor proteins of the **kinesin** and **dynein** families (the kinesin- and dynein-related motor proteins) provide connections between overlapping microtubules. These microtubule-binding motor proteins bind to and move along microtubules in an ATP-dependent manner; kinesins toward the plus end and dyneins toward the minus end. These motor proteins can bind to more than one microtubule and their activity leads to structural changes in collections of microtubules and movement of the mitotic spindle. For example, the action of proteins of the dynein family will tend to bring microtubules to a focus, with all their individual minus ends in proximity (Figure 8.15a). Similarly, plus end-directed motor proteins linking interpolar microtubules will change the morphology of the spindle by causing the overlapping microtubules at the equator of the spindle to move relative to each other, thereby lengthening the spindle (Figure 8.15b). We will discuss motor proteins and the mechanism of their action in more detail in Chapter 12.

Kinetochore proteins, which are bound to the centromere of each sister chromatid pair, bind microtubule ends, serving to stabilize them (Figure 8.15c). When microtubules, extending at their plus ends as they grow from the MTOCs at each pole, encounter a kinetochore, they bind to it, sideways on. The kinetochore also contains kinesin-related motor proteins which then bind to the captured microtubule.

○ In which direction will the kinetochore-attached kinesin-related motor protein move?

● It will move towards the minus end, that is toward the MTOC, which is positioned at the pole of the cell.

In moving along the microtubule towards the MTOC, the kinetochore–microtubule interaction changes to an end-on configuration, exposing the kinetochore on the other chromatid to microtubules extending from that pole. These microtubules attach to this exposed kinetochore and motor action by its kinesin-related motor proteins directs this second kinetochore toward the opposite pole. Since the chromosome is now held between two microtubules originating from opposite poles, it comes under tension and gradually stabilizes at the equator of the cell. This process occurs for each sister chromatid pair within the cell, with all of them eventually occupying a position in the cell referred to as the **metaphase plate**. Generally, this is midway between the spindle poles, but in cases where cell division is asymmetric, the metaphase plate lies closer to one pole than the other.

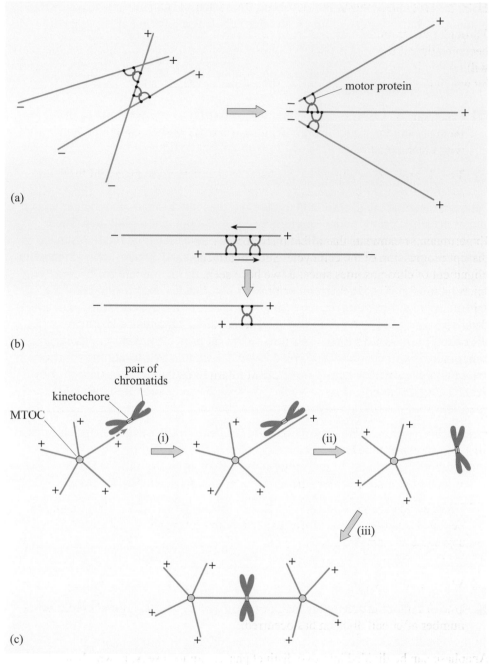

Figure 8.15   Spindle microtubules interact with motor proteins. (a) End-directed motor
proteins can each bind more than one microtubule. As each motor protein moves towards the
minus (−) end, the ends of the bound microtubules are brought together into a focus. (b) Plus (+)
end-directed motor proteins can bring about the sliding of two microtubules over each other.
Actions such as this lead to the lengthening of the mitotic spindle, where overlapping antiparallel
microtubules are linked by plus end-directed motors. (c) (i) Microtubules extending from one
spindle pole contact a kinetochore on one chromatid of a pair. (ii) Subsequent motor action
results in the chromatid pair being rotated, allowing microtubules from the opposite pole to attach
(iii). Motor action by the kinetochore along microtubules from both poles results in the sister
chromatid pair being held under tension between the spindle poles. This results in formation of the
metaphase plate.

8.2.5 The segregation of chromosomes in anaphase

Through the combined action of microtubules and motor proteins, chromosomes become aligned at the metaphase plate in preparation for their segregation. Anaphase will not begin until this arrangement has occurred. We will discuss the mechanisms by which the cell ensures that the chromosomes are in place later in this chapter.

○ Colchicine is a drug that that affects the structure of microtubules by causing them to depolymerize. What will be the effect on the cell cycle of treating cells with colchicine?

◼ The chromosomes will be unable to align at a metaphase plate and therefore to enter anaphase because, with the microtubules depolymerized, the mitotic spindle will be unable to form.

Experimental treatments that affect microtubules, such as the addition of colchicine, disrupt progression of the cell cycle. Such treatments inhibit the correct equatorial alignment of chromosomes since, as we have seen, this alignment requires normal microtubule function. In these circumstances, a **mitotic arrest** results. In part, the mitotic arrest occurs because anaphase itself requires microtubule function. However, detailed analysis indicates that the separation of sister chromatids is inhibited because the condition required for continuation, i.e. the correct alignment of chromosomes, is not met. This is due to a checkpoint that is used by the cell to regulate correct progression through the cell cycle. We will return to discuss its mechanism in more detail in Section 8.3.

If this checkpoint is disrupted (for example by mutation or by experimental intervention) chromosomes can be forced to undergo premature anaphase before they are all properly attached to kinetochore microtubules.

○ What are the likely consequences of undergoing such a premature anaphase?

◼ Unattached chromosomes will be left at the spindle midpoint when anaphase begins. Chromosomes that are attached by microtubules to only one pole will segregate asymmetrically.

○ What is the consequence of asymmetric segregation of chromosomes?

◼ One or both of the resulting daughter cells will have an abnormal chromosome number after cell division has occurred.

Anaphase can be divided into two distinct phases: **anaphase A**, in which an initial poleward movement of chromosomes occurs, and **anaphase B**, in which the spindle poles move further apart. These phases are illustrated in Figure 8.16a.

Anaphase A

As we have seen, at the end of metaphase, sister chromatids are held together by protein–protein interactions between cohesin complexes (Figure 8.8). Anaphase begins abruptly by the synchronous dissociation of the cohesin linkage between sister chromatids and their separation. This transition from metaphase to anaphase is triggered by the activation of the **anaphase promoting complex (APC)** by components of the cell cycle machinery. The cohesin linkage, and hence sister chromatid pairing, is broken by a protein called **separase** which is itself inhibited by

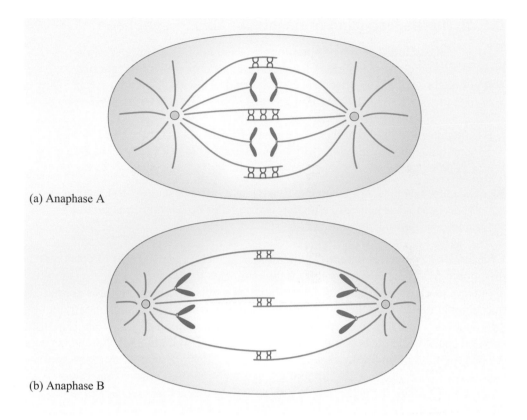

(a) Anaphase A

(b) Anaphase B

Figure 8.16   The two distinct phases of anaphase. (a) During anaphase A, the chromosomes are initially pulled poleward. (b) In anaphase B, the spindle poles themselves contribute to chromosome separation by moving apart. This separation is driven by the action of plus end-directed motor proteins on the overlapping interpolar microtubules and the shortening of astral microtubules through the action of minus end-directed motor proteins in the cell cortex (not shown).

another protein, called **securin**. Securin is cleaved by APC, which thereby releases the inhibition of separase activity, allowing it to cleave the cohesin complex; thus the chromatids become separated (Figure 8.17). As anaphase A proceeds, the chromosomes are pulled poleward through the action of the kinetochore motor proteins, with kinetochore microtubule disassembly occurring at the plus end and tubulin heterodimers being released.

Anaphase B

In anaphase B, the spindle poles themselves now move further apart, in a process dependent on two sets of motor proteins, one at the spindle poles and the other on the central spindle (Figure 8.16b). Plus end-directed motor proteins bind overlapping interpolar microtubules at the spindle equator and cause the microtubules to move relative to each other. A second contribution to spindle pole separation is from minus end-directed dynein-related motors that link astral microtubules to the cell cortex. The activity of these minus end motors serves to pull the spindle pole towards the cell cortex.

The combined effect of the kinetochore motors on the kinetochore microtubules, of the kinesin motors on the overlapping interpolar microtubules and of the dynein-related motors attached to the astral microtubules of the cell periphery is to move the MTOCs and the chromosomes to opposite ends of the cell.

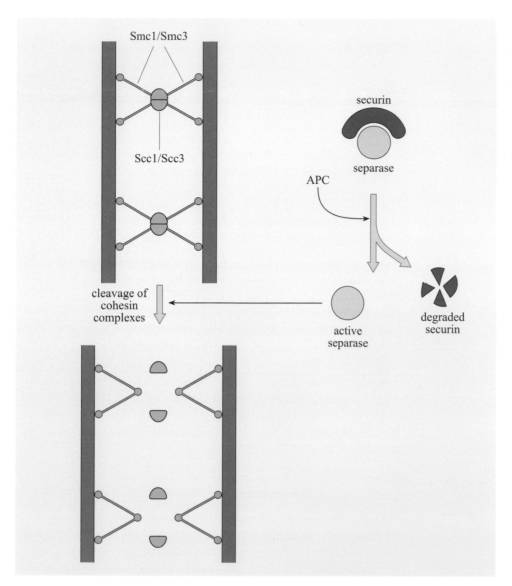

Figure 8.17
Separation of sister chromatids through the action of separase. At the onset of anaphase A, the cohesin complex responsible for sister chromatid association in metaphase is abruptly cleaved by separase. The activation of separase is brought about by the action of APC which cleaves securin, a separase inhibitor.

8.2.6 Telophase: cytokinesis and re-formation of the nuclear envelope

In telophase, the nuclear envelope re-forms, initially around individual chromosomes or groups of chromosomes. As nuclear envelope reassembly occurs, the cell begins to separate into daughter cells, by a process known as **cytokinesis**. This process is illustrated for animal cells in Figure 8.18 and for plant cells in Figure 8.19.

Cytokinesis in animal cells

The first visible change in the cell as it undergoes cytokinesis is a furrow in the cell membrane known as the cleavage furrow. This gradually becomes deeper, and more pronounced, until finally the two cells are connected only by a thin canal, which is finally pinched off to yield daughter cells. In animal cells, cytokinesis is brought about by the **contractile ring**, a structure that assembles beneath the cell membrane, roughly at the spindle equator. The contractile ring itself is composed of actin filaments, myosin II filaments, and a host of other structural and regulatory proteins.

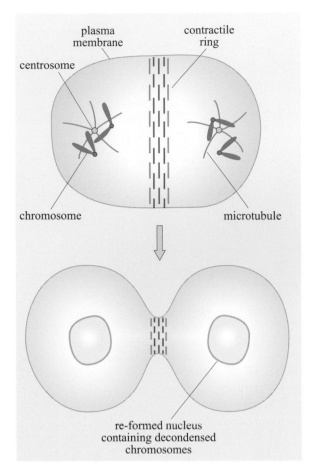

plasma
membrane

contractile
ring

centrosome

chromosome

microtubule

re-formed nucleus
containing decondensed
chromosomes

Figure 8.18   Cytokinesis in animal cells. During
telophase, the nuclear envelope re-forms, and the daughter
cells separate by cytokinesis. The contractile ring forms
underneath the cell membrane, and cytokinesis proceeds
by the contraction of the contractile ring to pinch the two
cells apart.

Microtubules determine the position of the contractile ring

Clearly, the location of the contractile ring is of paramount
importance in the successful completion of cell division.

☐ What would be the consequences of the contractile ring
forming in the wrong place?

■ At one extreme, the production of anucleate (without a
nucleus) and binucleate (with two nuclei) cells; at the other, the
formation of daughter cells of inappropriate size.

These outcomes can be seen in systems where cytokinesis is
disrupted by experimental intervention, or by mutation of genes
that encode essential contractile ring components.

In many cases, the relative sizes of the daughter cells are
important, such as in the early cleavages of vertebrate embryos.
What, then, determines the location of the contractile ring? It
appears that in some specific cases, this is determined by the
mitotic spindle: the contractile ring always forms in the same plane
as the metaphase plate. Physical manipulation of dividing large
embryonic cells indicates that the contractile ring forms midway
between the two sets of astral microtubules and does not require
the metaphase plate to be assembled on a spindle. However, this
does not appear to be universal – in other cell types, the astral
microtubules appear to play no role in the positioning of the
contractile ring.

Many cells divide asymmetrically

Many cell types do not divide to yield equal-sized cells; that is, they
divide asymmetrically. For example, the early cleavage divisions
in many embryos result in daughter cells of different sizes. How is
asymmetric division achieved? In cells where the location of the
contractile ring (and hence the location of the plane of division
between the daughter cells) is determined by the spindle or the
astral microtubules, it is possible that the position of the contractile
ring is determined by the location of the spindle within the mother
cell. In turn, the position of the spindle and astral microtubules is determined by a
combination of astral microtubule lengths and the activity of microtubule-binding
motor proteins located in the cell cortex. Note that this mechanism not only
determines the symmetry or asymmetry of cleavage, but also the orientation of the
cleavage plane.

Force is generated in the contractile ring

Contractile force in the contractile ring is generated by the interaction between the
proteins actin and myosin II. These proteins are normally organized in a network in
the cell cortex (which we will discuss in more detail in Chapter 12), but as the cell
begins mitosis, the network disassembles: the actin is reorganized, and myosin II
filaments are released. The released proteins reassemble to form the contractile ring.

The sliding filament model of force generation and the roles of actin and myosin in this process are discussed in S204 Book 3 *The Core of Life*, Vol. II, Section 7.5.

It is believed that it is the interaction between actin and myosin II that provides the contractile force required, in a similar manner to the contraction of smooth muscle. The contraction begins when a myosin light-chain kinase is activated by the Ca^{2+}– calmodulin complex. It is interesting to note, however, that the process by which the ring constricts does not appear to consist solely of the sliding of actin and myosin filaments relative to each other, for the diameter of the ring remains the same as it constricts.

○ Why does this observation indicate that the contraction of the contractile ring most likely involves other processes in addition to sliding filaments?

● If the contraction were due solely to sliding filaments, the thickness of the ring would be expected to increase. Since the contractile ring remains the same diameter, some material must presumably be lost, or altered in degree of compaction during this process.

The means by which the cell regulates contractile ring formation and coordinates this process with the other events in the cell cycle remain unclear. In some cases, at least, it appears that particular kinases of the polo-like kinase family are required. The first polo-like kinase to be identified was the gene product of the *Drosophila* gene *polo*. Mutants in this gene show defects in spindle arrangement. Polo-like kinases have been identified in most organisms examined; humans have three and *Drosophila* appears to have only one. It is also likely that, of the many components of the contractile ring, some are involved in its regulation.

Cytokinesis in plant cells

Much of the description of cytokinesis presented above pertains to animal cells. Cytokinesis in plant cells, however, differs significantly from that in animal cells.

○ Can you suggest why daughter plant cells separate via a different mechanism from that seen in animal cells?

● A typical plant cell is surrounded by a rigid cell wall, so cytokinesis by the contractile ring mechanism used by animal cells would be impossible.

Effectively, the process of cytokinesis in plant cells is the reverse of that in animal cells; that is, rather than occurring from the outside in, it occurs from the inside out (Figure 8.19). In G2, before any other signs of impending mitosis are apparent, a band of microtubules and actin filaments assembles at the position that eventually become the site of the post-mitotic cell cleavage. This assembly is known as the **pre-prophase band**, and it gradually narrows to become localized at the metaphase plate. By the time that the chromosomes have segregated, i.e. at telophase, the only remains of the mitotic spindle are the overlapping interpolar microtubules which span this region. These now form part of a structure known as a **phragmoplast**. The phragmoplast directs the accumulation of membranous vesicles carrying cargoes of cell wall components. These components give rise first to the cell plate, and subsequently to the complete cell wall between the daughter cells.

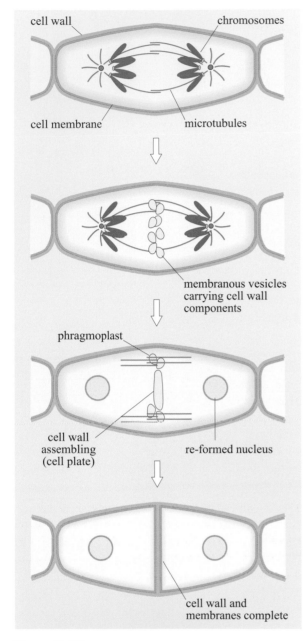

Figure 8.19
Cytokinesis in plant cells differs from that in animals due to the presence of the rigid cell wall. The phragmoplast assembles at the midbody of the mitotic spindle, where the remains of the overlapping interpolar microtubules lie at the end of mitosis. Membranous vesicles carrying cell wall components assemble at the phragmoplast; these components are used to assemble a cell wall that separates the daughter cells.

Reassembly of the nuclear envelope

Perhaps more remarkable than the breakdown of the nuclear envelope is its capacity to re-form after anaphase. Reassembly commences along the chromatids, and the fusion of vesicles and cisternae results in the reconstitution of the envelope. The nuclear pore complex reconstitutes soon after the envelope forms, and signs of nuclear lamina re-formation can be seen in late anaphase, when A type lamins appear associated with chromatids. Despite this observation, A type lamins can still be detected in the cytosol after cell division, well into G1 phase within daughter cells. The B type lamins are also still being imported and assembled into the lamina at this point. Thus full NE reassembly does not occur until G1.

Some cells undergo incomplete cytokinesis

In some cell types, cytokinesis is incomplete, the daughter cells remaining interconnected by cytoplasmic bridges. Incomplete cytokinesis is found in many organisms where there is rapid movement of cell contents between neighbouring cells. Examples include the germ-line mitoses in premeiotic stages in *Drosophila*, and various syncytial systems, such as fungal hyphae and insect embryos. Mammalian examples include osteoblasts, the cells responsible for bone remodelling throughout life.

8.2.7 The duplication, division and segregation of organelles

The sections above have described how the two daughter cells are assured of receiving the correct complement of chromosomes. However, it should be clear that the chromosomes are not the only cellular components that must be distributed between daughter cells. We have already seen how the centrosomes of an animal cell undergo duplication, ensuring that each daughter cell receives a functional MTOC. Other organelles such as mitochondria and chloroplasts must also be partitioned.

In eukaryotic cells, there are two types of organelle that contain their own genome: mitochondria (in all eukaryotes) and chloroplasts (only in plants). These structures represent cytoplasmic compartments in which defined processes are carried out: oxidative phosphorylation in mitochondria and photosynthesis in chloroplasts. Both organelles are membrane-bound and, as discussed in Chapter 1, are thought to have arisen from incorporation of symbiotic organisms within the early primordial cells, as they share many features with prokaryote cells. One of these features is their circular genome. Note, however, that most of the organelle's protein components are encoded by the nuclear genome.

Mitochondria

The mitochondrial genome varies in size between species. Most animal species have mitochondrial genomes that are between 14 and 40 kb in size, with the human mitochondrial genome being 16.5 kb. Plant mitochondrial genomes are commonly around 300 kb, although the mitochondria of some species, such as *Cucurbitaceae* (cucumbers) have genomes of up to 2400 kb. Fungal mitochondrial genomes range from 19 kb in *S. pombe* to 75 kb in *S. cerevisiae*. A mitochondrion contains multiple copies of its genomic DNA, which are organized as nucleoids attached to the inner membrane of the organelle.

Although mitochondria are often seen as discrete organelles in cell sections, they exist as membrane-bound networks in the cell. In fact, mitochondrial morphology is quite plastic and, as shown in Figure 8.20, this organelle can undergo both fusion and fission. In *S. cerevisiae*, mitochondria can fuse to form a reticulate (i.e. net-like), morphologically dynamic structure lying immediately under the plasma membrane. The fission of mitochondria is quite complex, since the organelle is bound by a double membrane and the relationship between the two membranes must be maintained for correct mitochondrial function.

Chloroplasts

Chloroplasts are organelles characteristic of mature plant cells. They are derived from immature, non-photosynthetic precursor organelles called **plastids**. Cell division in plants is confined to non-photosynthetic meristem tissues, which are the proliferative tissues of plants and do not have mature chloroplasts. We will therefore consider the replication of plastids, although in mature plant cells, division of chloroplasts does occur.

Plastid genomes are circular, and contain genes encoding about 100 plastid proteins. As with mitochondria, the great majority of plastid proteins are encoded by the nuclear genome. Plastids divide by a process called **binary fission**, which is also seen in prokaryotic cells, and is perhaps an indication of their evolutionary ancestry. We will discuss binary fission in more detail later in this chapter.

Binary fission of plastids seems to occur via a constriction of the organelle's bounding membranes, set up by a ring-shaped structure called the **plastid dividing ring**. This ring is composed of an internal ring, on the stromal (internal) side of the double membrane, and an outer ring on the cytosolic face of the double membrane. The precise details of plastid fission remain obscure.

Organelle segregation

Clearly, appropriate partition of mitochondria and plastids to daughter cells in mitosis and meiosis is important for viability.

⬜ Why do you think correct partition of mitochondria between daughter cells is important?

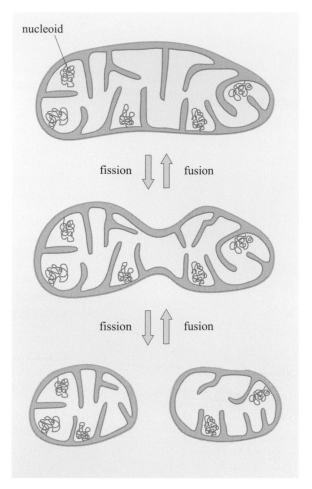

Figure 8.20
The fission and fusion of mitochondria. Mitochondrial morphology is quite variable, and mitochondria can fuse as well as divide. Each mitochondrion contains many copies of its genome within nucleoids.

■ Cells with insufficient mitochondria might be expected to be impaired with respect to respiration.

Since organelles such as the mitochondria and chloroplast replicate their DNA and duplicate independently of the cell cycle, they have a high copy number and can be relied upon to partition evenly between daughter cells without any specific mechanism being required.

Summary of Section 8.2

1   Chromosome condensation occurs in prophase and results in a pair of highly compacted sister chromatids held together by the cohesin complex.

2   The nuclear envelope is a highly complex double-membrane structure that separates the chromosomes from the cytoplasm. It breaks down at the start of mitosis, permitting the subsequent stages to proceed.

3   The mitotic spindle is principally composed of microtubules and is a highly dynamic structure. Each microtubule consists of many subunits of tubulin dimers which bind GTP, and has a polar nature, with defined plus and minus ends.

4   Spindle microtubules are nucleated at the centrosomes, complex organelles containing γ-tubulin ring complexes and which have their own division cycle, tied to the mitotic cycle. Movement of and along microtubules occurs through the action of motor proteins.

5   Anaphase is triggered by APC, the action of which leads to cohesin cleavage. Chromosomes separate to the cell poles through the combined action of motor proteins with microtubules which pull the chromosomes and spindle poles apart.

6   Cytokinesis in animal cells occurs via a contractile ring, which is composed largely of actin and myosin molecules. In plant cells, cytokinesis is assisted by the phragmoplast. Unequal division can generate cells of unequal size.

7   Independently replicating organelles are generally equally partitioned between daughter cells by virtue of their high copy number.

You should now go to the *Cell division* section of the *Movie gallery* on the CD-ROM, where you will find five short movies showing the dynamic nature of cell division.

8.3 Checkpoints and the regulation of the cell cycle

It is evident that as complex and important a process as cell division requires sophisticated control mechanisms. Cells that receive abnormal complements of genetic material are generally inviable, or behave abnormally. Typical abnormalities resulting from an unequal segregation of chromosomes include aneuploid cells, where there are deviations from the normal diploid chromosome complement (e.g. one chromosome too few or to many) and **polyploid** cells, where there are extra complete sets of chromosomes (e.g. tetraploids, in which there are four copies of the entire chromosome complement). As we shall see in Chapter 19, abnormalities such as these can represent a step toward the development of tumours.

The complexity of the cell cycle leads to a requirement that each step involved (e.g. DNA replication, the alignment of chromosomes at the metaphase plate and cytokinesis) must be monitored for completion before the next stage proceeds. Failure at any of these crucial points leads to the production of defective daughter cells. To ensure that all the required activities are completed before moving to the subsequent stages, the cell monitors its progress through the cell cycle with a series of checks, known as checkpoints (introduced in Section 8.1.1). Considerable progress in the overall understanding of cell cycle control has been obtained by the application of genetics, biochemistry and cell biology to the study of these checkpoints.

8.3.1 General characteristics of checkpoints in mitosis

Mitosis is a cyclic process, and while the individual phases may vary in duration, they must all occur in strict temporal sequence. Each cell cycle checkpoint operates via negative signalling, where the next mitotic event is inhibited until the conditions for accurate progression are met, whereupon the inhibition is lifted.

⬜ Why do you think the use of negative control signals is advantageous to the cell?

⬛ It is a safer way of ensuring that the prerequisites for successful cell division have been met; failure to generate a signal to proceed with the cell cycle will lead to arrest. If, on the other hand, a cell proceeds through mitosis unless made to stop by a signal to halt, any failure in the cell's systems that removed that signal would allow the cell to carry on through the cell cycle, possibly leading to mitotic errors.

As we shall see, correct regulation of the cell cycle is intrinsic to avoiding uncontrolled cell division. As might be expected, a number of genes that are involved in tumorigenesis encode proteins with roles in these regulatory processes (to be discussed in Chapter 19).

In the eukaryotic cell cycle, there are three stages at which progression is monitored and controlled: the G1/S transition (G1 checkpoint), the G2/M transition (G2 checkpoint) and the metaphase/anaphase transition (spindle checkpoint). These checkpoints are shown diagrammatically in Figure 8.21. The G1 checkpoint assesses whether growth conditions are appropriate for the cell to begin cell division and whether the genome is ready to be replicated. If these conditions are met, the cell proceeds into S phase. The G2 checkpoint assesses whether the genome has been fully replicated and is undamaged and that environmental conditions are appropriate.

Figure 8.21
The cell cycle checkpoints. The three points at which progress through the cycle is controlled by checkpoints are indicated by bars, with the appropriate trigger event shown for each.

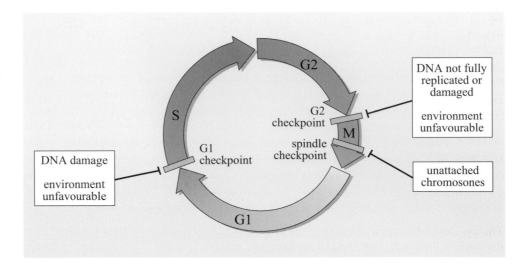

If these conditions are met, the cell proceeds into mitosis. The spindle checkpoint assesses whether all the kinetochores are correctly attached to the spindle. Note that two of these checkpoints assess the integrity of the genomic DNA.

This system of checkpoints utilizes an evolutionarily conserved set of protein components, but in general, higher eukaryotes possess a greater variety of each component. In order to understand the mechanism by which checkpoints operate, we first need to examine the proteins that regulate progression through the cell cycle.

Progress through the cell cycle is achieved through the cyclic activation and inactivation of a series of proteins. Many of these proteins activate other downstream effectors and inactivate upstream components, ensuring a progressive chain of signalling. The core components of this cell cycle machinery are linked to the checkpoint system through the activities of two families of proteins that are central to the operation of the cell cycle. Together, these families form what are called the cyclically activated kinases.

8.3.2 Cyclically activated kinases

In common with many biological processes, control of the cell cycle is crucially dependent on reversible phosphorylation events.

○ Which two opposing enzyme activities control the level of protein phosphorylation?

● The two activities are those of kinases (which phosphorylate proteins) and phosphatases (which dephosphorylate proteins).

The cell has numerous kinases and phosphatases, each with characteristic specificity as to its target molecule or molecules.

○ How does phosphorylation regulate protein structure and function?

● It can change the conformation of a protein, alter its interactions with other proteins or alter the protein's enzyme activity in several different ways (Section 3.6.2).

Key to the function of the cell cycle and its checkpoints are a family of **cyclin-dependent kinases (Cdks)**. Typically, the enzymatic activity of a Cdk rises and falls as the cell cycle proceeds, whilst its concentration remains constant. The activity of each Cdk is regulated and this regulation is achieved by a second protein with which the Cdk interacts, called a **cyclin**. Cyclins are so named because they were originally identified as proteins whose abundance in the cell rises and falls *cyclically* through the cell cycle. Cyclins are synthesized and degraded at specific points in the cell cycle.

Before we discuss specific examples, we will first outline the principle of how these two proteins, Cdks and cyclins, regulate the cell cycle. As the cell cycle proceeds, the appropriate cyclin is synthesized and binds to its partner Cdk to form what is termed a **cyclin–Cdk complex**. It is the activity of the complex that regulates progression through the cell cycle through the activation or inhibition of various other proteins.

The cyclin–Cdk complexes we will be considering are best described according to the phase of the cell cycle in which they are active:

▸ *G1 cyclin–Cdk complex*: Required for progression through G1 and to commit the cell to proceed into S phase for the synthesis of DNA.

▸ *S cyclin–Cdk complex*: Required for initiating and completing DNA synthesis in S phase.

▸ *M cyclin–Cdk complex*: Required to trigger progression into mitosis and to inhibits entry into the next G1 phase after cell division.

While all systems that have been studied use these cyclin–Cdk complexes to monitor or regulate cell cycle progression, they each differ in their complexity. First, there are several classes of cyclins, distinguished by their amino acid sequence and grouped by the period of the cell cycle when they are present within the cell. Each class may have several representatives in any single species. Typically, more complex eukaryotes, such as vertebrates, have a greater number of cyclins than do less complex eukaryotes, such as yeast. An example is seen in human cells, where no fewer than 10 cyclins are known, some of which are listed in Table 8.1.

Secondly, the number of Cdks also varies. For example, the budding yeast has only one Cdk, which binds to each of the cyclins as they are synthesized at the different stages of mitosis, and which is therefore involved in every checkpoint. In contrast, cells of vertebrates are more complex: they have multiple distinct Cdks. These Cdks can each bind different cyclins, with each cyclin–Cdk complex being responsible for different checkpoints. The diversity of kinase function is possible because not only does the phosphorylation state of the cyclin–Cdk complex determine the *level* of its kinase activity, but the cyclin component also determines the *target* of the kinase activity. Examples of human Cdks that partner specific cyclins are shown in Table 8.1.

Table 8.1 The human cyclin proteins with known roles in cell cycle regulation, their partner Cdks and period of activity.

Cyclin	Cdk partner	Phase of the cell cycle where active
cyclin A	Cdk2, Cdk1	S and G2
cyclin B	Cdk1	M
cyclins D1, D2, D3	Cdk4, Cdk6	G1
cyclin E	Cdk2	G1/S

8.3.3 Cyclin–Cdk complex activity is regulated by several mechanisms

The activity of each cyclin–Cdk complex is regulated by three distinct mechanisms: the availability of each cyclin, the presence of inhibitory proteins, and the reversible phosphorylation of specific sites on the Cdk molecule. Table 8.2 lists the types of proteins involved in regulating cyclin–Cdk complex activity and summarizes the functions of each.

Table 8.2 Classes of cell cycle regulatory proteins.

Class of protein	Function
protein kinases (e.g. Wee1) protein phosphatases (e.g. Cdc25)	inactivation of cyclin–Cdk complexes activation of cyclin–Cdk complexes
Cdk inhibitory proteins (CKIs)	suppression of Cdk activity; different CKIs inhibit Cdks by direct binding at different phases of mitosis
ubiquitin ligase	ubiquitination of G1 regulatory proteins and regulatory proteins involved in controlling exit from mitosis (other proteins control the activity of these ubiquitin ligases, principally by phosphorylating them or their target molecules)
transcriptional factors	factors required for transcription of regulatory protein genes; factors required to govern transcriptional response to (e.g.) DNA damage

Cyclin availability

The rates of Cdk synthesis are of little importance in the regulation of cyclin–Cdk complex activity, since Cdk levels are relatively uniform through the cell cycle. In contrast, cyclin levels rise and fall throughout the cell cycle. These fluctuations in cyclin levels are achieved through a combination of transcriptional activation, which results in increased translation, and protein degradation, which removes the cyclin. The fluctuations in the levels of cyclin proteins are shown schematically for yeast and human cells in Figure 8.22.

Note that in the complex networks of protein interactions examined in the course, the stimulatory and inhibitory effects are represented by special notation, shown in Figure 8.23.

Cyclins are specifically targeted for degradation at specific points in the cell cycle through the attachment of a number of **ubiquitin** molecules, a reaction catalysed by enzymes called **ubiquitin ligases**. The ubiquitin degradation pathway will be discussed in more detail in Chapter 11; here we shall introduce its relevance to the control of the cell cycle. Proteins tagged with ubiquitin are rapidly degraded, thus removing their activity from the cell. Two complexes trigger the rapid degradation of cyclins. These are the SCF complex (named for three components of the yeast SCF complex: s̲kp1, c̲dc53 and f̲-box) and the APC (anaphase promoting complex) (Figure 8.23).

Figure 8.23   The interrelationships between factors that control or influence the activity of cyclin–Cdk complexes. Cdk–cyclin complexes are formed by the interaction of a Cdk and a cyclin, both of which are present at levels dictated by their rate of synthesis and, in the case of cyclin, by its rate of degradation. The cyclin–Cdk complex can exists in active or inactive states, dependent upon its phosphorylation status. Inactivation of the cyclin–Cdk complex is brought about by phosphorylation of the Cdk component by Wee1 kinase; this activation is reversed by the Cdc25 phosphatase. CKI proteins inhibit the activity of the cyclin–Cdk complex. See text for further details.

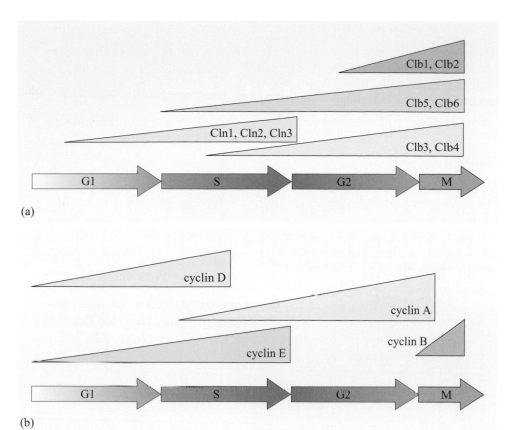

(a)

(b)

Figure 8.22
Cyclin formation and degradation
through the cell cycle in (a) yeast
and (b) human cells. The abundance
of each cyclin is plotted against time
as a wedge, the thickness at a given
time representing the abundance of
the named cyclin. Cyclin abundance
increases as the result of increased
synthesis and suddenly decreases
through rapid degradation. Thus,
for example, human cyclin E begins
to appear in G1, and increases in
abundance until it is rapidly degraded
when G2 begins.

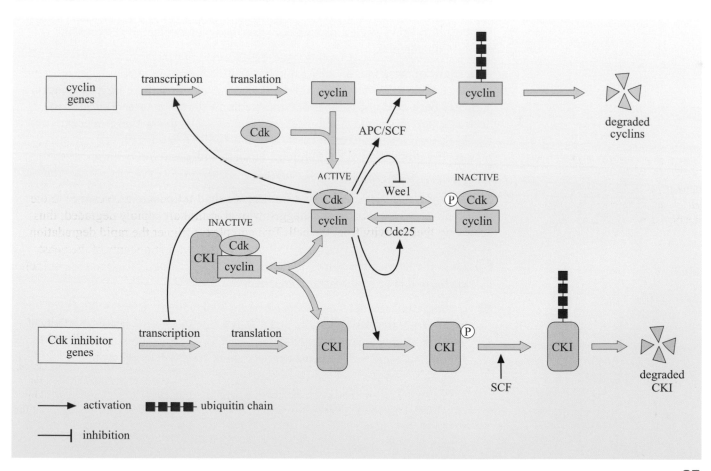

Inhibition of the cyclin–Cdk complex

There are several **cyclin kinase inhibitors** (**CKIs**) involved in the control of the eukaryotic cell cycle. CKIs inhibit cyclin–Cdk complex activity through direct binding (Figure 8.23). Just as there are more cyclins and Cdks in more complex eukaryotes than in less complex ones, so there are correspondingly more CKIs in the more complex eukaryotes. CKIs can also be removed by their being targeted for rapid degradation via ubiquitinylation.

Phosphorylation of Cdk

The phosphorylation status of several tyrosine and threonine residues close to the active site of Cdks regulates their function, with phosphorylation inhibiting kinase activity. Thus, cyclin–Cdk complex activity can be regulated through the phosphorylation status of the Cdk component (Figure 8.23). This situation provides a point at which regulation can occur. An example of the control of cyclin–Cdk activity by phosphorylation of the Cdk is shown by examining two proteins with opposing effects on the phosphorylation status of Cdks; the Wee1 ('wee-one') and Cdc25 proteins. The Wee1 protein is a kinase and is named for the reduced cell size phenotype that results from its genetic inactivation in fission yeast. Cdc25 is a phosphatase. Both these proteins modify the same site in their target Cdk. Thus, the action of Wee1 leads to phosphorylation of its target Cdk.

○ What effect will Cdk phosphorylation by Wee1 have upon the kinase activity of the target cyclin–Cdk?

■ It will inactivate the cyclin–Cdk complex.

Dephosphorylation of the Cdk by Cdc25 has the reverse effect: it activates the cyclin–Cdk complex.

As a result of these interactions, rapid but stable changes in cyclin–Cdk complex activity can be achieved through the cell cycle. A cyclin–Cdk in its active state activates both APC and SCF, and as these complexes (when active) lead to the destruction of the cyclin component (see Figure 8.23), this action is a negative feedback loop which serves to limit its own activity. Cyclin–Cdk activity also inhibits the production of CKI proteins through a block to transcription of their genes.

The activities of both the Wee1 and Cdc25 proteins are themselves regulated by the cyclin–Cdk complex, which inhibits its own phosphorylation by Wee1, while activating Cdc25 activity.

○ From the interactions shown in Figure 8.23, predict what effect the removal of a cyclin will have on the other components.

■ Cyclin removal will lead to reduced cyclin–Cdk activity, which will in turn lead to increased Wee1 activity and lowered Cdc25 activity, leading to further cyclin–Cdk inactivation through phosphorylation. Simultaneously, CKI synthesis will increase and SCF-targeted degradation of CKI will be prevented.

Now that the basic regulatory components of the cell cycle have been explained, we shall go on to discuss how these relate to the checkpoints themselves.

8.3.4 G1 checkpoints

The G1 checkpoints are used to check that conditions are favourable for the cell to commit itself to proceeding into S phase. We will discuss this checkpoint in budding yeast (*S. cerevisiae*), where it is known as **START**, and in mammals, where it is known as the **restriction point**.

START

Yeast cells that are experimentally deprived of nutrition or are exposed to mating pheromones will not enter mitosis unless they have already passed through the START checkpoint before these conditions are applied. This test provides the experimental definition of the G1 checkpoint in budding yeast. Thus, if a synchronous culture of yeast cells is transferred to a nutrient-poor environment before START, cells will arrest at this checkpoint. If, however, the culture has already passed START when nutritional restriction is applied, the cells will proceed through S, M and G2 phases before arresting at the following G1 START checkpoint. Experiments such as these led to the identification of a gene, *CDC28*, that is essential for correct function of the START checkpoint. This gene encodes a Cdk called Cdc28.

○ How many Cdks are present in the budding yeast?

■ Only one.

Cdc28 therefore forms complexes with all the yeast cyclins.

Budding yeast has three G1 cyclins, Cln1, Cln2, and Cln3, and the relationship between these and other components of the START checkpoint can be represented diagrammatically as shown in Figure 8.24.

The Cln3 protein is only synthesized when suitable nutritional conditions are experienced by the cell, hence the concentration of the Cln3–Cdc28 complex effectively serves as a monitor of cell growth. When growth is appropriate, the level of the Cln3–Cdc28 complex rises, stimulating the production of the other G1 cyclins, Cln1 and Cln2, through their increased transcription and translation. These cyclins in turn form complexes with Cdc28, which bring about the synthesis of a series of additional downstream (S phase) cyclins. This, in turn, induces the cell to begin DNA synthesis. On the other hand, should nutritional limitation restrict cell size and growth, Cln3–Cdc28 activity remains low because starvation prevents the synthesis and accumulation of Cln3. Consequently, Cln1 and Cln2 are not synthesized. In turn, the absence of Cln1 and Cln2 means the cell does not progress into S phase.

Mating pheromone, however, exerts its effect via a CKI called Far1, as shown in Figure 8.24.

Genetic screens carried out in yeasts to identify genes encoding proteins required for cell cycle progression resulted in the discovery of many genes. These genes were termed *CDC* in *S. cerevisiae* and *cdc* in *S. pombe* (for cell division cycle).

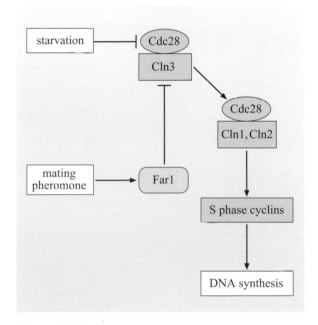

Figure 8.24
The interactions between regulatory components of the G1 START checkpoint in the budding yeast. The individual components of this checkpoint are shown. Both starvation and mating pheromone exert an inhibitory effect on the activity of the Cln3–Cdc28 complex. When this inhibitory influence is lifted by environmental change (such as addition of nutrients to the growth medium, or removal of mating pheromone), the Cln3–Cdc28 complex activates expression of the genes encoding Cln1 and Cln2. The action of these two cyclins in turn leads to progression into S phase.

○ What effect will mating pheromone have upon Cln2 and Cln3 levels?

● Mating pheromone leads to the production of the Far1 CKI, which in turn inhibits Cln3–Cdc28 complex activity, so Cln1 and Cln2 will not be produced.

Thus the effect of mating pheromone has the same end result as starvation; that is, the cell stalls in G1. This ensures that mating only occurs between two haploid G1 cells, creating a diploid cell.

Restriction point

The mammalian restriction point is similar to START, in that it represents a G1 checkpoint that is critical for mitotic progression (shown in Figure 8.25). Generally, it occurs 3–4 hours after the completion of mitosis in the original mother cell. In the period between completion of mitosis and the restriction point, during which time the cell has divided, growth factor deprivation leads to a delay of several hours before cell cycle progression can resume in the daughter cells. Treatment with cycloheximide, an inhibitor of protein synthesis, has the same effect. In both situations, these cells fail to synthesize cyclin D, one of the G1 cyclins (Figure 8.22). As a consequence, cyclin D concentration declines due to its degradation. Addition of growth factor or removal of protein synthesis inhibitors leads to a resumption of growth, but it takes several hours for cyclin D to accumulate to levels sufficient for it to have an effect.

Cyclin D interacts with the cell cycle via a protein known as the **retinoblastoma protein (Rb)**. In its active state, Rb inhibits cell proliferation through the inactivation of transcription factors required for the expression of the genes encoding cyclins A and E, and by generally inhibiting protein synthesis. The cyclin D–Cdk complex inactivates Rb by phosphorylation.

○ Suggest a consequence for the cell of loss of the Rb protein.

● Loss of Rb would release one of the controls that inhibit cell proliferation (Figure 8.25), and inappropriate proliferation may result. You will see later how this can contribute to the formation of tumours (Chapter 19).

Figure 8.25
The restriction point in mammalian cells. Reduced levels of growth factors bring about a reduction in cyclin D levels, thereby reducing cyclin D–Cdk complex activity. The cyclin D–Cdk complex normally acts to stimulate phosphorylation of the Rb protein, causing its inactivation, thereby removing the inhibition of cell proliferation. Loss of cyclin D–Cdk activity therefore leads to a build-up of active Rb, inhibiting cell proliferation.

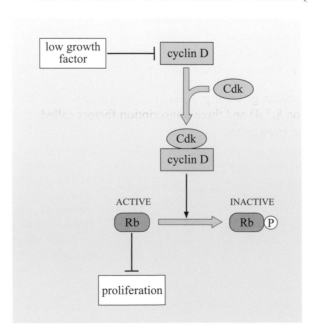

8.3.5 The response to DNA damage

One significant check that must be made before a cell commits itself to division is that of the integrity of the genome.

○ What might be the consequences of a failure to monitor DNA damage before S phase begins?

● If DNA synthesis begins before all damage to the DNA has been repaired, any base sequence changes will be copied in the newly synthesized DNA. Furthermore if there are breaks in the DNA molecules, these may disrupt replication and/or lead to chromosome breakage.

We will discuss the pathways of DNA damage detection and repair in detail in Chapter 9; here we focus on how these signals are relayed to the cell cycle checkpoints. In yeast, proteins that detect DNA damage interact closely with components of the cell cycle machinery, as shown in Figure 8.26.

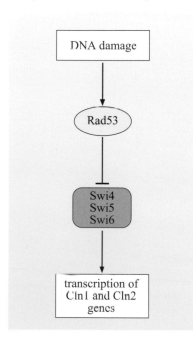

Figure 8.26
Arrest at the START checkpoint in response to DNA damage in yeast. Damage to DNA can result from many causes, such as chemical attack, irradiation and replication failure. DNA damage leads to activation of Rad53. This protein inactivates three transcription factors, Swi4, Swi5 and Swi6, which are required for transcription of the genes encoding the cyclins Cln1 and Cln2. Thus inactivation of Swi4, Swi5 and Swi6 leads to reduced levels of Cln1 and Cln2, so the cycle stalls at G1/S.

Transcription of the Cln1 and Cln2 cyclin genes is promoted by the combined activity of the Cln3–Cdk28 complex (Section 8.3.4) and three transcription factors called Swi4, Swi5 and Swi6. DNA damage triggers the activation of a protein called Rad53, which inhibits the activity of Swi4, Swi5 and Swi6. Thus, synthesis of Cln1 and Cln2 will be reduced if damage to DNA is detected. The absence of Cln1 and Cln2 in turn leads to arrest at the START checkpoint.

Mammalian cells have a similar pathway to monitor genomic integrity, which is shown schematically in Figure 8.27. This system acts in both G1 and S phase. In this case, cells respond to double-strand breaks by the activation by phosphorylation of two proteins, called ATM and ATR, and the cell's response to sites of blocked DNA replication is activation of ATR. Activated ATM and ATR both signal directly to components of the DNA repair pathways, and also activate two proteins, Chk1 and Chk2, which bring about the phosphorylation of Cdc25 protein, thereby inactivating it and targeting it for destruction. This leads to cell cycle arrest.

Figure 8.27
Checkpoint activation in response to
DNA damage in mammalian cells.
DNA damage (such as double-strand
breaks) activates the ATM and ATR
proteins, which act via a series of steps
to bring about the phosphorylation
of Cdc25 (a phosphatase). Because
phosphorylated Cdc25 is inactive,
the cyclin–Cdk complex becomes
phosphorylated, and therefore inactive,
and cell cycle progression is prevented.
Activation of p53 (by phosphorylation)
also leads to cell cycle arrest and the
induction of DNA repair or apoptosis
pathways. Activation activities are
indicated by black arrows.

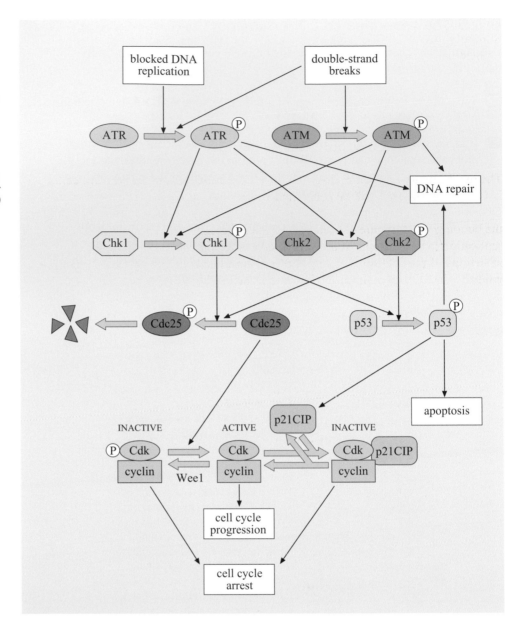

In addition, the activation of Chk1 and Chk2 leads to phosphorylation of a protein
called p53, which leads to cell cycle arrest via a separate route. In this case, a protein
called p21CIP is activated, which in turn inactivates the cyclin–Cdk complex by
binding to it. The p53 protein also acts as an inducer of downstream pathways of
DNA repair and (if repair is unsuccessful) apoptosis.

8.3.6 The initiation of DNA replication

It is obviously important that a cell replicates its genome both accurately and
to completion, and exactly once per cell cycle. The early indications that DNA
replication is under tight cell cycle control were derived from mammalian cell
fusion experiments, in which cells at different phases of the cell cycle were induced
to fuse, and the consequences of that fusion monitored. In brief, it was observed
that the fusion of G1 and S cells causes the G1 nucleus to begin DNA replication.

Following the fusion of G2 and S cells, the G2 nucleus did not initiate replication. Similarly, fusion of G1 and G2 cells did not result in any induction of DNA replication.

⬜ What do the results of these cell fusion experiments suggest?

⬛ That factors required for activation of DNA replication are present in S phase cells, and absent in G1 and G2 cells. Furthermore, G2 nuclei are insensitive to these factors, while G1 cells are sensitive to them.

The biochemistry and cell biology of DNA replication will be discussed in detail in Chapter 9. Here we will be concerned with the means by which the cell triggers DNA synthesis before entering mitosis. Again, this process is best understood in the budding yeast. Figure 8.28 illustrates the key steps in the regulation of DNA replication in yeast. Replication is initiated at specific sites in the genome, known as **origins of replication**. A complex of proteins, known as the **origin recognition complex (ORC)**, recognizes and binds to these origins. Cdc6, a protein that is normally present only at very low levels during most of the cell cycle, increases in concentration transiently in early G1. It binds to ORC, enabling the recruitment of other replication proteins to the complex.

When conditions are appropriate for DNA replication to commence, the G1 cyclin–Cdk complex activity results in the synthesis of S phase cyclins, and hence S cyclin–Cdk complexes form. These trigger the phosphorylation of both the Cdc6 protein and ORC. This modification causes the phosphorylated Cdc6 to dissociate from the complex, triggering the initiation of DNA synthesis. The released, phosphorylated, Cdc6 is immediately removed by degradation. Thus, each replication origin initiates DNA synthesis during S phase in response to the production of S phase cyclins.

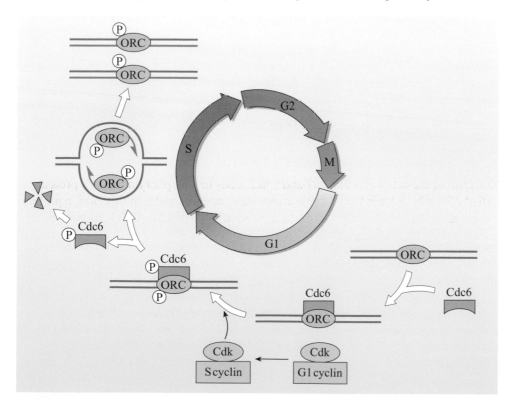

Figure 8.28
S cyclin–Cdk activity regulates the initiation of DNA replication in yeast. Replication origins are bound by ORC and Cdc6. When G1 conditions are appropriate, S cyclin–Cdk activity is activated, triggering the phosphorylation of Cdc6 and ORC. The phosphorylated Cdc6 dissociates and is degraded, allowing DNA synthesis to begin.

8.3.7 The G2 checkpoint

The control of entry into mitosis requires cyclin B-dependent kinase activity (cyclin B–Cdk1). This cyclin–Cdk complex was originally identified as **M phase promoting factor (MPF)**. MPF is initially present in the cell as an inactive form, called pre-MPF, in which the Cdk1 component is phosphorylated. Cdk1 phosphorylation is determined by the balance of Wee1 kinase and Cdc25 phosphatase activities. In the presence of DNA damage, activation of Chk1 and Chk2 leads to decreased Cdc25 activity, leading to the accumulation of inactive pre-MPF and so preventing the G2/M transition (Figure 8.29).

Figure 8.29
The G2/M checkpoint operates by preventing MPF activation. The detection of DNA damage before the G2/M transition results in activation of Chk1 and Chk2, which leads to decreased Cdc25 activity. Thus the level of pre-MPF rises, so the G2/M transition cannot occur.

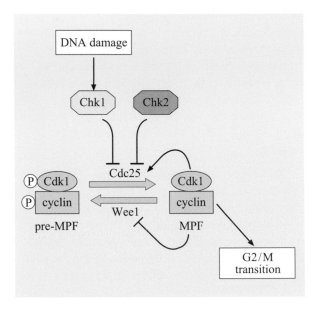

In the absence of DNA damage, or upon its completed repair, Cdc25 activity increases, pre-MPF becomes activated and the cell exits G2 and enters M phase. At this control point, there is a positive feedback loop: MPF activates more Cdc25 while also inactivating Wee1, thereby stimulating its own activation.

8.3.8 The spindle checkpoint

As we saw earlier, the mitotic spindle is complex, not only in its structure and operation, but also in its interaction with the condensed chromosomes. As a high rate of inaccurate chromosomal segregation would be detrimental, cells have a metaphase/anaphase checkpoint, usually known as the spindle checkpoint, which ensures that chromosomes have aligned correctly at the midpoint of the mitotic spindle prior to their segregation. This checkpoint can be induced experimentally; for example, by treating cells with colchicine. Mutational analysis in yeast has shown that the cell monitors the state of the kinetochore–spindle interaction through proteins that localize to the kinetochores or spindle poles. Precisely how these serve as sensors is unknown. The spindle checkpoint acts via Mad2: when the kinetochore–spindle association is complete, Mad2 is no longer activated and inhibition of APC is relieved (Figure 8.30). APC activates separase, thereby initiating anaphase.

○ How does separase activation play a role in triggering anaphase?

● Recall from Section 8.2.5 that sister chromatids are held together by cohesin proteins and that these interactions are removed by the action of separase, through release of the inhibitory action of securin (Figure 8.17).

Similar studies reveal that this spindle checkpoint operates at both the metaphase/anaphase transition, and the anaphase/telophase transition, highlighting the importance of accurate chromosome segregation.

An additional property of APC is that it brings about the destruction of cyclin B by targeting it for ubiquitinylation and proteolysis (Figure 8.30). Recall that along with Cdk1, cyclin B is a component of MPF. As one of the functions of MPF is to activate APC, destruction of cyclin B causes the loss of APC activity at the end of mitosis. APC therefore triggers its own loss, acting as a short-lived switch. This is another example of how the cell cycle contains self-regulating loops that allow rapid and stable transitions to occur.

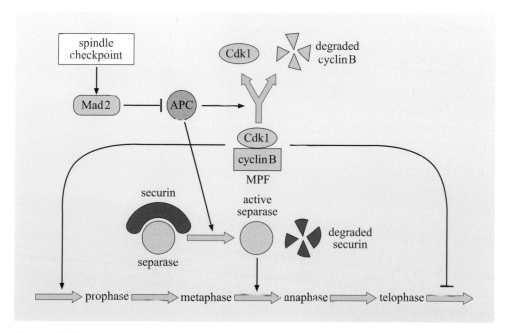

Figure 8.30   The anaphase promoting complex (APC) and the control of the metaphase/anaphase transition. Mad2 is one of a number of proteins identified by genetic screens for mutants that do not arrest mitosis (<u>m</u>itosis <u>a</u>rrest <u>d</u>eficient) in response to specific drug treatments. Mad2 is activated by unattached kinetochores (which signal that metaphase has not yet been completed) and inactivates APC. The central role of APC is clear: not only does it degrade securin, resulting in the activation of separase, which in turn terminates the cohesion of sister chromatids (as shown in more detail in Figure 8.17), but it also acts to degrade cyclin B, and therefore eliminates MPF activity. Inhibitors of APC therefore inhibit both the inactivation of MPF and chromosome separation.

Summary of Section 8.3

1   The cell cycle is regulated through a sequential formation of a series of cyclin–Cdk complexes, each containing a cyclin and a cyclin-dependent kinase. Fine control of this activity is achieved via reversible phosphorylation, protein synthesis and degradation, and the presence of specific Cdk inhibitors, CKIs.

2   Progression through the cell cycle is regulated by a series of checkpoints, which monitor a variety of parameters including cell growth, DNA damage, DNA replication progression and chromosome alignment. Failure to satisfy a checkpoint results in cell cycle stalling.

3   There are three main checkpoints: the G1 checkpoint at G1/S, the G2 checkpoint at G2/M and the spindle checkpoint at the metaphase/anaphase transition.

4   The G1 checkpoint (START in yeast, restriction point in mammals) assesses growth conditions and genome integrity, and commits the cell to proceed into S phase.

5   The G2/M checkpoint assesses whether the genome has been completely replicated, and permits the entry to M phase.

6   The spindle checkpoint restricts cell cycle progression at the end of metaphase, and only allows entry to anaphase once all the chromosomes are correctly aligned on the spindle.

7   The presence of DNA damage results in activation of proteins (Rad53 in yeast, ATM/ATR in mammals) that lead to cell cycle stalling.

8.4 Meiosis

Meiosis is described in S204, Book 2 *Generating Diversity*, Section 3.2.

Meiosis and mitosis share many features.

○   Why are similar molecular mechanisms used in mitosis and meiosis?

■   The two cell divisions share one main feature: the duplication of genomic DNA and subsequent segregation of chromosomes.

It might be expected, therefore, that many of the cellular components used in meiosis are the same as, or similar to, those used for the related cell division, mitosis. This is generally so; however, there are differences between the two processes, and in many cases, these are brought about by the use of different (albeit related) components. The main ways in which meiosis differs from mitosis are:

▶ Meiosis is a reductional process which occurs via two separate chromosome separation events, meiosis I and meiosis II.

▶ Before meiotic division, the chromosomes undergo genetic recombination.

We shall consider here just two cases where similar control systems exist in meiosis and mitosis.

Cohesins and chromosome cohesion in meiosis

An example of a related, but distinct, component is the cohesin complex. While chromosome cohesion in meiosis shares much in common with that in mitosis, some differences are inevitable, given the different segregational processes in the two divisions. To permit genetic crossovers in meiosis I, the cohesion between chromatids must be weakened, but critically, cohesion between the centromeres must be maintained to allow for chromosome segregation to occur accurately. This is reflected in slight differences between the proteins concerned with cohesion in mitosis and meiosis.

A crucial step in the establishment of the spindle is the attachment of microtubules from opposing poles to paired centromeres. The chromosomes congregate at the metaphase plate in response to tension from both poles.

○ What would be the consequences of a loss of centromeric cohesion at metaphase?

● If the centromeres were not paired, two possible consequences might be expected to ensue. Firstly, chromosomes might move prematurely towards the spindle poles, and secondly, segregation might be random.

Further subtle differences appear in the checkpoints controlling meiosis, with MPF playing a central role. Meiotic regulation uses the same or similar pathways to those used in mitosis, but often with subtle differences related to specific meiotic events.

Cdc25 and the regulation of meiotic progression

In many species, oocytes are arrested in prophase of meiosis I, and remain suspended until activation or fertilization. Examples include humans, in which all oocytes are differentiated at puberty, and are arrested in meiosis until maturation. This is believed to underlie the increased incidence of Down syndrome (trisomy 21) as maternal age increases, and is related to the increased likelihood of damage occurring to the stalled meiotic apparatus. Resumption of meiosis from prophase I arrest results from the activation of MPF. Recall that MPF comprises a cyclin and a cyclin-dependent kinase, and that the activity of MPF is controlled by the opposing activities of a phosphatase, Cdc25, and a kinase, Wee1. Mammalian cells possess more than one Cdc25 phosphatase and one of these Cdc25 homologues, Cdc25B, appears to have a specific role in the release of the meiotic prophase I arrest. Female transgenic mice unable to synthesize Cdc25B are sterile and exhibit a failure to complete meiosis.

Summary of Section 8.4

1   Meiosis shares many of the structural and regulatory components used in mitosis, but with subtle differences associated with events specific to meiosis.

2   Protein components involved in chromosome cohesion are subtly different from those utilized in mitosis, allowing events specific to meiosis to take place.

3   Component proteins of meiotic checkpoints are related to, but distinct from, those of mitotic checkpoints. For example, a specific Cdc25 homologue is required for correct progression from prophase I.

8.5 Cell division in prokaryotes

Broadly speaking, the account of mitosis presented in Sections 8.1–8.3 applies to all eukaryotes. In contrast, there are a number of major differences in the processes of cell division in prokaryotes. Firstly, the prokaryotic genome is usually a single circular entity and is not compacted into chromatin as is the case in eukaryotes, although some bacteria do have more than one chromosome. There is no nuclear envelope, and a spindle is not utilized for segregating the newly replicated copies of the genome. Regardless of these differences, prokaryotes face the same challenges in division as do eukaryotes – they must only divide when appropriate, they must ensure accurate genome replication, and the replicated genomes must be equally partitioned between the daughter cells. As a model for prokaryotic cell division, we will consider the bacterium *Escherichia coli*.

Prokaryotic cells divide by binary fission. We can, broadly speaking, think of the *E. coli* cell cycle as having two components: growth and division of the cell, and replication and segregation of the chromosome.

Chromosome replication

The *E. coli* genome is slightly more than 4.5 million base pairs long, and is circular. Replication is initiated at a single origin of replication, known as *oriC*, and proceeds bidirectionally to terminate diametrically opposite the origin. This process is discussed in more detail in Chapter 9. The rate of DNA synthesis in *E. coli* is approximately 920 bp per second, and complete replication takes approximately 40 minutes at 37 °C.

○ To the nearest 5 minutes, how long does it take to replicate a bacterial chromosome of 4 500 000 bp at this rate?

● 4 500 000/920 = 4891.3 seconds = 4891.3/60 minutes = 81.5217 minutes. Divide by 2 (because replication is bidirectional), which gives 40.761 minutes. When rounded to nearest 5 minutes, this equals 40 minutes.

Interestingly, the length of time required to fully replicate the chromosome is relatively insensitive to growth conditions. A further 20 minutes is required to form the septum that splits the two daughter cells.

Cell growth

E. coli cells are rod-shaped, the cell wall being cylindrical in shape with hemispherical caps. As the cell grows, it does so by enlarging the cell wall longitudinally; that is, the cylinder grows longer. Growth continues until a point is reached at which the cell forms a septum and divides into two daughters of equal size. The restriction of growth to cell lengthening is a consequence of the mechanisms of cell wall growth. In contrast to chromosome replication, the rate of cell growth is very much dependent on the nutrients available in the medium. In a poor culture medium, cells may double in mass in perhaps 60 minutes, whereas in a rich culture medium, doubling will take as little as 20 minutes. How, then, does the prokaryotic cell manage its affairs such that cell growth does not outstrip its capacity to replicate the chromosome?

The signal to initiate chromosome replication depends upon cell mass. When the cell reaches the critical mass (called M_i), DNA replication is triggered. If cell growth is such that cell mass reaches four times the critical mass ($4M_i$), then a further round of chromosomal replication will be initiated. This can be observed experimentally if stationary phase cells (i.e. cells grown to saturation in a depleted medium and which are typically half the critical mass, i.e. $0.5M_i$) are transferred to a rich culture medium. As they are now in a medium with unrestricted nutrients, they will double in mass every 20 minutes. Twenty minutes after transfer, the cells will reach M_i and chromosome replication will be initiated. Cell growth will continue at the same rate. By 40 minutes, therefore, $2M_i$ will have been reached, and a second round of chromosome replication will begin, while the first round is only half completed. By 60 minutes, $4M_i$ will be reached, the first round of replication will be complete, and a third will be initiated. The first round of septation begins, and is completed at 80 minutes. Thus, there is a clear relationship between replication and fission. This relationship is shown graphically in Figure 8.31.

○ What cell mass is reached before the cell placed in rich medium completes septation for the first time and what is the mass of each of the daughter cells that results from this division?

● The cell reaches a mass of $8M_i$, and then divides to produce two daughter cells of mass $4M_i$.

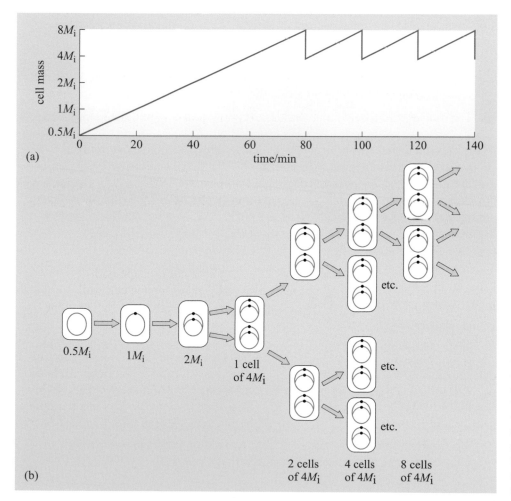

Figure 8.31
The relationship between bacterial cell growth, chromosome replication and binary fission. Stationary phase cells transferred into a rich medium will grow at a rate such that they will initiate replication after 20 minutes. Growth continues, triggering subsequent rounds of replication to be initiated before cell separation via septation has occurred. Note that the cells are not drawn to scale.

49

Chromosome segregation

Prokaryotes such as *E. coli* lack the mitotic apparatus with which eukaryotic cells ensure accurate segregation of chromosomes. The molecular pathways by which prokaryotes achieve precise chromosome segregation is not yet fully understood. Each bacterial chromosome is arranged in the form of a nucleoid. In an unreplicating cell, the nucleoid lies roughly at the centre of the cell, but after chromosome replication, the two copies are located equidistantly from the septation site. At present, it is unknown how the cell moves the nucleoids, although it is clear that *oriC* and the terminus region are both associated with the cell wall, and it is likely that these associations form part of the chromosome segregation machinery.

Binary fission

After the chromosome has been copied and partitioned within the cell, the cell must divide to yield the two daughter cells. Binary fission is brought about by the FtsZ protein, a GTPase related in structure to tubulin. Filaments of FtsZ assemble a ring structure at the point in the mother cell where fission is to occur, and are responsible for the accumulation of the components necessary for the ingrowth of the cell wall and cell separation. FtsZ is crucial; should a cell lack FtsZ, none of the subsequent events leading to binary fission will occur. A second protein called FtsA, which is similar to eukaryotic actins, associates with the FtsZ ring. Another protein, ZipA, is a transmembrane protein that interacts with FtsZ, and is thought to anchor the ring to the membrane. There are further proteins that are required for the formation and function of the cytoplasmic ring. Mutation of the genes encoding these proteins causes cytoplasmic ring defects.

○ What do you think would be the consequence for a bacterial cell of a mutation in the gene that encodes the FtsZ protein?

● The mutant cells would fail to divide, and instead would form elongated filaments.

It is interesting to note that in *Arabidopsis thaliana* the nuclear genome contains two genes that encode homologues of the prokaryotic cell division protein FtsZ. These proteins are required for the binary fission of chloroplasts (Section 8.2.7). One of them is localized to the stromal face, the other to the cytosolic face of the chloroplast double membrane. It may be speculated that these proteins represent important components of the inner and outer plastid dividing ring respectively. Many organelle proteins, including FtsZ, are encoded in the nuclear genome; it is thought that the transfer of such genes has occurred since the symbiotic uptake of mitochondria and chloroplasts into early cells.

Summary of Section 8.5

1   Prokaryotes such as *E. coli* divide by binary fission. While prokaryotes face the same challenges in cell division as do eukaryotes, they carry out cell division differently.

2   The rate of cell growth and division is determined by the availability of nutrients in the medium.

3   The bacterial genome is circular and is replicated bidirectionally from the replication origin. In the case of *E. coli*, replication takes approximately 40 minutes. The chromosome is attached to the cell wall.

4   The signal to initiate bacterial DNA replication derives from the mass of the cell.

Learning outcomes for Chapter 8

When you have studied this chapter, you should be able to:

8.1 Define and use each of the terms printed in **bold** in the text.

8.2 Explain how cellular cytoskeletal elements function in cell division.

8.3 Describe how the stages of the cell cycle and cell cycle checkpoints are controlled at a biochemical level.

8.4 Outline the biological consequences of errors in the cell cycle.

8.5 Explain the degree of evolutionary conservation of components of the cell cycle machinery and the relevance of studies in simple organisms to the understanding of cell cycle processes in higher organisms.

8.6 Describe the similarities and differences between mitosis and meiosis.

8.7 Describe how prokaryotic cells divide and the similarities and differences with eukaryotes.

8.8 Explain the techniques described and their application in studying the cell cycle.

Questions for Chapter 8

Question 8.1

What is the most visually obvious cytoskeletal element in mitosis, and of what is it composed? Which organelle is instrumental in establishing this structure?

Question 8.2

What is a cell cycle checkpoint and why are checkpoints important?

Question 8.3

Name the two principal components of the cell cycle checkpoint machinery. What biochemical activity do they have when complexed?

Question 8.4

Colchicine is a drug that inhibits microtubule polymerization. Consider a culture of mammalian cells and describe the likely consequences on the cell cycle of inhibiting microtubule assembly.

Question 8.5

Which organelle is the microtubule organizing centre (MTOC) in a typical animal cell? What are the MTOCs in yeast cells?

Question 8.6

What is START in the yeast cell cycle and what is its counterpart in mammalian cells?

Question 8.7

Describe the three classes of spindle microtubules.

Question 8.8

Outline the main characteristics of anaphase A and anaphase B.

Question 8.9

How does cytokinesis differ between animal and plant cells? Why do animal and plant cells undergo cytokinesis differently?

Question 8.10

What triggers DNA replication in the *E. coli* cell cycle?

Further sources

Alberts, B., Johnson, A., Lewis, J., Raff, M., Roberts, K. and Walter, P. (2002) *The Molecular Biology of the Cell* (4th edn), Garland Science, New York.

Murray, A. and Hunt, T. (1993) *The Cell Cycle*, OUP, Oxford.

Novák, B., Sible, J. C. and Tyson, J. J. (2002) Checkpoints in the Cell Cycle, in *Nature Encyclopedia of Life Sciences*, London: Nature Publishing Group.

9 DNA REPLICATION AND REPAIR

9.1 Introduction

In this chapter, we will be exploring the molecular basis of DNA replication, the process by which organisms copy their genomes. As DNA is the common genetic storage system used in all free-living life forms on Earth, it is perhaps not surprising that the basic mechanics of the replication process and many of the protein components are evolutionarily highly conserved. As you saw in Chapter 8, in preparation for cell division, the genome is first copied, which means that each daughter cell will receive a complete set of the parental DNA. For some organisms, this is a large amount of DNA. Once DNA replication has been initiated, the cell is committed to fully replicating its genome, but for obvious reasons, division cannot occur until full replication has been achieved. The cell controls and regulates the process very tightly by means of several built-in cell cycle checkpoints, as described in Chapter 8.

In this chapter, we will examine how replication is controlled through initiation at specific sites, or origins, and how the replication machinery is intimately associated with components of DNA repair to ensure that when errors of DNA synthesis occur or when DNA damage is detected or encountered by various cellular machineries, it is dealt with appropriately. We will also examine the temporal nature of replication at the level of the whole genome by studying patterns of replication in both yeast and *Drosophila*. These studies combine various investigative approaches that exploit the availability of complete genome sequences of several organisms and reveal contrasting relationships between replication and gene expression.

All replicative DNA synthesis is semiconservative; that is, the resultant two daughter helices consist of one old template strand and one newly synthesized strand. DNA synthesis always occurs in one direction, and because the two strands within the double helix run in opposite orientation, the precise mechanisms by which each strand is copied are different, a process we will examine in some detail. As you saw in Chapter 5, eukaryotic genomic DNA is associated with many different chromatin proteins, which can exist in different states along a chromosome, and these proteins serve to regulate genes. This **epigenetic** information must also be copied, so that the recipient daughter cells receive appropriately regulated and packaged regions of the genome. The DNA in cells is constantly being subjected to damaging agents or processes, and in this chapter we will be examining how various repair pathways detect and rectify base modification and misincorporation, as well as strand breaks.

In most cases, what we know or infer about replication in the mammalian cell is based upon what we have learnt through many years of study of bacterial, yeast and viral DNA replication. In these simpler systems, it has obviously been easier to study DNA replication and repair, sometimes in exquisite detail, because of the power of their genetics or through the use of *in vitro* reconstruction experiments. In this chapter, we will utilize what is known from various model systems to illustrate how replication and repair occur and what we can learn about these processes in the eukaryotic cell.

9.2 Initiation of DNA replication

Replicative DNA synthesis is initiated from specific sites along a chromosome, termed **replication origins**, and the regions of the genome copied from forks originating at any particular origin are called **replicons**. In *E. coli*, all genomic replication is initiated from a single site, whereas in other organisms there can be many thousands of replication origins. The most likely reason for having such defined starting points for synthesis is that DNA replication during S phase is a major commitment for a cell; one cycle must be precisely initiated and controlled prior to cell division and the initiation at specific sites presumably allows for easier and more regulatable replication.

☐ What eukaryotic cell cycle checkpoints are in place that precede S phase?

◼ We described two such checkpoints in Chapter 8. The first is START (yeast) or restriction point (mammalian cells), in which the cell assesses the nutritional conditions. The second is the G1 DNA damage checkpoint, which functions via the ATM and p53 proteins (Section 8.3.5).

Here we will consider the properties of replication origins by examining what is known about initiation and its regulation in both bacteria and eukaryotes.

9.2.1 Properties of replication origins in different organisms

The origin of replication in *E. coli* is well characterized. By contrast, amongst eukaryotes, with the exception of yeasts, only a small number of replication origins have been analysed in detail. It is unclear whether the sites that have been analysed in human, hamster and *Drosophila* are typical structures for these organisms. We shall start by discussing what is known about replication origins in *E. coli* and *S. cerevisiae*.

As we saw in Chapter 8, the *E. coli* genome of over 4 Mb of DNA is replicated from a single origin, termed *oriC*. The *E. coli* genome can be considered as one single replicon, in which replication proceeds in both directions from the *oriC* site at a synthesis rate of almost 920 bp per second, completing the replication of the entire genome in just over 40 minutes. The replication origin itself is 240 bp in length and contains several repetitive sequences rich in A and T bases that are bound by an initiator protein called dnaA, as shown schematically in Figure 9.1. The binding of dnaA protein to the origin leads to the bending of the helical backbone, untwisting of the local helix and disruption of the local base-pairing. A **DNA helicase** protein, called dnaB, is subsequently recruited and proceeds to unwind the flanking helix in a 5′ to 3′ direction in an ATP-dependent manner.

Illustrated within this example are two properties of replication origins that are believed to be important. The first is the untwisting of the helical structure of DNA and the second is the localized breaking of the hydrogen bonding between paired bases. This allows further localized untwisting and melting of the helix from this single point.

☐ Can you suggest the properties of the DNA at *oriC* that facilitate this process?

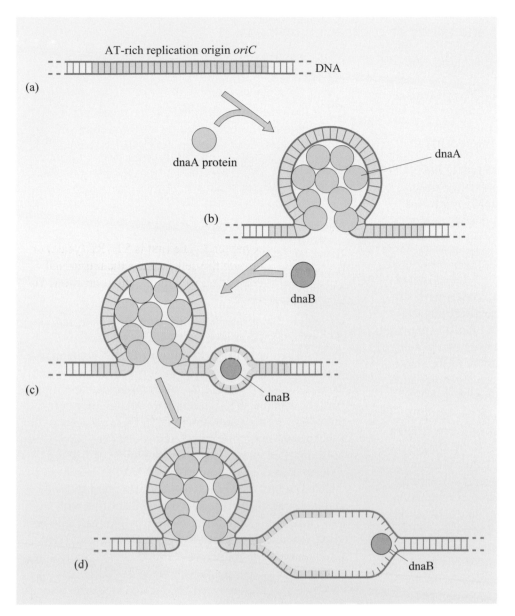

Figure 9.1   Events during the initiation of genomic replication at the single *E. coli* chromosomal replication origin *oriC*. (a) *oriC* contains AT-rich regions. (b) Binding of initiator protein dnaA to the replication origin leads to bending and local untwisting of the helix, whereupon (c) the DNA helicase dnaB binds, leading to unwinding and opening of the replication origin (d).

● The process is facilitated by the presence of AT-rich DNA regions. Recall from Chapter 5 that AT-rich regions have lower base stacking energies (see Table 5.2, Section 5.2.2) and the bases are paired by only two hydrogen bonds. The easier unwinding of the helix is an essential element in initiation of replication by origin proteins.

Several different laboratory techniques have been developed to identify replication origins and to study replicating DNA, as outlined in Box 9.1, and we shall see examples of their application throughout this chapter.

Box 9.1   Identification and study of replication origins

Replication origins can be identified using several experimental techniques that either measure or detect replication intermediates or measure their functional activity.

The incorporation of labelled nucleotides

By allowing DNA to undergo replication in the presence of modified nucleotides, it is possible to either directly visualize or isolate newly replicated DNA. Three examples of this approach are described here.

The first example is a classical experiment performed in 1957 by Meselson and Stahl, which demonstrated that DNA replication is indeed semiconservative, as predicted from the B-form helical structure suggested by Crick and Watson. Meselson and Stahl's experiment is summarized in Figure 9.2. Bacteria grown in culture medium in which all nitrogen atoms are of the stable isotope ^{15}N ('heavy' medium) possess DNA in which the nitrogen atoms in the bases are ^{15}N. This DNA is denser than normal DNA (in which the nitrogen atoms are ^{14}N) and is known as 'heavy' DNA. Heavy DNA can be separated from normal 'light' DNA by centrifugation. Meselson and Stahl cultured bacteria in heavy medium, and then transferred the culture to normal, 'light' medium, and one round of replication was allowed to occur. While the template DNA is of the heavy form, newly incorporated bases are of the light form. They then isolated the newly replicated DNA using a centrifugation technique that would separate the resulting duplex DNA according to its density. They found that all newly replicated DNA had a density intermediate between fully heavy and fully light densities (i.e. HL) and none was HH or LL. The conclusion from these observations is that newly replicated daughter DNA duplexes are hybrids of one old and one new strand.

- ⬜ If the experiment described in the preceding paragraph was continued for a second round of replication, which density forms of DNA would you expect, and in what proportions?

- ⬛ HL and LL, in equal proportions.

Microscopic assays

Using microscopy it is possible to directly visualize sites of replication initiation. This approach utilizes a technique called **pulsed labelling**, in which cells undergoing replication are briefly exposed to a nucleotide that is labelled with some form of tracer (Figure 9.3a). This pulse of labelled nucleotide results in short stretches of the chromosomal DNA containing the modified nucleotide. Labelling is usually performed using a nucleoside analogue called bromodeoxyuridine (BrdU), which is incorporated into DNA in place of thymidine. In the example shown in Figure 9.3b, a synchronous culture of *S. cerevisiae* cells has been pulse-labelled with BrdU at the beginning of S phase so as to detect replication origins. DNA has then been isolated and its fibres stretched out on a glass slide and the areas of BrdU incorporation identified with an anti-BrdU antibody. The replication origins can then be visualized and their relative spacing determined. Here, four areas are stained across a 200 kb region, indicating the presence of four active origins in this particular chromosomal region. Newly replicated DNA can also be analysed using PCR after precipitating of DNA fragments containing BrdU with an anti-BrdU antibody (Figure 9.3c).

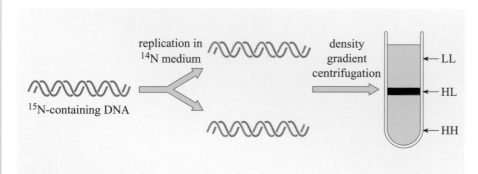

Figure 9.2
Schematic representation of the Meselson and Stahl's classical experiment in which 'heavy' and 'light' nucleotide incorporation into replicating DNA was used to demonstrate that DNA replication is semiconservative.

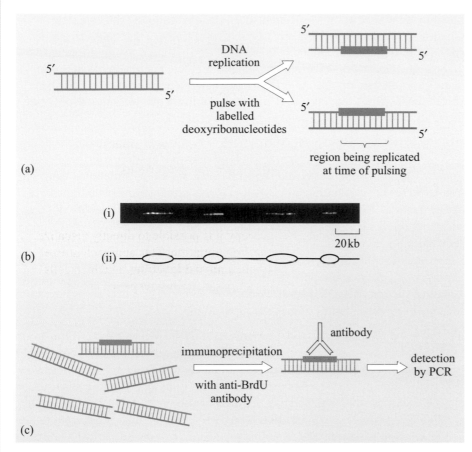

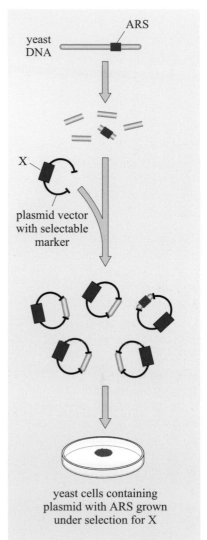

Figure 9.3 Pulsed labelling of newly replicated DNA with bromodeoxyuridine (BrdU). Regions of active replication are frequently detected by incorporation of the nucleoside analogue BrdU. (a) A region of DNA is pulse-labelled, resulting in a short stretch of BrdU-containing DNA. This is detected by applying a fluorescently labelled antibody directed towards BrdU onto the extended chromosomal DNA (b). In (i) four sites of fluorescence are detected on this single DNA fibre, which are interpreted as four origins of replication (ii). The second method of detection commonly used in mammalian cell studies involves immunoprecipitation of BrdU-containing DNA, followed by PCR detection (c).

Figure 9.4 The detection of replication origins in yeast using a functional assay. Chromosomal DNA from yeast is fragmented into small segments and cloned into a circular plasmid DNA vector that carries a selectable marker gene (X). This library of DNA fragments is introduced into yeast cells. A colony of many millions of cells will only grow from single cells that received a plasmid carrying DNA elements that can support plasmid DNA (and hence selectable marker) replication. These cells will carry plasmids that contain an ARS element.

Functional assays

Sequences capable of supporting replication in the yeast *S. cerevisiae* can also be identified using a functional assay; that is, testing for their ability to permit a segment of DNA to undergo replication. Random segments of the yeast genome are cloned in a circular plasmid DNA vector carrying a selectable marker, and introduced into yeast cells. Plasmids that have had a segment of DNA inserted into them that can support the initiation of DNA replication are selected as they allow the yeast cells to grow under selection. In these cases, the DNA segments are called **ARS** (<u>a</u>utonomously <u>r</u>eplicating <u>s</u>equence) **elements** and they allow the DNAs to remain stable within the cells (Figure 9.4).

In eukaryotes, which generally have larger genomes than those found in *E. coli*, replication is initiated at many different sites, thereby allowing the complete replication of the genome within a reasonable time frame. Thus, these larger genomes are divided into multiple replicons. As we shall discuss later, this multiplicity of replicons provides an opportunity to regionally regulate genome replication. An obvious question that arises from this observation is whether these origins share some consensus DNA sequence or structure in common that might provide a clue as to their function.

One of the best-studied organisms with regard to replication is that of the budding yeast *S. cerevisiae*. In this organism, it has been possible to study most replication origins by both functional assay and sequence analysis. Using functional assays to detect ARS elements, as outlined in Box 9.1, it was possible to isolate regions of the yeast genome that allow replication to be initiated. Sequence analysis of these elements revealed a consensus sequence rich in A and T bases. However, the presence of sequences that are functional as ARS elements in yeast does not necessarily mean that they are all replication origins in the yeast chromosome; rather, replication origin use appears to depend upon other factors, which most likely include local or regional chromatin structure. We will discuss chromosomal replication origins further when we examine real-time studies of genome replication.

Studies of yeast ARS elements did, however, lead to the identification of the group of proteins that bind to replication origins, called the origin recognition complex. ORC was introduced in Chapter 8 and we will consider its role in replication in more detail in the following section. For now, you should note that similar complexes exist in other eukaryotes. A typical budding yeast replication origin and the site for ORC binding are shown in Figure 9.5a. ORC binds at a site immediately adjacent to the site of replication initiation. The *S. pombe* replication origin and typical examples of origins from *Drosophila*, human and hamster are shown for comparison (Figure 9.5b and c). Sites for ORC binding have been identified in both *S. pombe* and *Drosophila*. For mammalian cells, no consensus site for a replication origin has been identified; some origins have been found to be highly localized, whereas others have only been localized to regions of tens of kilobases of DNA and no similar assay to the yeast ARS assay exists for such cells. In the case of the human β-globin gene, a well defined origin has been identified in a 1kb region from which replication of the entire β-globin complex is initiated. In contrast, replication of the hamster DHFR (dihydrofolate reductase) gene is known to be initiated at several possible sites that span tens of kilobases.

We still have limited understanding of what factors determine the choice and use of any particular region of a chromosome as a replication origin. Site-specific factors play a role in yeast where a consensus DNA sequence is found. It is possible that sequence-specific factors also exist in other eukaryotes, although none has yet been identified. What is known is that most active origins are found in intergenic regions, i.e. regions that are not within transcription units. This fact could indicate that the binding of ORC to DNA (which remains bound throughout the cell cycle) is incompatible with the passage of RNA polymerase. Also known to be important is the local chromatin structure; alteration in the positioning of nucleosomes near an origin can disrupt its function. Several studies in human cells have identified ORC-interacting proteins known to be histone acetyltransferases, which modify local chromatin structure.

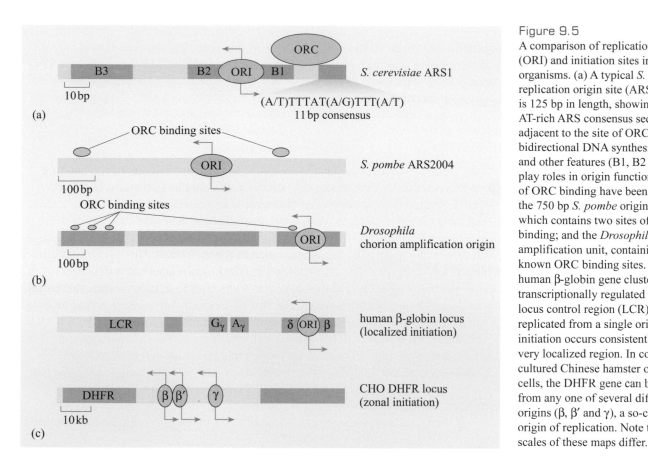

Figure 9.5
A comparison of replication origins (ORI) and initiation sites in various organisms. (a) A typical *S. cerevisiae* replication origin site (ARS1), which is 125 bp in length, showing the AT-rich ARS consensus sequence, adjacent to the site of ORC binding, the bidirectional DNA synthesis (arrows) and other features (B1, B2 and B3) that play roles in origin function. (b) Sites of ORC binding have been identified in the 750 bp *S. pombe* origin ARS2004, which contains two sites of ORC binding; and the *Drosophila* chorion amplification unit, containing four known ORC binding sites. (c) The human β-globin gene cluster is transcriptionally regulated from the locus control region (LCR) and is replicated from a single origin where initiation occurs consistently in a very localized region. In contrast, in cultured Chinese hamster ovary (CHO) cells, the DHFR gene can be replicated from any one of several different origins (β, β' and γ), a so-called zonal origin of replication. Note that the scales of these maps differ.

How might the factors just described exert effects upon ORC binding or the use of any particular region of DNA as a site of replication initiation?

These factors could influence replication activity in several different ways. The positioning of a nucleosome could influence the recognition of specific DNA sequences through blocking access to the major groove. The compaction of local chromatin structure could act in similar manner across larger regions. As replication origins are sites of local DNA untwisting and base unpairing, regions with high positive supercoiling, such as occur within transcriptionally active regions, might also prove unsuitable as origins.

Once bound at an active replication origin, the role of ORC in initiation and its interactions with the cell cycle machinery are better understood.

9.2.2 Yeast ORC interacts with cell cycle components to prevent re-initiation

Although there are many origins of replication along a typical eukaryotic chromosome, they allow the initiation of replication at each site only once per cell cycle. Obviously, an error in initiation frequency could be disastrous for the cell, as it could lead to duplication of genetic material in the daughter cells or damage to whole chromosomes. Studies in *S. cerevisiae* have shown that the initiation of synthesis at each replication origin is controlled by components of the cell cycle machinery, as was discussed in Chapter 8.

A complex of proteins bind to an origin in the G1 phase of the cell cycle to form what is called a **pre-replication complex**. Only origins with this complex bound to them will form active replication origins at the next round of DNA synthesis (Figure 9.6). Amongst this complex of proteins is the ORC. Together this complex acts as a loading system for components of the DNA replication machinery. The components of this pre-replication complex also interact with the cell cycle machinery to trigger the start of DNA synthesis.

○ Can you recall how DNA synthesis is triggered by the cell cycle machinery?

● At the start of S phase, an S phase cyclin–Cdk complex phosphorylates both ORC and the Cdc6 protein. The dissociation of phosphorylated Cdc6 from the complex triggers DNA synthesis (Section 8.3.6, Figure 8.28).

DNA synthesis commences only from replication origins that are bound by pre-replication complexes. ORC assembles on the origins of the two new daughter strands immediately after synthesis and, in doing so, plays a major role in preventing the re-initiation of replication from these two new origins while the present round of DNA synthesis is underway. Once initiation has occurred, although ORC remains bound to the origin, it is still phosphorylated, which prevents other components of the pre-replication complex from binding. During late M phase, cell cycle components dephosphorylate ORC and allow the formation of new pre-replication complexes at those origins that have ORC bound to them. This process is completed during G1 in the two daughter cells; thus each origin is 'set' for replication. In this way, ORC status is used to ensure that only one round of DNA synthesis is initiated from each origin.

The functional role of the ORC complex in replication origin activity has been conserved across eukaryotes, and many ORC-related proteins have been identified in organisms ranging from yeast, to plants to humans; however, the level of amino acid conservation of many of the individual proteins is low.

Figure 9.6
The role of ORC in the regulation of replication initiation. In G1, replication origins are bound by both the pre-replication complex and the Cdc6 protein. At the start of S phase, phosphorylation of Cdc6 and ORC by S phase Cdks triggers release of the phosphorylated Cdc6 and the start of DNA synthesis. ORC remains bound to the origin in its phosphorylated state, but new pre-replication complexes are prevented from binding until late M phase, after ORC dephosphorylation.

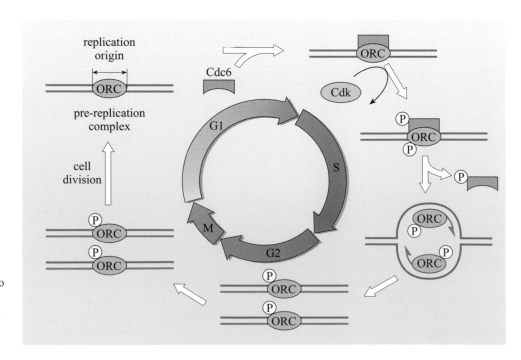

9.2.3 The dynamics of replication across the eukaryotic genome

As a typical eukaryotic genome is large, multiple origins of replication are required to ensure that the entire genome is duplicated before mitotic cell division. Based upon estimates of the rate of DNA polymerization, it is probable that there are around 50 000 origins in a typical mammalian genome. Each of these origins will nucleate DNA synthesis at the beginning of S phase, with synthesis occurring at replication forks that extend to complete the copying of between 50 and 250 kb of the flanking genomic DNA in each replicon. However, the rate of polymerization – only 30–40 bases per second – is much slower than that in *E. coli*. This rate would suggest that the average mammalian genome could be replicated in about 1 hour, but in fact S phase takes between 6 and 8 hours to complete, on average, in mammalian cells. One explanation for this unexpectedly long S phase is that not all regions of the genome are replicated at the same time or have the same speed of fork progression, with some replicons being initiated earlier than others in the cell cycle and with only about 1000 forks actively replicating at any one time during S phase. In addition, DNA repair processes, chromatin breakdown and its reassembly have to accompany DNA synthesis in eukaryotic cells, making the whole process much lengthier.

Until recently, our ability to analyse the dynamics of replication across the entire genome had been limited to microscopic approaches (Box 9.1). The availability of complete genome sequences has, however, allowed us to get a detailed glimpse of how dynamic replication is across a genome as a whole during a single cell cycle. We will examine two such studies: those of *S. cerevisiae* and *Drosophila*.

Temporal replication across the yeast genome

The complete analysis of replication across the entire genome of an organism during a single cell cycle requires a combination of several investigative techniques. Using a combination of DNA pulsed labelling, microarray hybridizations (Box 5.2) and ChIp studies (Chapter 5, Box 5.3), it has been possible to construct dynamic replication profiles of the entire *S. cerevisiae* genome. One approach, shown in Figure 9.7, exploits a strategy similar to that used originally by Meselson and Stahl (Box 9.1) to incorporate 'heavy' isotopes of carbon and nitrogen (^{13}C and ^{15}N respectively) into the entire genome of yeast cells. The culture is then synchronized; that is, the cells are treated so that they are all held stationary in G1. Then, before the start of S phase, the yeast are transferred to growth medium that contains only 'light' components (i.e. ^{12}C and ^{14}N), and released from the cell cycle block. The cells are then sampled at various time points through S phase, and their DNA isolated and cleaved with enzymes to generate small fragments. These fragments are separated by centrifugation according to their density.

Two types of genomic DNA fragment are isolated from the gradient, heavy–heavy (HH) and heavy–light (HL), which represent unreplicated and newly replicated DNA respectively.

☐ In which density fractions will genomic DNA from segment B appear, in samples collected at the second and third time points?

■ At the second time point, genomic DNA from segment B will be in the unreplicated, HH fraction, whereas at the third point it will be in the replicated, HL fraction.

Figure 9.7
Replication analysis of the entire yeast genome using a combination of Meselson–Stahl pulsed labelling and microarrays. (a) Synchronized yeast cells growing in 'heavy' medium are transferred to 'light' medium at the start of S phase. Replication is then allowed to proceed through the entire genome. Samples are collected at four time points. (b) Bidirectional synthesis in one hypothetical region of a chromosome, through DNA segments A–E, which contains two replication origins (black) is shown at four time points: before S phase, after replication, and at two intermediate times. Newly synthesized DNA is shown in purple. (c) DNA is then isolated from each sample, the DNA cut into small pieces and these fragments separated according to their density. (d) Newly replicated (heavy–light, HL) and unreplicated (heavy–heavy, HH) DNA is then labelled with a fluorescent tag and used as a hybridization probe against whole yeast genome microarrays, shown here schematically. (Modified from Raghuraman *et al.*, 2001)

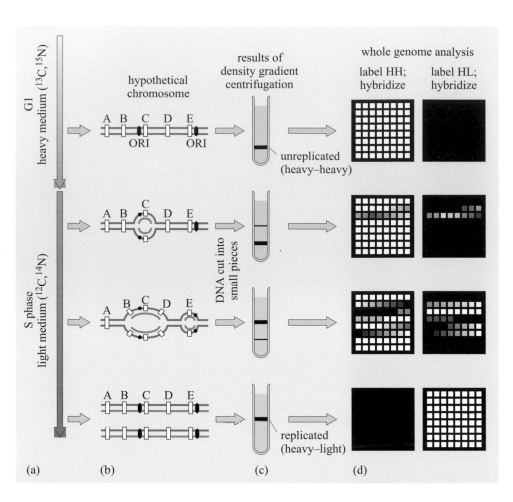

Each of these genomic DNAs is then labelled with a fluorescent marker and used as a hybridization probe to microarrays that contain DNAs spotted onto a glass slide, spots that represent the entire yeast genome. The amount of hybridization at any one spot on the microarray, an example of which is shown in Figure 9.7, will be directly proportional to the amount of DNA replicated at the particular time point the sample was collected, at that genomic location. By comparing which segment is replicated at which time point, it is possible to determine the order in which replication origins commenced replication. For example, in Figure 9.7, the replication origin adjacent to segment E initiates DNA synthesis after the origin adjacent to segment C.

○ Consider the hypothetical chromosome shown in Figure 9.7b. At the second time point shown, how many copies of segment C DNA will be present in a single yeast cell compared to DNA from segment E?

● At the second time point, replication in a single cell will have proceeded through the region of DNA containing segment C but segment E will still be unreplicated. There will therefore be two copies of segment C and one copy of segment E per cell.

○ What will be the relative amounts of DNA containing segments C and E at the third time point?

● By the third time point, segment E will have also been replicated, so there will be the same amount of segment E DNA as segment C DNA.

In this example, segment A is the last segment to be replicated.

By sampling cells throughout the entire length of S phase and by analysing an entire chromosome with many hundreds of markers using this approach, it is possible to say which DNA segment along any chromosome has been replicated at any particular time. By measuring when each DNA segment is first replicated relative to the start of S phase, it is possible to draw a 'replication map' of the entire chromosome. An example of such a map is shown in Figure 9.8 for yeast chromosome VI, which is 255 kb in length.

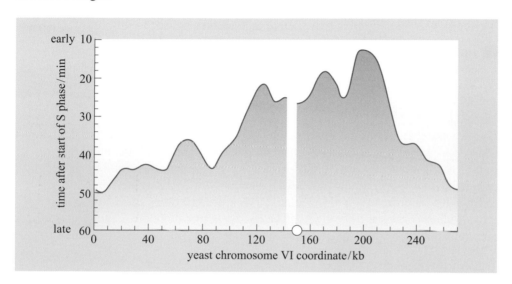

Figure 9.8
The replication map of yeast chromosome VI. The time of replication for segments on chromosome VI is shown in minutes after the start of S phase (vertical axis), relative to the position along the chromosome in kilobases of DNA (horizontal axis). Origins of replication appear as peaks on the graph. The analysis is incomplete around the region of the centromere (open circle on horizontal axis). (Based upon data presented by Raghuraman *et al.*, 2001)

We can utilize replication maps to tell us about the temporal order of replication across this chromosome.

○ Look at Figure 9.8. How much of chromosome VI has been replicated at 10 minutes after the start of S phase?

● None; that is, there are no peaks that reach the 10-minute time point on the graph.

○ Consider the situation at 22 minutes after the start of S phase. How many origins of replication have initiated DNA synthesis, in which regions of chromosome VI do they occur and what is the order in which they started?

● At the 22-minute point, there are three regions that have been replicated: (1) 122–130 kb, (2) 160–180 kb and (3) 190–215 kb. Replication is initiated from these three origins in the order: (3), (2), (1). (This can be determined by placing a ruler at the 22-minute point and noting the dissection with the replication graph. Peaks higher up the graph represent earlier origins.)

○ Can you suggest what the troughs on the graph represent?

● The troughs represent the position at which two replication forks moving in opposite directions meet. Replication will terminate at this point.

Overall, replication of the entire yeast genome takes almost 60 minutes, with replication forks being initiated as late as 45 minutes into S phase (e.g. in the region of 20 kb on Figure 9.8). The rate at which replication forks progress through different regions of the genome also differs, by over 10-fold, ranging from 1000 bp per minute to over 10 000 bp per minute.

The approach outlined above represents a visualization of replication based upon DNA duplication. These maps localize origins to regions relatively precisely, as positions that correspond to peaks on the graph, but a complementary approach has been exploited to isolate regions of a yeast chromosome that are active origins of replication. This approach utilizes chromatin immunoprecipitation (ChIp, Box 5.3).

○ Can you suggest which protein complex could be targeted with suitable antibodies for ChIp to identify active replication origins?

■ Antibodies against proteins in the ORC. Remember that this complex stays associated with the genomic DNA throughout the cell cycle. DNA segments bound by ORC will therefore represent active replication origins, at least those that were used in the last round of replication.

By comparing the results of the dynamic study outlined earlier with those from the ChIp approach, it is possible to estimate the number of active replication origins in the yeast genome as approximately 350. Most of the sites identified by these two methods also correspond to the ARS elements we discussed earlier. As three independent approaches – ARS cloning, DNA pulsed labelling and ChIp against ORC – identify the same sites, we can be confident that these are genuine sites of chromosomal replication initiation.

Temporal replication across the Drosophila *genome*

A similar approach has been taken to analyse the *Drosophila* genome, which is 10 times the size of that of yeast. Using a pulsed-labelling approach, *Drosophila* cells growing *in vitro* were transiently labelled with BrdU. Cells in early and late S phase were separated from each other by fluorescence-activated cell sorting (FACS, Box 9.2). From each of these cell pools, the newly replicated DNA was isolated using an antibody directed against BrdU. Finally, this DNA was labelled with a fluorescent marker and used as a hybridization probe against *Drosophila* whole genome microarrays. This procedure identifies all areas of the genome that are being replicated within the early and late time points, and a replication profile for each chromosome can be created. An example of how pulsed labelling has been used to create the replication profile of a *Drosophila* chromosome is shown in Figure 9.9a, which represents hybridization to 386 microarray DNA spots from genes distributed evenly along an 8000 kb segment of the *Drosophila* chromosome 2L. To confirm replication timing, several regions were also analysed by PCR, as shown in Figure 9.9b. For example, for gene CG3436, the amount of hybridization to the PCR product is high in the early (E) fraction and low in the late (L) fraction, indicating that CG3436 was replicated early in S phase. In contrast, CG2955 has the opposite profile, indicating late replication. As can be seen, the pattern of replication across the chromosome varies dramatically and, as with the yeast example discussed earlier, it is possible to delineate early replicating and late replicating regions quite clearly.

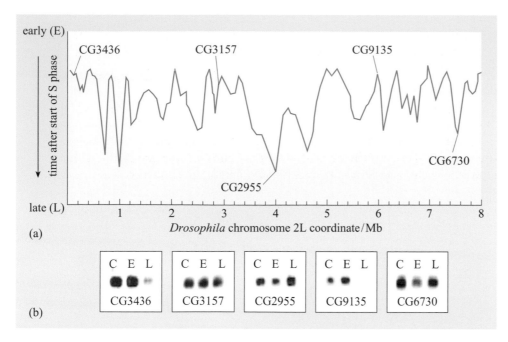

Figure 9.9
(a) Replication profile of a segment of *Drosophila* chromosome 2L that is proximal to the telomere. This graph was made by comparing the ratio of early to late replicating DNA; thus peaks represent early replicating DNA and troughs are late replicating DNA. The positions of the five genes shown as examples in (b) are indicated. (b) Examples of the PCR detection of five genes in pulse-labelled early (E) and late (L) DNA fractions, compared to control (C) DNA made from non-FAC-sorted cells, visualized after electrophoresis and Southern blot detection. These panels represent quantitative Southern blots of PCR products for each of the genes, with a darker signal indicating more DNA; thus the amounts of each gene's DNA can be estimated relatively accurately. (Based upon the study of Schubeler *et al.*, 2002)

When the pattern of replication profiles was compared to transcription within these cultured *Drosophila* cells, it became apparent that a strong correlation exists between genes that replicate early and those that are actively transcribed.

Box 9.2   Analysing replication profiles in cultured cells

Fluorescence-activated cell sorting (FACS) is an automated process whereby cells can be analysed and sorted according to the level of fluorescence they show in response to excitation by a laser at a particular wavelength. This technique can be exploited in many ways. For example, a fluorescent tag can be added to a specific antibody and the cells sorted according to the amount of expression of the protein carrying the epitope recognized by that antibody.

In order to study the cell cycle and DNA replication, a dye that fluoresces when it intercalates into duplex DNA is used, similar to ethidium bromide. In most cases, the dye used is propidium iodide. Using this approach, it is possible to analyse a population of cells that have been growing in culture. The cells will have an increasing level of fluorescence as they proceed through the cell cycle and increase their DNA content from G1 through S and into G2 phase. A typical example of this type of analysis is shown in Figure 9.10a for a population of asynchronously growing cells in which cells at all stages of the cell cycle are present, where peak height reflects the relative proportion of cells in each phase.

○ What is the difference in DNA content between cells in G2 and those in G1?

● G2 cells contain a duplicated genome and therefore have twice the DNA content of G1 cells.

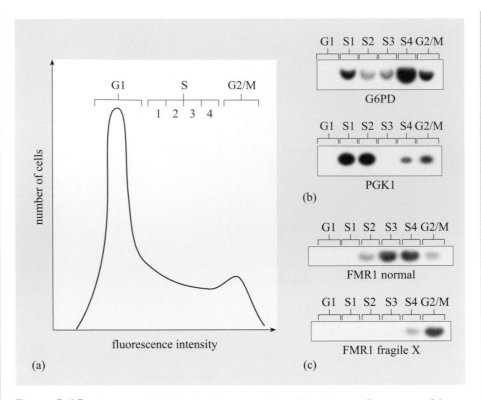

Figure 9.10   The use of FACS to isolate mammalian cells at intermediate stages of the cell cycle. (a) A typical replicative FACS profile of asynchronously growing human cells stained with the DNA dye propidium iodide, in relation to their stage in the cell cycle. The lowest level of fluorescence is in G1 cells. As DNA is synthesized in S phase, the fluoresence level increases (from S1–S4), reaching a peak as cells accumulate in G2. (b) and (c) show the results of PCR analysis of BrdU pulse-labelled DNA isolated using an anti-BrdU antibody after electrophoresis and Southern blot detection. (b) Genes from the human X chromosome (G6PD and PGK1) are analysed in a human female cell line in G1, S1–S4 and G2/M phases. In each case, the active X chromosome is replicated in early S phase, the inactivated X chromosome later. (Adapted from Hansen *et al.*, 1996) (c) Analysis of human FMR1 gene replication in normal (top) and fragile X (bottom) male cells. In normal cells, the FMR1 gene is replicated in late S phase, whereas in fragile X cells its replication profile is shifted into G2/M. (Adapted from Hansen *et al.*, 1997)

A population of asynchronously growing cells can be pulse-labelled with BrdU (as described in Box 9.1) and samples of cells collected from the different portions of the cell cycle by FACS according to the intensity of fluorescence with propidium iodide. This process allows cells to be collected from many subdivisions of the cell cycle, including four segments of S phase, numbered S1 to S4. When DNA is isolated from these cell fractions, an anti-BrdU antibody can be used to isolate newly replicated DNA, which can be quantified easily by PCR analysis. An example of quantitative PCR detection is shown in Figure 9.10b, which shows analysis of several X chromosome DNA markers in a female human cell line. In this case, it is clear that half the DNA is replicating early and the rest late, reflecting the presence of one active and one inactive X chromosome. One particular X-linked human disease is associated with an alteration in the replication profile of a gene, FMR1 (fragile X mental retardation), which becomes very late replicating, as is shown in Figure 9.10c. This shift is associated with transcriptional silencing and extensive localized histone tail deacetylation.

Although it has not yet been possible to analyse a mammalian genome with the accuracy achieved with yeast and *Drosophila*, it has been known for many years that some regions are replicated earlier than others. At a global level, the differential between early and late replicating regions of the mammalian genome reflect both the structural components of chromosomes (such as heterochromatin at centromeres and other areas) and the transcriptional activity of genes within a replicon, with heavily transcribed regions frequently being replicated, on average, earlier in S phase. As described in Box 9.2 (Figure 9.10b), in female human cells, the inactivated and transcriptionally inert X chromosome replicates very late in S phase compared to the active X chromosome.

Summary of Section 9.2

1   Replication is initiated at specific points along the chromosome called replication origins. These are well defined in bacteria and yeast, where they contain AT-rich elements.

2   Replication and replication origins can be studied using functional assays and through the incorporation of nucleotide analogues during DNA synthesis.

3   A protein complex called ORC binds to replication origins and is involved in the initiation of replication, interacting with components of the cell cycle machinery.

4   The time course of replication can be investigated by whole genome studies, which combine the differential labelling of newly replicated DNA and hybridization to genome microarrays. These analyses demonstrate a range of replication origin properties in eukaryote cells, in terms of their time of initiation and fork progression.

5   There is a general association between transcriptionally active regions and early replication.

6   Various techniques to analyse replication at the genome level include pulsed labelling, PCR, microarrays and FACS.

9.3 The mechanics of DNA replication

In this section we will be focusing on several specific features of the replication machinery. A general overview of replication can be found in S204 Book 3, *The Core of Life*, Vol. II, Chapter 8.

Before we discuss the specific components and mechanics of the replication machinery, there are three important points to note about all DNA synthesis, which are shown schematically in Figure 9.11. Firstly, as a universal rule, all DNA synthesis occurs in the 5′ to 3′ direction through the formation of a phosphodiester bond between adjacent nucleotides (Section 5.2, Figure 5.3) and all DNA synthesis requires a 3′-OH on the deoxyribose sugar from which to initiate polymerization. Secondly, DNA synthesis requires a single-stranded nucleic acid chain to serve as the template on which synthesis occurs, and which directs which nucleotide is added to the extending chain. For the most part, duplex DNA provides its own template, the 3′ to 5′ oriented strand. We will examine how DNA polymerase is able to ensure that this process occurs with a high fidelity when we look at its structure and function in detail. Finally, as double-stranded DNA consists of antiparallel

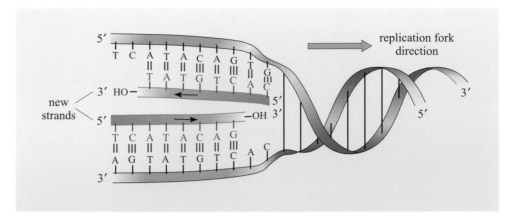

Figure 9.11   Important features of DNA replication. A new DNA strand is always synthesized in the 5′ to 3′ direction on a nucleic acid template and DNA polymerase requires a 3′-OH for polymerization. This schematic representation of the replication fork illustrates how the synthesis of each new strand is in the 5′ to 3′ direction, although the direction of synthesis of one of the strands is apparently in the opposite direction to replication fork movement.

strands, synthesis on one strand has to occur apparently in the opposite direction to fork progression. This paradox will be resolved when we detail the mechanism by which the synthesis of the two strands is coordinated within the replication complex.

Both prokaryotes and eukaryotes contain several different DNA polymerases and a very large number of ancillary proteins that play essential roles in the process of replication. Many of these proteins are evolutionarily highly conserved, both at the level of their function and at the level of their amino acid sequence. As with many other cellular processes, we have learnt most of what we know about replication at the molecular level from studies on *E. coli*, so we will start by describing how genomic replication is achieved in this bacterium, highlighting important similarities seen with eukaryotes, before describing important differences from eukaryotes.

We will start by discussing the control of initiation. We saw earlier how components of the cell cycle interact with ORC to regulate the initiation of DNA synthesis in eukaryotes, preventing re-initiation. A similar outcome is achieved in *E. coli* through a very different mechanism.

9.3.1 The initiation of replication in *E. coli*

We discussed earlier the process of replication initiation through the action of proteins at the *E. coli* genomic origin, *oriC* (Figure 9.1). This first stage in initiation, involving localized disruption of the helical structure of the DNA and separation of paired bases allows the enzyme **DNA primase** to synthesize two short RNA chains, one on each strand (Figure 9.12). This short primer chain serves to provide the necessary 3′-OH from which replicative synthesis by DNA polymerase will commence. We will discuss the polymerization process in more detail shortly, but first we will consider how *E. coli* controls this pathway to prevent the re-initiation of synthesis at the two newly formed daughter *oriC* sites, one on each new chromosome.

The binding of the 20–40 copies of these initiator proteins at the *E. coli* replication origin serves as a critical control point during genomic DNA replication. This control point is achieved by exploiting the timing of post-replicative DNA methylation, as described below.

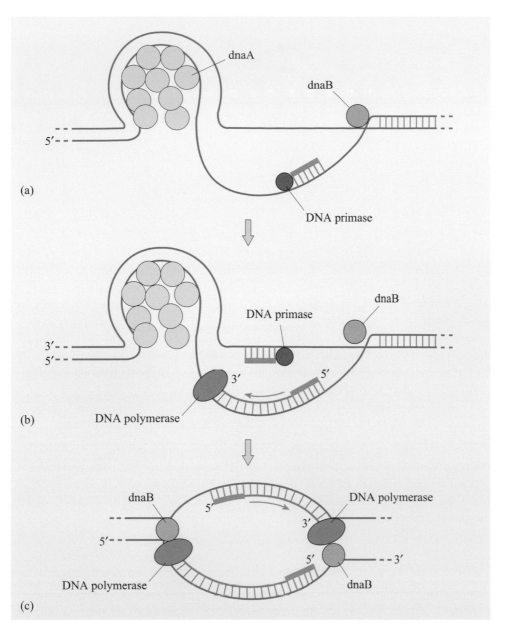

(a)

(b)

(c)

Figure 9.12
Initiation of DNA synthesis at the *E. coli* origin. Binding of the replicative proteins dnaA and dnaB to the *oriC* Site (see Figure 9.1) promotes the opening of the helix. A short primer RNA chain is synthesized by the enzyme DNA primase (a) and serves as a 3'-OH start site from which the main replicative DNA polymerase will proceed (b). DNA primase action on the opposite strand establishes bidirectional synthesis (c).

E. coli genomic DNA is normally modified by a protein called dam methylase, which recognizes and methylates the adenosine residue (to form N^6-methyladenosine; see Figure 5.4c) within each short sequence 5'-GATC (Figure 9.13). Immediately after replication, each new daughter helix contains one old and one newly synthesized strand. As methylation of the new strand occurs only 10–15 minutes after DNA synthesis has occurred, newly synthesized DNA is transiently a hybrid of methylated and non-methylated strands, and is described as being **hemi-methylated**. The dnaA protein only binds to the replication origin site *oriC* when it is methylated on *both* strands. Therefore, for a short period of time immediately after replication has proceeded from the origin, no dnaA protein can bind to the replication origin. This mechanism serves to prevent the assembly of new competent replication origins on the two new daughter chromosomes and reduces the risk of re-initiating replication before the cell requires it to go ahead.

Figure 9.13
The role of N^6-adenosine methylation of genomic DNA in the regulation of initiation at the *E. coli* origin. As the replication forks progress from *oriC*, 5′-GATC sites in the newly synthesized strand remain unmethylated, preventing the binding of dnaA proteins to the two new daughter chromosomes. After 10–15 minutes, the action of dam methylase upon 5′-GATC sites on the newly synthesized strand of the hemi-methylated daughter duplexes results in restoration of full methylation. This delay in the binding of dnaA to *oriC* ensures that initiation of synthesis is delayed, preventing re-initiation, which would be damaging to the cell.

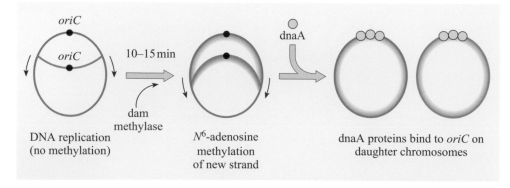

DNA replication (no methylation)

dam methylase

N^6-adenosine methylation of new strand

dnaA

dnaA proteins bind to *oriC* on daughter chromosomes

10–15 min

○ What is the major determinant of whether DNA replication will be initiated in *E. coli*?

■ The growth status of the cell, which determines the critical mass (Section 8.5).

Whilst differing in how replication initation is achieved, you will no doubt recognize the similarity between the control of initiation in *E. coli* and the control point in the eukaryotic cell cycle that is mediated through ORC. The observation that replication initiation is so tightly controlled in both prokaryotes and eukaryotes serves to highlight the importance of replication initiation as a critical point during the cell's preparations for cell division.

9.3.2 The elongation of DNA chains by DNA polymerase

The enzymes that synthesize new DNA strands on existing templates are termed **DNA polymerases** and as we mentioned earlier, both bacteria and eukaryotic cells contain several different forms of these proteins. Those involved in replication of *E. coli* genomic DNA are detailed in Table 9.1, which also highlights some of their important features.

Table 9.1   DNA polymerases involved in genomic replication in *E. coli*.

Name	Estimate of number present in each cell	Subunit structure	Rate of nucleotide addition / nt min^{-1}	Exonuclease function	Major role in replication
DNA polymerase I	300–400	single polypeptide with both polymerase and 3′–5′ exonuclease activities	600	3′ to 5′ 5′ to 3′	processes lagging strands
DNA polymerase III	20	10 polypeptides; major subunits are: 'core' subunit (3 polypeptides) α: a polymerase ε: a 3′–5′ exonuclease θ: (function unknown) β clamp subunit (2 polypeptides)	30 000	3′ to 5′	major replicative polymerase

We will focus here on the two DNA polymerases that function in *E. coli* replicative DNA synthesis, but you should note that there others that play roles in specialized synthetic stages, which we will not discuss. DNA polymerase I consists of a single polypeptide, whereas DNA polymerase III is a multisubunit enzyme. The complementary properties of these two polymerases allow them to cooperate in genomic DNA replication. As you might guess from the properties of these two polymerases, listed in Table 9.1, the considerably higher synthesis rate for DNA polymerase III suggests that this enzyme is responsible for the bulk of replication. DNA polymerase I, however, plays an important role in the processing of DNA chains synthesized by DNA polymerase III, to allow ligation into a single strand. Before we discuss the role of specific DNA polymerases in genomic replication, we will first consider some of their general properties.

General features of DNA polymerases

All DNA polymerases catalyse the reaction between a free deoxyribonucleoside triphosphate (dNTP) and the hydroxyl group attached to the C3′ atom (C3′-OH) at the end the polydeoxyribonucleotide chain. This results in the linkage shown in Figure 5.3. Recall that each dNTP has three phosphate groups attached via an oxygen to the C5′ atom of the deoxyribose sugar (PPP–O–C5′) (Figure 2.20 and Figure 5.4). The polymerization reaction, in which the C3′-OH is joined to the phosphate group nearest the C5′ atom (the α phosphate) of the dNTP, releasing inorganic diphosphate (PPi), can be represented by the following equation:

$$(DNA)_n–C3'\ OH + PPP–O–C5'—deoxyribonucleoside \rightarrow (DNA)_{n+1}–C3'–OH + PP_i$$

Breakage of a high-energy phosphoanhydride bond in the incoming dNTP provides the energy required to drive this reaction (Section 5.2.1). The outcome of the reaction is the formation of a phosphodiester linkage and an increase in the length of the DNA chain by an additional nucleotide. The newly incorporated nucleotide provides the C3′-OH for the next polymerization reaction. During replication initiation in *E. coli*, the short primer synthesized by the DNA primase provides this C3′-OH.

In addition to catalysing phosphoester bond formation, DNA polymerases and other components of the replication machinery play key roles in ensuring that only the base that matches the template is inserted during the polymerization process. Two factors contribute to this accurate matching. The first is an intrinsic feature of the DNA bases involved.

◻ Can you suggest what features of duplex B-DNA contribute to the choice of the correct nucleotide?

◼ Hydrogen bond formation between the incoming nucleotide and the complementary base on the template strand and also steric features of the new base pair (as discussed in Section 5.3.1).

If, however, the accuracy of DNA replication were to rely exclusively upon the discrimination between the different bases at this level alone, we would expect that errors would occur at the frequency approaching 1 per 10 000 bases. The error rate is actually much lower than this, being closer to 1 in 10^7 bases.

The explanation for this low error rate is that the DNA polymerases have what is called 'proofreading' activity, which allows the enzyme to recognize a mispaired base, reverse itself and remove the wrongly inserted base before continuing synthesis. This function is provided by an exonuclease activity which operates by sequentially removing deoxyribonucleotides from the end of the chain in the 3′ to 5′ direction. This proofreading activity is present in all DNA polymerases. To illustrate the process, we will consider *E. coli* DNA polymerase I, which contains both polymerase and 3′–5′ exonuclease activities as separate domains in a single polypeptide (Table 9.1). This proofreading ability is extremely important for the fidelity of replication and serves as the first line of defence against mutation. To see how DNA polymerase carries out its proofreading activity, we will now examine its structure in more detail.

As you can see from the schematic representation of DNA polymerase I in Figure 9.14, the sites in which polymerization (P) and exonuclease activity (X) occur are in separate regions of the protein. In addition, the single-stranded template and the duplex product strands lie within a groove that extends across the polymerase. The first stage in maintaining fidelity results from the structure of the catalytic region. The incoming dNTP and the base from the exposed template strand form a nascent base-pair within a binding pocket adjacent to the 3′-OH. The geometry of this binding pocket in the P site is such that it ensures that only appropriately Watson–Crick-paired bases are accommodated. This discriminatory ability depends upon multiple non-covalent interactions between the nascent base-pair's individual components (base, sugar and phosphate) and the amino acid residues that form the walls of the pocket. When mispaired bases are joined by mistake, they are 'sensed' and the nascent pair is slid into the adjacent exonuclease (X) site, where the base is removed and the free 3′-OH returned to the polymerase (P) site.

In some cases, mispairing does go undetected, as is the case when the nascent base-pair geometry closely resembles that of a normal Watson–Crick base pair. For instance, if the incoming dNTP contains 8-oxoguanine (a damaged base that arises by metabolic activity in the cell, Section 5.5.1), this base will form a pair with a template strand adenine. This base pair is satisfactorily accommodated within the binding pocket and thus goes undetected, leading to a mutation in the DNA sequence. This example emphasizes the importance of other proteins that protect the cellular pool of dNTPs from such damage.

DNA polymerase III is the major replicative polymerase in E. coli

In contrast to DNA polymerase I, DNA polymerase III is a complex of 10 polypeptides (Table 9.1). The 'core' subunit of DNA polymerase III is made of three polypeptide chains that together essentially function like DNA polymerase I described above. The other major subunit of *E. coli* DNA polymerase III protein we shall discuss is a specialized structure that acts to hold the 'core' polymerase onto the DNA. This protein, the β subunit, which consists of two polypeptide chains, is also called a 'sliding clamp', or 'β clamp', because it forms a ring of protein assembled around the DNA helix, as shown in Figure 9.15.

The β clamp in *E. coli* consists of a ring made from two polypeptide chains, which locks onto duplex DNA. This structure acts to supports the core polymerase ahead of it on the single-stranded DNA template chain, sliding along behind it as new DNA is synthesized. The interaction between the clamp and the core polymerase

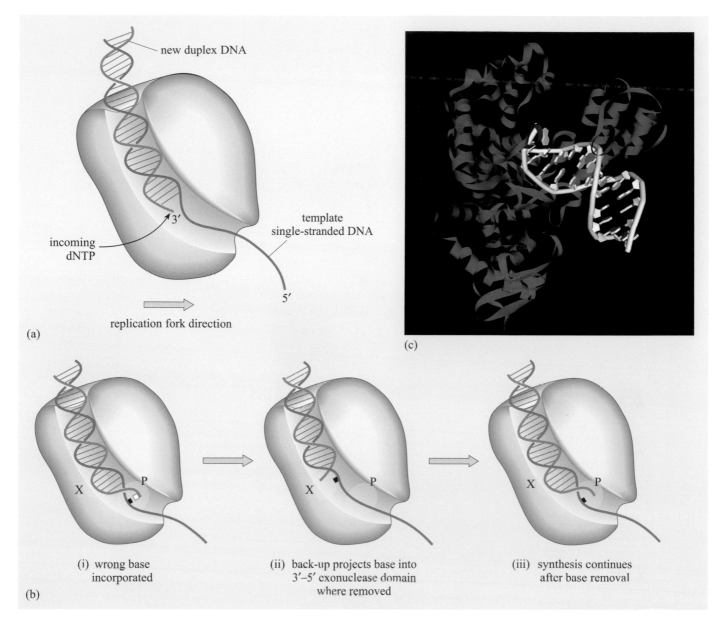

Figure 9.14 The structure of the *E. coli* replicative DNA polymerase I protein and its role in polymerization and error correction. X-ray diffraction studies have provided structures of both the polymerase and 3′–5′ exonuclease functions in action on a DNA template. (a) In this schematic representation of the polymerase, a channel can be seen through which the DNA strands run, single-stranded template entering the protein on the right and newly synthesized duplex exiting on the left. (b) Within the core of the protein are two catalytic sites, the first for polymerization (P), where the incoming dNTPs react with the 3′-OH on the extending strand, the second for 3′–5′ exonuclease (X) activity. If a base is misincorporated (white box) (i), the mispaired region is translocated into the exonuclease site (ii), where it is removed and synthesis can continue (iii). (Based on Beese *et al*., 1993) (c) The tertiary structure of *E. coli* DNA polymerase I with its DNA substrate bound. Note that it is rotated relative to the schematic in (a) to highlight the polymerase groove in cross-section. (pdb file 1kln).

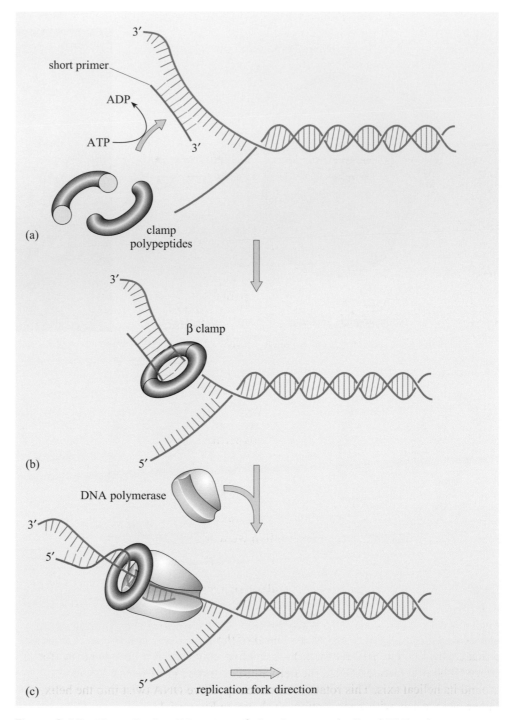

Figure 9.15   The replicative sliding clamp (β clamp) supports the *E. coli* DNA polymerase III core on the DNA template. (a) and (b) The β subunit of DNA polymerase III forms around duplex DNA in an ATP-dependent manner. The duplex DNA, which is required for β clamp assembly, is provided by the short RNA–DNA duplex made by DNA primase. (c) The β clamp–core polymerase complex is assembled with the clamp directly behind the polymerase, positioning the central groove of the polymerase along the single-stranded template and allowing synthesis to proceed along it.

dramatically increases the processivity of the polymerase (i.e. the rate at which polymerization occurs). We have already mentioned that the components of DNA polymerases are highly conserved; it is therefore not surprising that the structure of this clamp molecule is also very highly conserved. As can be seen in Figure 9.16, the eukaryotic homologue of the *E. coli* β clamp, termed PCNA (proliferating cell nuclear antigen), comprises three polypeptide chains, but has a very similar three-dimensional structure.

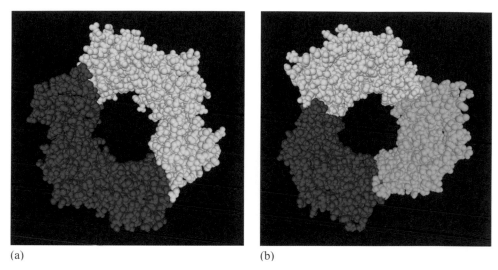

(a)   (b)

Figure 9.16   Sliding clamp structures. (a) Structure of the β clamp from *E. coli* (based upon pdb file 1b8h). (b) The equivalent structure from eukaryotic cells, which is composed of three identical polypeptide chains of the PCNA protein (based upon pdb file 1axc).

Elongation requires the concerted action of enzymes that unwind duplex DNA

The final component of the elongation machinery we will consider here comprises two proteins that aid in the unwinding of the double-stranded DNA helix to expose the template strand. The first protein we will consider is a DNA helicase, which serves to unwind the DNA duplex immediately in front of the clamp–core polymerase complex as it moves along the DNA helix (Figure 9.17a); in *E. coli*, this is the dnaB protein. The helicase slides along the strand oriented in the 5′ to 3′ direction and its action requires ATP. Such replicative helicases are capable of unwinding as many as 1000 bases per second. As this unwinding process occurs, a build-up of superhelical stress occurs ahead of the fork. Remember from Chapter 5 that each complete helical turn of B-form DNA contains 10 bases; therefore, for every 10 bp of replicated DNA, the helix must be turned through one full rotation around its helical axis. This rotation introduces positive DNA twist into the helix, rather like we saw with transcription, as shown in Figure 5.11.

☐ Which class of enzyme is capable of relieving such helical stress?

◼ A DNA topoisomerase.

As the replication fork proceeds, one strand of the template duplex is cleaved by a second protein, DNA topoisomerase I. As outlined in Section 5.3.2 and shown schematically in Figure 9.17b, this enzyme cleaves one of the strands of the duplex, allowing rotation of the template helix to occur, releasing built-up helical stress.

Figure 9.17
The action of the *E. coli* replicative DNA helicase (dnaB) and DNA topoisomerase I at the replication fork. (a) DNA helicase acts to unwind the DNA duplex and reveal the template strand for the β clamp–polymerase machinery. Positive DNA twisting leads to the build-up of positive superhelical stress ahead of the replication fork. This stress is released by the action of DNA topoisomerase I, which breaks the sugar–phosphate backbone of one strand, allows rotation and ensures resealing (b).

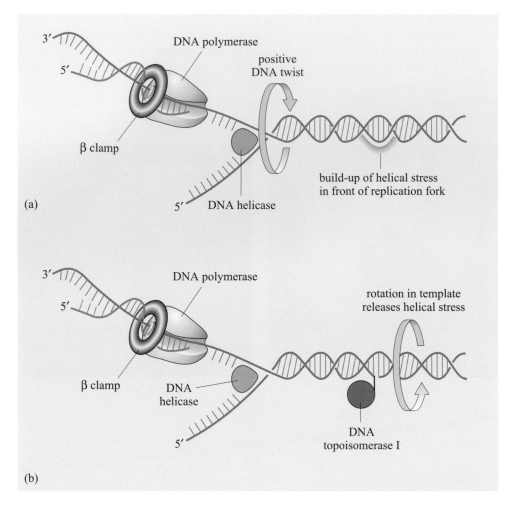

Breaking the backbone of a chromosomal DNA chain could be potentially damaging to the cell if the ends of this break were 'lost'. However, topoisomerase I has a novel strategy to ensure that the nick is resealed. It binds to the end of the chain via a covalent linkage to a tyrosine residue in the protein, and once strand rotation has been completed, rejoining occurs, utilizing the energy released from breaking the tyrosine–DNA bond. This reduces the helical stress, restores the helix and the whole process requires no energy input.

9.3.3 Coordinated strand synthesis

As described earlier, the antiparallel structure of DNA, combined with the requirement for synthesis to be in the 5′ to 3′ direction, means that the polymerase machinery at the replication fork has to coordinate synthesis in both 'directions' (Figure 9.11). In this section, we will describe how this **coordinated synthesis** is achieved.

If we consider the replication fork shown in the inset of Figure 9.18, we can see that the DNA strand that is oriented in the same direction as the fork movement (i.e. left to right; top) can be synthesized continuously as the replication fork progresses, and in the same direction as the fork is moving. This strand is commonly termed the **leading strand**. The other strand, known as the **lagging strand**, must somehow be synthesized in what appears to be the 'opposite' direction to fork progression. Thus, as the replication fork proceeds along the chromosome, synthesis must occur in two directions. The situation is complicated by the fact that the replication machinery itself remains fixed.

To resolve this paradox, we shall see how the replication machinery utilizes two DNA polymerase units and synthesizes the lagging strand in small segments, but in the same 'direction' as the leading strand. An elegant model explaining how this is achieved *in E. coli* is shown schematically in Figure 9.18. The coordination within one replication fork between synthesis on two strands is achieved through the use of two DNA polymerase III units that lie in the same orientation and synthesize in the same direction. As synthesis of the leading strand proceeds (top polymerase unit in Figure 9.18), the lagging strand template is displaced outwards and a short RNA primer is synthesized on it by the DNA primase enzyme. A single-stranded binding protein (SSBP, not shown) binds to this exposed template strand, preventing both damage and secondary structure formation. A second β clamp unit binds around the primer–template duplex region, wherein the full DNA polymerase III unit assembles and extends it, displacing SSBP, until it reaches the end of the previously synthesized section. At this point, synthesis terminates and the β clamp–polymerase dissociates,

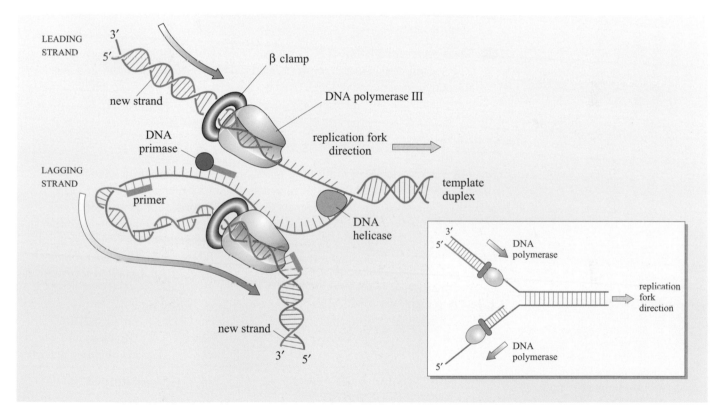

Figure 9.18   Coordinated synthesis of leading and lagging strands at the replication fork. A model for coordinated strand synthesis in *E. coli*. Both strands are synthesized through a static replication machinery containing core polymerases. Leading strand synthesis is performed by one complete DNA polymerase III unit and as it proceeds, single-stranded lagging strand template is extruded. A short RNA primer is synthesized on this template by DNA primase. The unit synthesizing the lagging strand assembles on this primer–template duplex and initiates synthesis until the 5′ end of the previously synthesized fragment is reached. At this point, the DNA polymerase III dissociates and translocates onto the next primer–template duplex. Thus, the direction of both polymerase units is from left to right, in the same direction as the replication fork movement. Note that, although not shown on this diagram, the exposed single-stranded lagging strand DNA template is bound by a single-stranded binding protein (SSBP) which protects it from damage or from forming secondary structures. *Inset:* At a replication fork proceeding along the chromosome from left to right in this diagram, the apparent direction of synthesis for the polymerase on the lagging strand appears to be opposite to the direction of the replication fork.

relocating to the next primer site. You should note that at this stage, whilst the leading strand is a continuous DNA chain, the lagging strand consists of DNA chains interspersed with short RNA primers.

The RNA primer in the lagging strand is removed through the action of DNA polymerase I, which has a 5′–3′ exonuclease activity, synthesizing DNA in its place, and the two adjacent segments are joined through the action of DNA ligase. At the *E. coli* replication fork, these lagging strand sections, termed **Okazaki fragments** (after the scientist who first reported them), are approximately 1000–2000 bp in length. Synthesis of the lagging strand lags behind that of the leading strand as lagging strand synthesis cannot commence until sufficient template has been generated and an RNA primer synthesized. In order to achieve an almost continuous synthesis at the replication fork, the clamp–polymerase is continuously relocated to the next short RNA primer, but both polymerases are working in the same overall direction, and thus the fork progresses along the template.

After the replication fork has progressed through a region, the duplex undergoes further processing.

○ What post-replicative processing occurs on two newly replicated *E. coli* chromosomes?

● The first is methylation of 5′-GATC sites by Dam methylases (Figure 9.13). The second is the association with bacterial chromosomal proteins and the introduction of negative DNA twist by the enzyme DNA gyrase, which serves to introduce negative superhelical stress into the duplex (Chapter 5).

9.3.4 Replication of genomic DNA in eukaryotes

Most of our knowledge of replication in eukaryotes has come from studies in the yeast *S. cerevisiae* and of the replication of the SV40 virus in mammalian cells. It is believed that the same basic mechanism for DNA replication is utilized by all eukaryotes, and furthermore that most of the component proteins are very similar to those in *E. coli*, with a few notable exceptions. The first of the exceptions are the various DNA polymerases required for replicative DNA synthesis in eukaryotes. These polymerases are listed in Table 9.2.

Table 9.2 Replicative DNA polymerases in eukaryotes.

Yeast	Human	Primase activity	Direction of exonuclease activity
DNA polymerase I	DNA polymerase α	yes	5′ to 3′
DNA polymerase III	DNA polymerase δ	no	5′ to 3′ and 3′ to 5′

In humans, the primase function is performed by DNA polymerase α, which has an intrinsic primase activity. Primase activity is triggered by phosphorylation of the polymerase by a cyclin–Cdk activity. On the single-stranded lagging strand template, which is bound by a protein analogous to SSBP called RPA, DNA polymerase α initially synthesizes an RNA chain, before switching synthesis to DNA incorporation for a short stretch until the replication clamp–polymerase complex takes over.

The second major difference is that during synthesis of the lagging strand, specialist proteins are responsible for the removal of the RNA primers. In eukaryotes, this job is performed by a protein called FEN1 which binds to these junctions and removes the RNA primer, allowing DNA synthesis to fill in the missing nucleotides and leaving flush ends suitable for DNA ligase activity.

A major difference between replication in *E. coli* and that in eukaryotes is that the replication machinery has to negotiate a more highly structured chromatin within the nucleus of a eukaryote. DNA here is packaged into chromatin through the association with nucleosomes, as described in Section 5.7. Every 180–200 bp of DNA is packaged around a nucleosome, and the replication fork must proceed through these obstacles. This continued requirement for processing of nucleosomal DNA is believed to be the reason why Okazaki fragments in eukaryotes are considerably shorter than those in *E. coli*, at only 150–200 bp. The fact that eukaryotic Okazaki fragments are shorter almost certainly contributes to the slower overall rate of synthesis.

Recall that ahead of the replication fork there is a build-up of DNA twist due to the activity of DNA helicase.

◯ What is the nature of this twist and what do you predict its effect will be upon nucleosomes?

◼ It is a positive twist, which will create positive supercoiling in the duplex. Nucleosomes create negative DNA supercoils as the DNA wraps around the core octamer, as described in Section 5.7. Thus, positive twist ahead of the replication fork will destabilize nucleosomes.

Replication through regions containing highly compacted DNA presents particular problems.

◯ What modifications to histones are likely to be found in such areas?

◼ Generally, these regions would be expected to contain histones with decreased levels of acetylation of the H3 and H4 tails, and may also contain H1 (as described in Section 5.7.3).

Progress of the replication machinery through areas of highly compacted chromatin, which make up a large proportion of the mammalian genome, probably requires additional local decondensation. This function is likely to be performed by complexes of proteins called chromatin remodelling factors, which utilize ATP to reorganize nucleosomes without altering the histone content.

Finally, at the end of S phase, the two newly replicated genomes undergo further packaging and condensation in preparation for mitosis and cell division, stages of which were outlined in Chapters 5 and 8.

Summary of Section 9.3

1   Re-initiation of DNA synthesis in *E. coli* is prevented by delaying the establishment of *OriC* initiation complexes through DNA methylation.

2   DNA polymerase fidelity is achieved through a nascent base-pair pocket which detects sterically appropriate Watson–Crick base pairs. Mispaired bases are removed by an exonuclease activity.

3   Polymerase processivity is enhanced by the structurally supportive sliding clamp subunit of the polymerase. DNA helicase and topoisomerases play key roles in unwinding the helix, releasing helical stress and retwisting the DNA.

4   Coordinated strand synthesis within the replication fork is achieved using two clamp–polymerase units. The unit synthesizing the lagging strand undergoes repeated disassembly–relocation–assembly–synthesis cycles.

5   The disassembly of nucleosomes ahead of the replication fork in eukaryotes is enhanced by positive DNA twisting. Compacted areas of the mammalian genome most likely require additional chromatin remodelling factors to allow the replication machinery to progress.

9.4 Maintenance of local chromatin structure

Following the replication of duplex DNA, each of the two daughter duplexes is a hybrid of a new and an old (parental) strand and any nucleotide modifications present on the original duplex will now only be present on each of the parental strands. We have already seen how hemi-methylated 5′-GATC sites in *E. coli* are modified to contain methyladenine after chromosomal DNA replication.

○ What is the major modified base in the genomic DNA of many eukaryotes?

● 5-methylcytosine (shown in Figure 5.4).

In eukaryotes that methylate their genome after DNA replication, the parental strand (upper strand in the diagram below) remains methylated at cytosine bases within a 5′-CG sequence. Methylation of the highlighted cytosines in the newly synthesized (lower) strand is dependent upon enzymes that recognize hemi-methylated DNA. The site of modification is always a 5′-CG dinucleotide.

In eukaryotes, newly replicated DNA has also to be reassembled into mature chromatin. As discussed in Chapter 5, there are regional differences in the modifications found to the core histone proteins H3 and H4, and these modifications have roles in regulating accessibility and chromatin compaction.

○ Can you list examples of regionalized chromatin modifications you have encountered in the course?

● We have used several examples: the *S. pombe* centromere (Figure 5.37), the chicken β-globin gene (Figure 5.34) and the inactivated mammalian X chromosome (Figure 5.36).

In all these examples, such epigenetic information must be re-established after replication. How is this achieved? Although the precise details are still not known at the single nucleosome level, the general process is understood and is shown schematically in Figure 9.19.

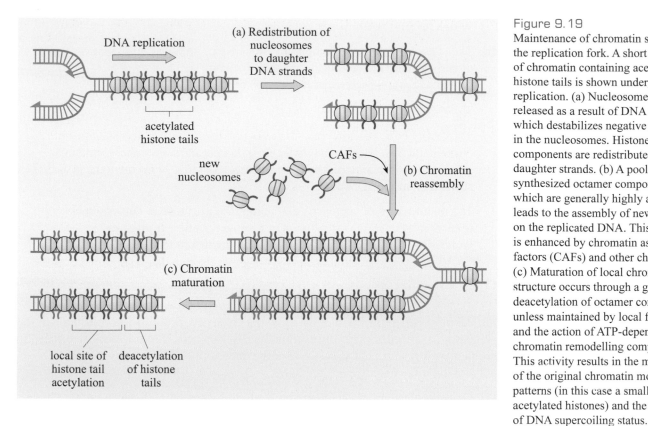

Figure 9.19
Maintenance of chromatin status at the replication fork. A short region of chromatin containing acetylated histone tails is shown undergoing replication. (a) Nucleosomes are released as a result of DNA untwisting, which destabilizes negative supercoils in the nucleosomes. Histone octamer components are redistributed to both daughter strands. (b) A pool of newly synthesized octamer components, which are generally highly acetylated, leads to the assembly of new chromatin on the replicated DNA. This process is enhanced by chromatin assembly factors (CAFs) and other chaperones. (c) Maturation of local chromatin structure occurs through a generalized deacetylation of octamer components, unless maintained by local factors and the action of ATP-dependent chromatin remodelling complexes. This activity results in the maintenance of the original chromatin modification patterns (in this case a small region of acetylated histones) and the restoration of DNA supercoiling status.

As mentioned in the previous section, as the replication fork proceeds along the chromosome, it encounters and must displace the nucleosomes. As the replication fork proceeds through a region of DNA, the nucleosomes upon it are displaced evenly to both daughter strands and this process is assisted by proteins called chromatin assembly factors or CAFs. New nucleosomes are then assembled to reach the required density of packaging.

○ What effect does the formation of nucleosomes have upon DNA topology?

● It introduces negative DNA twist into the newly replicated genomic DNA through the formation of negative supercoils.

Most of the newly assembled nucleosomes have histones with acetylated tails. These histone tails undergo a gradual deacetylation unless their acetylation is actively maintained. The degree to which deacetylation occurs is most likely influenced by the local density of modifications on the nucleosomes redistributed from the original DNA template. It is also influenced by DNA methylation and the presence of other regulatory proteins, possibly including transcription regulators and ATP-dependent chromatin remodelling complexes.

Continued packaging of the newly synthesized chromatin proceeds, permitting compaction of the chromosome in preparation for mitosis, as described in Section 5.8.3 and shown in Figure 5.43. The two daughter chromatids are maintained in close proximity to each other.

○ Which proteins perform this function?

● The cohesin complexes, comprising Smc1/Smc3 subunits, bind the chromatids directly and are linked together by a bridge comprising pairs of Scc1/Scc3 subunits (Section 8.2.1).

Summary of Section 9.4

1   DNA methylation – N^6-methyladenine in *E. coli* and 5-methylcytosine in eukaryotes – is maintained by enzymes that recognize hemi-methylated targets in newly synthesized DNA.

2   The maintenance of epigenetic chromatin modifications in nucleosomes is ensured through the distribution of histone octamers from ahead of the replication fork to the newly synthesized daughter strands.

9.5 Replication of telomere DNA

For the most part, replication of the bulk of a eukaryote genome proceeds through the processes described above. However, in the case of linear chromosomes, one special problem arises: how can the very end of the duplex (the telomere) be replicated without the loss of genetic information?

Why is the replication of a telomere problematic? Recall that three essential features of DNA synthesis are: (1) it requires a primer with a 3′-terminal hydroxyl group (as we have seen, usually provided by small RNA primers); (2) synthesis always proceeds from 5′ to 3′; and (3) it requires a single-stranded template. These features mean that the very end of the chromosome cannot be synthesized, as lagging strand synthesis requires a primer site to be available (see Figure 9.20).

The problem of the loss of genetic information from the ends of linear chromosomes has been counteracted by a novel mechanism that adds DNA to the ends of each chromosome in a manner that does not require the normal replication machinery. Without such mechanisms, the progressive loss of terminal DNA sequences could trigger DNA damage signals and could ultimately prove lethal to the cell.

Figure 9.20
The telomere end-replication problem. The requirements of normal DNA synthesis are such that the 3′ end of each of the strands of the duplex cannot be synthesized due to the lack of a suitable priming site. In this schematic representation of the end of a chromosome (a), the terminal Okazaki fragment with its RNA primer is shown; its removal during lagging strand processing will lead to loss of DNA in each replication, either through loss of DNA directly or as loss in the next round of DNA synthesis (b).

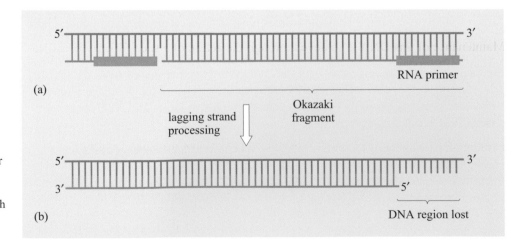

9.5.1 The structure of telomeres

The majority of eukaryotic telomeric DNA consists of highly repetitive blocks of short G-rich sequences.

◻ Can you recall the sequence of the telomere repeat in humans?

⬛ The sequence is 5′-TTAGGG, as described in Section 5.3.3 and Figure 5.15.

These simple telomere repeats are highly conserved between organisms, as shown in Table 9.3.

Table 9.3 G-rich telomere repeat sequences in various organisms.

Sequence (5′–3′)	Organisms
TTAGGG	humans (and many other vertebrates) *Neurospora crassa* (a fungus)
TTGGG	*Tetrahymena thermophila* (a protoctist)
TTTAGGG	*Arabidopsis thaliana* (a plant)
TTACAGG	*S. pombe*
$A(G)_{1-8}$ e.g. AGGGGG	*Dictyostelium discoideum* (a slime mould)
$T(G)_{2-3}(TG)_{1-3}$ e.g. TGGTGTGTG	*S. cerevisiae*

The number of repeats present at telomeres varies between organisms, but can range from blocks of 1–2 kb to over 200 kb. The end of the DNA chain within these telomere repeats consists of a single-stranded G-rich region.

◻ What unusual structure is this DNA believed to form?

⬛ G-quadruplex structures, as described in Section 5.3.3.

Bound to this telomeric DNA are telomere binding proteins which are involved in telomere maintenance and in chromosome regulation. During S phase, this telomeric complex is removed and the single-stranded portion is present as a 3′ overhang. Maintenance of this DNA is achieved through the action of a specific enzyme called telomerase.

9.5.2 Telomerase-directed DNA synthesis of telomeric repeats

Telomerase is a specialized enzyme that is capable of synthesizing new telomeric DNA at the ends of a linear chromosome. The mechanism by which it does this is by effectively extending the 3′ end of a chromosome, as shown schematically in Figure 9.21. It uses the 3′-OH of the existing parental strand, synthesis is 5′ to 3′ and the enzyme provides its own template in the form of an RNA chain. This RNA template is encoded by a separate gene to the telomerase. This extended strand provides a template upon which lagging strand synthesis occurs.

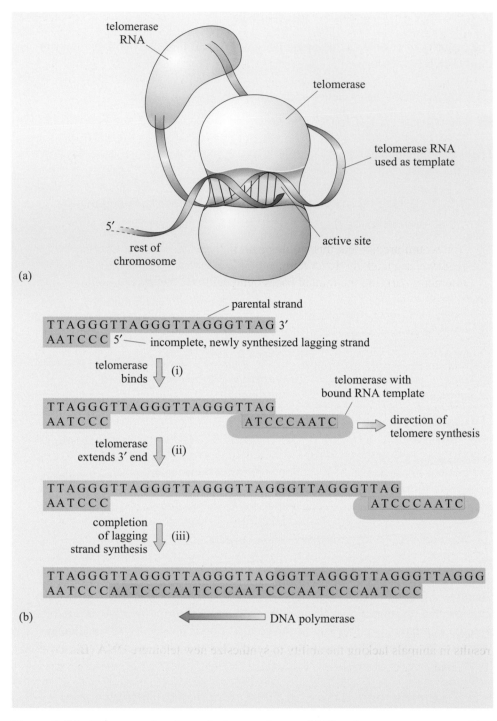

Figure 9.21   Telomerase function at the human telomere. (a) The telomerase enzyme resembles other polymerases in having a groove within which the template RNA and the newly synthesized DNA strand lie. (b) Telomere DNA synthesis is shown in several stages as described. (i) Annealing of the template RNA in register with the 3′ overhang on the parent strand aligns the template for synthesis of a repeat unit (ii), after which telomerase translocates and continues synthesizing. Once complete, lagging strand synthesis can be continued on the newly extended parental strand (iii).

The RNA template contains a short region that serves as the template for synthesis of each new telomeric DNA repeat. The template region contains one and a half copies of the telomere repeat sequence, such that annealing to the end of the parental strand aligns the repeat template RNA in register with the repeat on the chromosome. When the parental strand has been lengthened in this way, primer synthesis by DNA polymerase I (yeast) or α (human) (Table 9.2) can initiate lagging strand synthesis to complete replication of the region.

The overall secondary structure of the RNA template is evolutionarily highly conserved, although the sequence of the template region itself obviously varies between species.

○ Based upon the mechanism of action of Figure 9.21, what would you predict would be the consequence of mutating the RNA template's repeat region?

■ You would predict that this would result in the addition of telomeric DNA repeats that match the RNA template. This is indeed what happens, with 'new' telomeres carrying the mutant bases being added to the existing ones.

Polymerases such as telomerase, which synthesis DNA chains on a RNA template, are called **reverse transcriptases**. Telomerase is, therefore, a novel reverse transcriptase that carries its own template. Telomerase action is an evolutionarily highly conserved process, occurring in all eukaryotes with simple repeat-based telomeres.

The length of telomeric repeat DNA found at the end of a linear chromosome varies considerably between organisms. For example, *S. cerevisiae* chromosomes carry 1–2 kb of telomeric repeat DNA. For multicellular organisms, the length of repeat present in somatic cells is dependent upon the replicative history of the cells and tissues, because the expression of telomerase in somatic cells is dependent upon the developmental stage and cell type. Germ-line cells have high levels of telomerase activity, as would be expected in order to maintain the integrity of chromosomes to be inherited. Telomerase activity is also present in early, highly proliferative, stages of development in mammals, but within somatic cells in the adult it may be limited to certain populations of continuously dividing cells such as stem cells in various lineages. Investigation of the role of telomerase in mouse development has been made possible by the creation of a transgenic mouse that is deficient in the telomerase RNA template (Box 9.3 overleaf).

Deletion of the mouse telomerase RNA template gene by homologous recombination results in animals lacking the ability to synthesize new telomere DNA (Blasco *et al.*, 1997) and progressive telomere loss occurs. As the normal mouse chromosomes present in the ES cells carried many thousands of telomeric repeats, the process of loss takes more than six generations for the telomeres to erode to a point where signs of chromosome damage start to accumulate in cells. This damage arises due to the fact that, in addition to counteracting the erosion of genetic information through the direct loss of DNA, telomeres also provide an essential structural element to a linear chromosome, so that the cell does not mistake it as a broken DNA end (as would occur, for example, in radiation- or chemical-induced DNA breaks) and attempt to repair it. As you can see from the example of the telomerase knock-out mouse in Box 9.3, the eventual erosion of telomeres results in rearranged chromosomes (Figure 9.23), as the DNA ends are recognized as breaks and processed by the cell repair machinery. We will discuss how this repair occurs later in the chapter.

Box 9.3   Creation of a telomere-deficient mouse by homologous recombination

Gene manipulation of the mouse is commonly achieved by a direct alteration of the genomic locus in cells cultured *in vitro* through a technique called **homologous recombination**, which is outlined in Figure 9.22. The mechanism of recombination will be discussed in detail later (Section 9.9). Recombination allows two DNA duplexes of identical sequence to interact, and in the case of homologous recombination in embryonic stem (ES) cells, allows one DNA fragment to become inserted into the other at the point of homology.

First, the desired gene fragment is engineered using recombinant DNA techniques. This procedure commonly involves the creation of recombinant plasmids which, when integrated into the endogenous gene, create mutations by altering reading frames, deleting segments of genes or introducing premature stop codons. The mouse DNA containing the desired sequence changes is included in the plasmid and is homologous to the target sequence in the mouse genome. In addition, a method of selection – commonly a gene that confers resistance to a drug called G418 – is included so that cells carrying the altered target gene can be easily isolated. The engineered DNA is introduced into cultured ES cells, a process called transfection, and those carrying a suitably altered mouse gene selected on the basis of antibiotic resistance. These cells are then introduced into a developing blastocyst (an early embryonic stage), where they form part of the inner cell mass which will form the fetus. A proportion of transgenic mice born will carry the manipulated gene in their germ-line cells, and these animals can then be maintained by breeding.

Mice carrying genes that have been destroyed using this technique are commonly called **'knock-out'** animals; where the gene has been modified in some way but remains functional, the animals are described as **'knock-in'**.

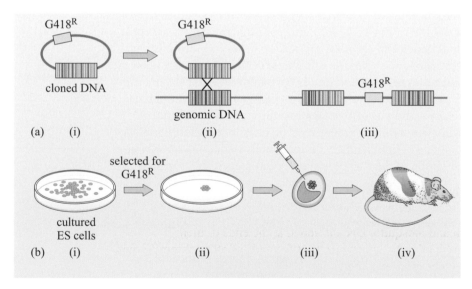

Figure 9.22   Schematic representation of the key stages of homologous recombination in mouse embryonic stem (ES) cells. (a) (i) Cloned DNA is engineered *in vitro* to match a target gene in the mouse genome. (ii) This DNA is introduced into mouse ES cells in culture and (iii) a small number of cells will allow this DNA to integrate by recombination between the incoming and genomic target DNA strands. This results in the mutated gene being created. (b) (i) ES cells are transfected with the construct DNA carrying the G418 resistance (G418R) gene. (ii) Cells in which homologous recombination has occurred will grow as a colony after selection for resistance to the drug G418. (iii) Cells carrying the mutation in the mouse gene are inserted into a mouse blastocyst and the mice isolated (iv).

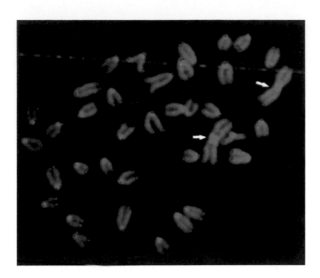

Figure 9.23
Chromosome fusions via end-joining in telomere-deficient transgenic mice. Chromosomes from the sixth generation of telomerase-deficient mice are shown analysed by FISH to the telomere probe TTAGGG (red). Note that mouse chromosomes have one long chromosome arm and one very short chromosome arm – a structure known as an acrocentric chromosome. End–end fusion chromosomes are visible in these cells (white arrows) against the background of normal smaller acrocentric chromosomes.

At this point, it is important only to note that, without telomeres, chromosomes can undergo rearrangements. Telomeres are therefore essential in maintaining chromosomal integrity. Broken DNA can also trigger programmed cell death, or apoptosis, which we will examine in more detail in Chapter 14. Finally, telomeric DNA appears to be involved in the proliferative capacity of cells, a subject we will return to in Chapter 18 when we discuss cell senescence and in Chapter 19 when we deal with tumorigenesis.

9.5.3 Telomerase-independent maintenance of linear chromosomes

So far, we have discussed how simple telomeric repeats are used to stabilize the ends of linear chromosomes. There are several eukaryotes, however, that do not have a telomerase enzyme, and do not utilize short repeats to maintain their linear DNA; examples include *Drosophila*, the onion and the mosquito.

In the case of *Drosophila*, telomeres consist of blocks of DNA called HeT elements. These are a type of DNA called **retro-elements**, which are capable of copying themselves through the action of reverse transcriptase on their mRNA and then inserting these copies back into chromosomal DNA. HeT elements appear to insert at telomeric regions and serve to counteract DNA erosion.

In the case of the onion and mosquito, DNA is added at the ends of their chromosomes by recombination between repeats at the ends of other chromosomes. We will discuss the mechanism of recombination later in this chapter.

Summary of Section 9.5

1   Telomeres are specialized structures that lie at the ends of linear chromosomes and prevent their erosion.

2   In most eukaryotes, telomeric DNA consists of large blocks of simple repetitive G–rich sequences maintained by telomerase, a reverse transcriptase that carries its own template.

3   Alternative mechanisms exist to maintain DNA ends, including retro-elements and recombination.

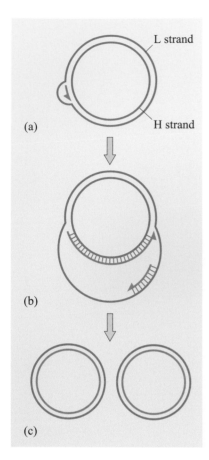

(a)   L strand

      H strand

(b)

(c)

Figure 9.24
The replication of mitochondrial DNA.
The human mitochondrial genome is
approximately 16.5 kb in length and its
strands (called H and L) are replicated
separately. (a) DNA synthesis is
initiated at the D-loop region on the
H strand template. (b) As the
replication fork passes the second
initiation site, synthesis then proceeds
in the opposite direction using the
displaced L strand as template.

9.6 Replication of mitochondrial DNA

As mitochondria contain their own genetic material, this DNA must also be copied
before cells divide, in order for new organelles to be created (as you saw in Section
8.2.7). Mitochondria actually contain many copies of their circular genome and DNA
synthesis is carried out by a polymerase dedicated to mitochondrial DNA (mtDNA)
maintenance.

In the case of mammalian mtDNA (see Figure 9.24), replication is carried out by
DNA polymerase γ, which has an intrinsic proofreading 3′–5′ exonuclease activity.
Each strand of the mitochondrial genome is synthesized separately from a different
initiation point. The process is believed to commence when replication is initiated
at what is called the D-loop region, by synthesis of a short RNA primer by RNA
polymerase. DNA polymerase γ continues synthesis until, at a point approximately
two-thirds the way around, the 16.5 kb circle, the synthesis initiation site for the
other strand is revealed. This site is then used to initiate synthesis of the second
strand. When both strands have been completed, the two molecules are separated.

9.7 Replication of viral DNA in mammalian cells

> The life cycles of viruses are described in detail in S204 Book 4 *Microbes*,
> Section 1.3.

Mammalian cells can be infected with different viruses, many of which have
been exploited for experimental studies or for therapeutic use in humans. These
applications will be discussed in later chapters. Here, though, we shall focus on
two differing strategies utilized for replication of the viral genome. The first is
for the virus genome to integrate into the host cell's DNA. The resultant virus is
then replicated by the host cell's replication machinery when the chromosome
is replicated. This is the strategy used by retroviruses such as the mouse virus,
Moloney murine leukaemia virus (MMLV) and the human immunodeficiency virus
(HIV). In the case of HIV, the first stage of infection results in the conversion of
the viral RNA genome into a DNA copy through the action of reverse transcriptase,
an enzyme that synthesizes DNA using an RNA template and is encoded in the
viral genome. This DNA copy then integrates into the host cell's DNA, which
can lead to the disruption or destruction of a chromosomal gene at the site of
integration.

The second strategy used by many viruses is to remain as a non-integrated genome
and undergo **extrachromosomal replication**. Viruses that use this approach carry
their own replication origins and their genome encodes several ancillary proteins that
modulate the virus's utilization of the host cell's replication machinery. Examples of
such viruses include the Epstein–Barr virus (EBV) and the human papilloma virus
(HPV), both of which have circular DNA genomes, and adenovirus, which has a
linear genome. These viruses can also integrate into the host cell genome in some
circumstances. For example, another commonly used virus, adeno-associated virus
(AAV), replicates extrachromosomally in the presence of adenovirus components,
but integrates when adenovirus is absent.

When host cell division occurs, the integrated retroviruses are segregated with the two sets of mitotic chromosomes. Extrachromosomal viruses must use an alterative strategy to ensure their genomes are distributed to both daughter cells. Firstly, these viruses are present in many copies within a cell. Secondly, the virus also encodes one or more proteins that serve to attach the viral genomic DNA directly to the host cell's chromosomes without DNA integration. This chromosomal attachment ensures that at cell division, viral genome copies are segregated to both daughter cells with the chromosomes during mitosis.

9.8 Repair of DNA damage

You saw in Chapter 5 the types of DNA damage that can arise either due to the action of normal by-products of cell respiration or through the action of extraneous chemical and physical agents on DNA. Some bacteria have a strategy of protecting their DNA from damage during inactive stages of their life cycle by adopting a highly compacted chemically inert structure (Section 5.7.1). Most cells, whether bacteria or eukaryotic cells, spend the majority of their existence in an active metabolic state, and exposure to a chemically damaging internal and external environment is therefore a normal state of affairs. DNA replication errors can also lead to genetic damage by the misincorporation of bases.

○ Can you recall the types of DNA damage that can occur?

● DNA damaging agents were discussed in Section 5.5 and include the formation of abasic sites, deamination, pyrimidine dimer formation, oxygen radical damage such as the formation of 8-oxoguanosine, alkylation damage and the covalent binding of 'bulky' agents such as BAP metabolites.

The consequences of DNA damage are obvious: the loss or alteration of the genetic information carried within the base order of the DNA chain. Damage can be at the level of the single base or involve larger amounts of DNA. If, for example, a break occurs in the sugar–phosphate backbone, it is essential that no DNA is lost through degradation from the free ends of the chromosome. We will see in this section how such ends are detected rapidly and rejoined appropriately. The breaking of the DNA backbone is especially dangerous to a cell if multiple ends are generated, as can be the case after exposure to some forms of ionizing radiation and where there is a potential to join together ends that were not originally contiguous, perhaps even on different chromosomes. In other cases, some forms of DNA damage can physically block the processes of replication and transcription, thus preventing normal cellular metabolism.

The detection and repair of all these types of DNA damage are of obvious importance for the viability of a single cell, for the whole organism if multicellular, and for the passage of genetic material between generations. In this section, we will concentrate on the cellular processes and systems that protect against the different types of DNA damage. This protection essentially involves a two-stage process: first, the detection of damage, and then the recruitment of effector proteins to carry out repair and halt cell cycle progression if necessary. In all cases, the ideal outcome of these different systems is to restore the DNA to its original state. We will see how this is achieved by repairing damage from the other strand in a duplex, the sister chromatid or the homologous chromosome. The accumulation of DNA mutations due to defective components of the DNA repair machinery is an important factor in many human diseases and in the development of tumorigenic cells.

9.8.1 The direct repair of damaged bases in DNA

Several specific forms of DNA damage have proteins dedicated to their repair.

◻ Can you recall an example of such a protein that you encountered in Chapter 5?

◼ O^6-methylguanosine methyltransferase removes a methyl group to regenerate guanosine (Section 5.5.1).

A family of proteins in *E. coli* called alkB proteins function to repair methylation damage at cytosine (3-methylcytosine) and adenine (1-methyladenine) to restore the bases *in situ* within the helix. A family of evolutionarily conserved proteins in eukaryotes perform the same function.

9.8.2 The removal of damaged bases from DNA

In the case of damaged nucleotides, it is often necessary to remove the entire base concerned and insert the correct base, a process called excision repair. Such repair can be of two types, depending upon what damage has occurred. Examples of base damage include the formation of dimers between adjacent T or C residues due to exposure to UV light, but more commonly include the products of chemical attack upon the bases, such as deamination, depurination or alkylation. The repair of this type of damage is performed by several different systems, all of which involve the removal or excision of the damaged base, followed by template-driven resynthesis.

Depurinated or deaminated bases are amongst the most commonly found types of damage in DNA, and specific proteins are dedicated to the scanning and removal of them in a process called **base excision repair**. The proteins detecting such damage belong to the family of enzymes called DNA glycolyases. An example of how glycolyases function is shown in Figure 9.25a.

The damage that these proteins detect does not lead to a distortion of the external dimensions of the double helix. Therefore, in order to detect the damaged bases, these proteins scan along the double helix and sense base damage by 'flipping' each base out from the helix. Some members of this protein family have a broad specificity that detects common forms of oxidative DNA damage, whereas others have a highly specific activity. For example, a specific glycolyase removes 8-oxoguanine bases, whereas another, illustrated in Figure 9.25a, removes uracil from DNA. Many of these proteins are evolutionarily highly conserved in eukaryotes. As can be seen in Figure 9.25a, the DNA glycolyase cleaves the base from the DNA backbone and recruits an endonuclease to remove the sugar–phosphate. The correct nucleotide is inserted by a DNA polymerase using the opposite strand as a template and the DNA backbone is re-formed through the action of DNA ligase.

Some DNA damage distorts the dimensions of the helix, such as with 'bulky' agents, pyrimidine dimers such as T–T, and some types of chemotherapeutic agents. In these cases, it is the distortion of the helix that triggers their detection, rather than the specific form of damage. As shown in Figure 9.25b, after detection of the damage, two endonucleases are recruited and a small region, ranging from several bases up to 10–12 bases in length, surrounding the lesion is removed and resynthesized. This process is termed **nucleotide excision repair (NER)**.

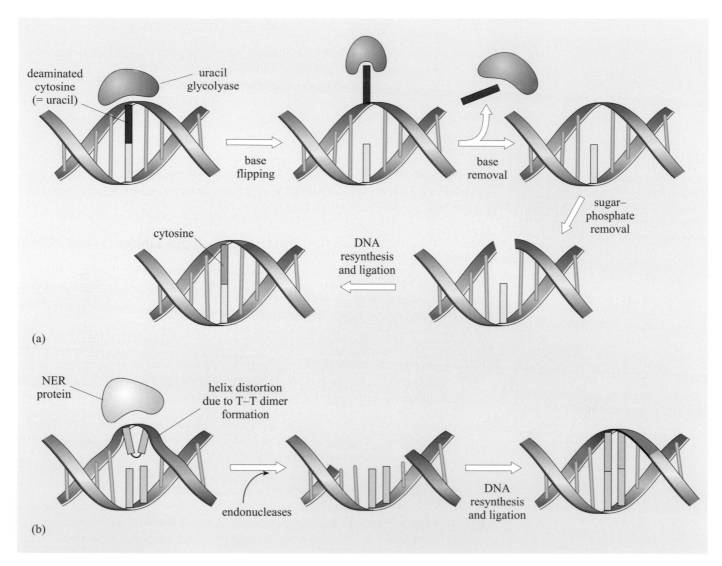

Figure 9.25   The mechanisms of excision repair. (a) Base excision repair. Detection of lesions
is effected by DNA glycolyases, which detect damaged bases directly by scanning each base using
a mechanism that 'flips' it from the helix. In this example, uracil glycolyase detects the presence
of uracil that has arisen through cytosine deamination. The glycolyase removes the base, leaving
the sugar–phosphate backbone intact. This abasic site is then processed by an endonuclease
that removes the sugar–phosphate unit. Subsequently, DNA polymerase and DNA ligase effect
a template-driven resynthesis. (b) DNA damage that distorts the helix structure, in this case a
thymidine dimer, is detected by nucleotide excision repair (NER) proteins, which trigger the
recruitment of two endonucleases that remove a portion of the affected DNA strand. New duplex is
completed by resynthesis and ligation.

9.8.3 The detection and removal of mispaired bases

We have already seen that during replication, the binding pocket of DNA polymerase allows the detection of mispaired bases and the exonuclease activity has the ability to remove them. This proofreading ability of the replication machinery is one of the first DNA integrity checking processes in place within the cell. Misincorporation of bases does occur and occasionally bases are added or deleted that are not corrected by the polymerase itself (see Figure 9.26).

Figure 9.26
DNA synthesis errors detected by the mismatch repair machinery: three examples of mutations that can arise during replicative DNA synthesis at the sequence 5′-ATGCTG.

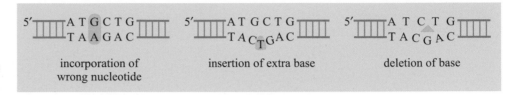

These types of DNA damage are detected by a group of specialized proteins physically associated with the replication machinery and are called the **mismatch repair** proteins. In *E. coli*, the error is detected by a dimer of the mutS protein (see Figure 9.27) which binds to it in association with a dimer of the mutL protein.

○ If we consider the errors shown in Figure 9.26, can you think of a mechanism by which the mutS/L complex could determine which strand the error is on? In other words, in the case of a mismatched base pair, which is the correct base?

■ In order to repair the error, the machinery must be able to determine the original parent strand. Recall that after bacterial replication, this parental strand is methylated and the new strand transiently non-methylated.

The repair complex 'scans' the newly synthesized duplex DNA until a hemi-methylated site allows a discrimination between the parent and new strands. At this point, the mutH protein binds and cleaves the newly synthesized strand and the region containing the mismatch is removed by an exonuclease. New DNA is synthesized in its place. In eukaryotes, this process is evolutionarily highly conserved, but the number of proteins involved is greater than in prokaryotes. There are six forms of mutS-related proteins, termed MSH proteins (for <u>m</u>ut<u>S</u> <u>h</u>omologue), in eukaryotes. The MSH proteins function as dimers to detect specific

Figure 9.27
DNA mismatch repair in *E. coli*. Errors in DNA synthesis (a), such as those in Figure 9.26, are detected in *E. coli* by the mutS protein which, together with mutL, binds to the error (b) and 'scans' locally (dashed arrows) to detect a site of hemi-methylation, which allows strand discrimination of parent and new strands. Binding of a third component, the endonuclease mutH, leads to the cleavage of the DNA backbone and removal of the mispaired region (c). Template-driven resynthesis and ligation complete the repair (d).

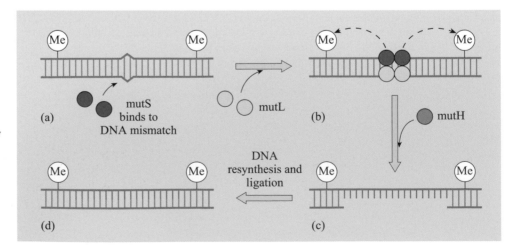

lesions, including single base insertions/deletions (MSH2 : MSH6 dimer) or insertions of 2–6 bp (MSH2 : MSH3 dimer). One MSH protein, MSH4, is a specialized mitochondrial DNA repair protein.

The cell's ability to distinguish the newly synthesized strand within a duplex is not always dependent upon DNA hemi-methylation as it is in *E. coli*, as many eukaryotic genomes are unmethylated. It appears that the persistence of non-ligated Okazaki fragments in most newly synthesized lagging strands allows for strand discrimination to permit appropriate excision and repair.

9.8.4 Copy repair

In the cases discussed above, once damage has been detected and removed, resynthesis is straightforward as it is based upon the use of the other strand as a template. Damage to the DNA strand is often encountered during DNA replication and in some cases, the replication fork simply skips over the damaged area, leaving it to be repaired after replication, as is shown is Figure 9.28. As a consequence, when the two daughter duplexes have been completely synthesized, the helix carrying the damage has a gap in its newly synthesized strand, immediately opposite the site of damage.

○   How do you think the repair systems discussed thus far would cope with such a configuration of DNA damage and a 'gapped' strand.

●   The damage can be excised, but a problem arises when it comes to resynthesizing the strand, as there is no template strand available.

If such damage had been detected before replication, repair resynthesis would have been directed from the strand opposite the damage. This strand is, after replication, now part of the other daughter DNA helix. The two daughter helices (sister chromatids) are, of course, identical to each other, except for instances of damaged DNA. So the other daughter helix is the only DNA chain that has the appropriate base order and is thus used as the template to resynthesize the DNA that is missing from the gapped region. This type of post-replicative repair, where one strand is repaired by copying from the other newly synthesized daughter strand,

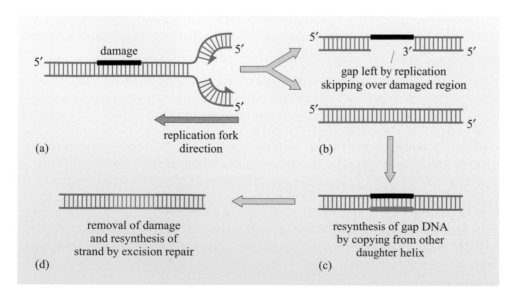

(a) damage · 5′ · replication fork direction
(b) gap left by replication skipping over damaged region
(c) resynthesis of gap DNA by copying from other daughter helix
(d) removal of damage and resynthesis of strand by excision repair

Figure 9.28
Bypass synthesis during replication requires repair from the sister chromatid. (a) and (b) During replication, damaged bases are occasionally bypassed by DNA polymerase, which leaves a gap in the newly synthesized strand. (c) After replication is complete, this gap is filled in by copying from the sister chromatid (this process is shown in Figure 9.32, if you want to jump ahead). (d) Once resynthesis is complete, excision repair (as shown in Figure 9.25) finishes off the repair process.

is termed **copy** or **recombinational repair**, and will be discussed in more detail in Section 9.9. Once synthesis from the other helix is complete, the normal processes of excision repair replace the damaged area.

9.8.5 Transcription-coupled repair

The other cellular process during which DNA damage is frequently detected is transcription, when the DNA helix is unwound for the synthesis of mRNA. If damaged DNA is detected during transcription, it can lead to the termination of RNA synthesis. RNA polymerase, however, has the ability to reverse, and when damage is encountered that prevents continued synthesis, ancillary proteins that are part of the transcription machinery trigger what is called **transcription-coupled repair**. These proteins recruit specific excision repair components to the region. This process favours repair of the coding strand, thus providing an additional level of protection against mutations in protein-coding regions.

9.8.6 Repair of double-strand breaks

Until now, we have been discussing damage to DNA bases or damage that has occurred on only one strand of the helix, in which case it has been possible to synthesize a replacement from the other strand, or from the other daughter helix after replication. Sometimes, however, the DNA helix backbone is broken in both strands to generate a double-strand break (DSB), such as happens during exposure to ionizing radiation or as a result of oxidative damage.

○ Can you recall from Chapter 5 the name of the histone variant that is incorporated at DNA breaks?

● Histone 2AX (Book 1, p. 238).

An unrepaired DSB could potentially be a very serious problem for the cell, as it could lead to the loss of genetic information, not only by the loss of bases at the ends of the DNA chains involved, but also by the formation of segments of chromosomes without a centromere. If many breaks are present, rearrangements of chromosomes could result if misjoining occurs (see Figure 9.29). The tendency for broken DNA ends to be joined together in error is one reason why the natural ends of a chromosome at telomeres are protected by specific chromatin structures that prevent such occurrences, or are unable to interact with any breaks that do occur in the cell.

The consequences of DSBs are potentially severe, so it not surprising that cells have a variety of detection and repair systems directed towards them. DSBs are generally dealt with in one of two ways, as shown schematically in Figure 9.30. As a first stage, specific proteins detect the presence of the breakage site and directly bind to both ends. At the same time, the DSB results in the activation of a sensor protein called ATM, which we will discuss in more detail shortly. The 'simplest' repair strategy is to directly rejoin the two broken ends and whilst this could result in loss of information, it does at least maintain the chromosome and allows the cell to repair a broken chromosome. In most cases, this is how breaks are processed and it can lead to the loss of genetic information or the generation of chromosome rearrangements. In diploid eukaryotic cells, another commonly used pathway relies upon a copy repair process rather like that we discussed with post-replicative repair between sister chromatids (Figure 9.28).

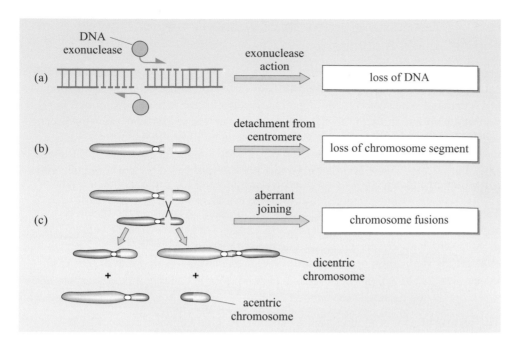

Figure 9.29
The consequences of double-strand breaks if not detected and repaired appropriately. Double-strand breaks in chromosomal DNA can result in the loss of genetic information through: (a) direct exonuclease removal of bases at the unprotected DNA ends; (b) if ends are not rejoined, the fragment without a centromere (acentric DNA) will be lost as it will not align or segregate properly in cell division because it cannot attach to the mitotic spindle; and (c) if multiple breaks are present, aberrant joining can result in the formation of new chromosomal fusions such as translocated or dicentric chromosomes which, upon cell division, will generate genetic imbalances within cells.

⬭ What template could be used for a copy repair process in a diploid cell that has not just undergone replication?

⬛ The only available molecule to serve as a template is the other chromosome. Remember that in diploid cells, there are two copies of each chromosome, one inherited from each parent. These will, of course, be potentially genetically different, but the order of genes and the majority of the sequence of DNA will be virtually identical.

This type of repair, called homologous end-joining or recombinational repair, utilizes machinery in the cell that is used for recombination, which we will discuss in more detail in Section 9.9. In eukaryotes, the presence of DSBs is potentially lethal as, if left unrepaired, they trigger cell death through apoptosis. A key protein in the detection of DSBs is called ATM. ATM is activated within a few minutes of exposure of human cells to radiation in both dividing and non-dividing cells. Although the precise mechanism of ATM activation is still unknown, it most likely involves the end-binding proteins and local alterations to chromatin structure, such as H2AX binding, that occur at the site of the DNA break. ATM is a kinase that activates many downstream targets, several of which we will discuss further in the following section.

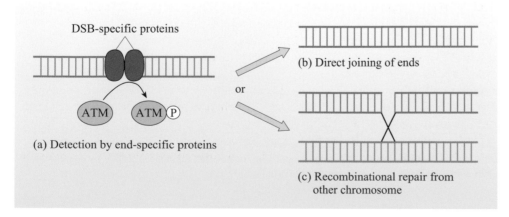

Figure 9.30
The detection and processing of double-strand DNA breaks. (a) A double-strand break is detected by proteins that bind to the free DNA ends. These complexes also interact with additional signalling proteins such as ATM. (b) Most repair is effected through a direct end-joining process. Alternatively, repair can utilize the other chromosome as a template across the break (c).

9.8.7 Interactions between DNA repair and components of the cell cycle machinery

Once the eukaryotic cell is committed to progress through DNA replication and into cell division, the process normally continues to completion. If, during replication, DNA damage is detected and not repaired, feedback mechanisms ensure that the cell does not continue through the cell cycle and into cell division. This prevents loss of segments of chromosomes that have become detached from their centromeres. As we have seen, much of post-replication repair relies upon the presence of the sister chromatid. Detection of DNA damage that has not undergone repair before a certain point in the cell cycle leads to its stalling until repair is completed.

Two proteins play key roles in regulating the interaction between the repair system and the cell cycle in mammalian cells (Figure 9.31). The first of these is the ATM protein, which as we saw earlier, is activated in response to double-strand breaks that arise during replication or as a result of radiation damage. Activation of the ATM kinase can lead to activation of the G1, G2 and spindle checkpoints, depending upon when breaks are detected (see Section 8.3).

The second protein is another kinase called ATR. This kinase can also trigger the same cell cycle checkpoints as ATM, and does so in response to UV damage (principally pyrimidine dimers) and in response to the presence of stalled replication fork complexes. Its ability to detect stalled replication forks depends upon its ability to interact with the RPA protein (introduced in Section 9.3.4). Thus, the persistence of incompletely synthesized lagging strands or the exposure of single-stranded DNA during DNA repair leads to ATR activation.

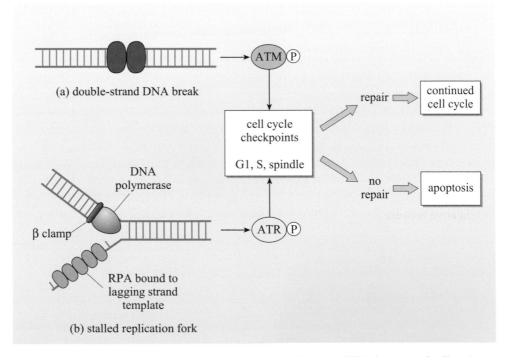

Figure 9.31 ATM and ATR proteins act as an interface between DNA damage and cell cycle checkpoints. Cell cycle checkpoints can be activated by (a) the presence of double-strand breaks, which activate ATM, or (b) DNA damage, resulting in a stalled replication fork, which activates ATR through persistent single-stranded DNA bound to RPA.

○ Can you recall the downstream targets for ATR and ATM activation?

● Both ATM and ATR activate two proteins called Chk1 and Chk2. These in turn signal cell cycle arrest through regulation of the cyclin–Cdk complex (Section 8.3.5, Figure 8.27).

Persistent ATM and ATR activation that does not result in suitable repair will eventually trigger cell death by apoptosis (discussed further in Chapter 14).

9.8.8 Human diseases and deficits in DNA repair

Deficits in the DNA repair process can lead to severe consequences through the accumulation of genetic damage, mutations in proteins and loss or duplication of genes. There are many inherited human diseases that result from specific deficits in components of the repair machinery and some of these are listed in Table 9.4. In many cases, defects in DNA repair proteins are involved in the process of tumorigenesis. Many of these defects allow the accumulation of chromosomal damage, which leads to imbalances in chromosome number after cell division or allows mutations to occur in key growth regulatory genes. This will be discussed further in Chapter 19. The other major effect is upon the response to DNA damage, either externally (radiation) or internally (oxidative or replication damage), all of which contributes to the accumulation of damage in cells that could lead to cell death. The clinical consequences of these deficits frequently involve sensitivity to irradiation or symptoms that resemble premature ageing.

Table 9.4 Examples of human diseases associated with the different DNA repair and detection pathways.

Repair system	Gene/protein	Cellular effect and disease	Disease
DNA mismatch repair	MutS and MutL homologues (MSH and MLH families)	accumulation of mutations	hereditary colon cancer and many other tumours
DNA nucleotide excision repair	XP family of 7 genes (XPA–G)	defective NER sensitivity to UV light	xeroderma pigmentosa skin cancer
double-strand break detection	ATM	X-ray sensitivity	ataxia telangectasia
recombinational repair	BRCA1	decreased repair	breast and ovarian cancer
replicative helicase	Bloom protein	elevated mitotic chromosome exchange	Bloom's syndrome (cancers and stunted growth)
replicative and repair helicase/exonuclease	Werner's protein	defective replication and repair	Werner's syndrome (cancer, premature ageing)
transcription-coupled repair	CS proteins	defective transcription-coupled repair	Cockayne's syndrome

9.8.9 The repair of RNA damage

As you may recall from Chapter 5, a large fraction of the nucleic acids in a cell is RNA. Until recently, very little was known about whether RNA was actively repaired. AlkB proteins, described earlier (Section 9.8.1), have been found to remove the methyl group from 3-methylcytosine and 1-methyladenine in RNA. This observation suggests that the structurally important RNAs in the cell may be maintained, or perhaps regulated, through the action of this group of proteins. AlkB proteins may also play roles in the repair of mRNA.

Summary of Section 9.8

1   The cell contains various specialized proteins dedicated to the detection and repair of damaged or misincorporated bases in nucleic acids. These proteins are evolutionarily highly conserved.

2   Specialized repair proteins exist to directly remove certain damaged bases, e.g. O^6-methylguanine and 8-oxoguanine.

3   Lesions that do not distort the helix structure are detected by damage-specific proteins that mediate repair by base excision repair (e.g. DNA glycolyases).

4   Larger lesions can be detected by proteins that recognize resultant distortions in the helix. Restoration of the short region near the lesion is mediated by nucleotide excision repair.

5   Mispaired bases, insertions and deletions are detected and repaired by the mismatch repair machinery.

6   In cases of gapped strands or DSBs, repair utilizes another template strand for restorative DNA synthesis. Examples include post-replicative copy repair and DSB repair.

7   DSBs are detected by proteins that recognize DNA ends, activating ATM. Repair is usually mediated through direct end-joining but can be through copy repair.

8   The presence of DNA damage that could cause genetic damage to a cell results in the activation of cell cycle checkpoints, a process that is mediated through the activation of ATM (DNA breaks) or ATR (pyrimidine dimers, stalled replication forks via RPA persistence).

9   Failure to repair DNA breaks can lead to loss of genetic material, chromosome rearrangement or loss of acentric fragments.

9.9 Recombination between DNA strands

As you have seen in this chapter, the cell goes to great lengths to maintain the integrity of the genetic information in its DNA, but the process of DNA repair seems directly at odds with the processes through which it is believed that molecular evolution has occurred; that is, through the mutation and subsequent selection for or against organisms carrying these mutations. Without mutation there would be no variation on which natural selection could act. We must, therefore, assume that mutations can and do escape repair.

A second process that is important in generating variety is that new combinations of chromosomes carrying mutations are generated in meiosis, leading to a diversity of genetic variation. Natural selection on a genetically diverse population leads to the removal of deleterious combinations of mutations and the persistence of favourable combinations. Although the detailed aspects and the genetic impacts of these processes are beyond the scope of this course, we will discuss here the molecular pathways by which genetic information is reassorted at the DNA level, a process called **recombination**.

Central to the process of recombination is the interaction between two DNA strands that have identical or almost identical DNA sequences. These are called homologous sequences. During meiosis, this interaction is between two homologous chromosomes; in recombination such as that described in Box 9.3, it is between the incoming genetically engineered DNA and the target genomic locus; and in post-replicative repair it is between the two newly synthesized sister chromatids. Recombination, therefore, not only plays a key role in both generating and maintaining diversity within a population at the genetic level through meiosis, but also has an essential role in maintaining the integrity of the genome through DNA repair.

9.9.1 Recombination is initiated by DNA breaks

We start our examination of recombination by focusing on this central feature: the interaction of two DNA duplexes of the same DNA sequence. The interaction is believed to be initiated through the formation of a double-strand break (DSB) in one of the DNA helices. We have seen examples of how DSBs can arise as a result of exposure to damaging agents or as a consequence of repair (Sections 9.8.4 and 9.8.5). To begin, we will consider how recombination is used to repair such a break.

Consider the DSB shown in Figure 9.32. In order for this DNA duplex to interact with another, DNA on both sides of the DSB is first removed by a 5′ to 3′ exonuclease to expose the bases of the remaining strand and to leave a 3′-OH end (Figure 9.32, step (ii)). Base pairing between this exposed strand and a stretch of homologous DNA then occurs and the free 3′-OH serves as a primer for the synthesis of a new DNA strand (step (iii)).

This **strand invasion** process is assisted by many proteins. In mammalian cells, these proteins include BRCA1 which, in humans, is frequently mutated in ovarian and breast tumours (Table 9.4).

As DNA synthesis proceeds, the other 3′ -OH in chromosome A can now anneal to the displaced strand of chromosome B and itself prime DNA synthesis (step (iv)). DNA synthesis is performed by DNA polymerases, assisted by DNA helicases which unwind the helix. As a result, DNA is synthesized for *both* strands that span the original DSB (step (v)). This structure is

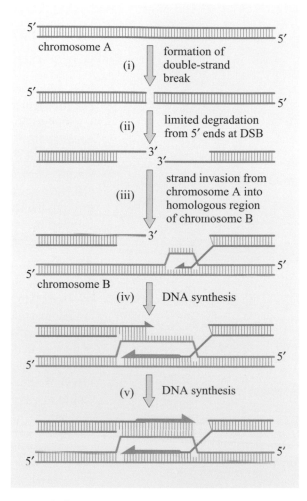

Figure 9.32   Recombination between two DNA duplexes in repair and meiosis. Recombination is initiated through the formation of a double-strand break (i) in chromosome A. Exonuclease activity exposes short stretches of single-stranded DNA with 3′-OH ends (ii). Strand invasion into chromosome B (iii) is enhanced by ancillary proteins. At the point of invasion, the strand anneals to the complementary strand of chromosome B, forming a heteroduplex region. DNA synthesis is now initiated from the invading 3′-OH (iv). As DNA synthesis proceeds, chromosome B DNA is displaced, to which the other 3′-OH end in chromosome A can now anneal and also begin DNA synthesis (v). Thus DNA synthesis fills in the DNA from across the DSB region on both strands.

resolved by specialized proteins that cleave the strands to restore the original chromosome A, now with the region across the DSB restored. Note that the section immediately flanking the original DSB on chromosome A is now a copy of the DNA sequence from chromosome B.

In the case of post-replicative repair, a similar invasion occurs, allowing the missing section of DNA to be regenerated. If you look back to Figure 9.28b, you can see that the DNA strand carrying the gap has an exposed 3′ end. Through a similar strand invasion and copying process to that shown in Figure 9.32, this 3′-OH is extended until the gap is filled, wherein the strand dissociates and is ligated to reform an intact segment. In the case of post-replicative repair, strand invasion occurs into the sister chromatid.

9.9.2 Recombination in meiosis

Recombination also occurs during meiosis to allow chromosomes to exchange genetic information. In meiosis, the DSB is created by meiosis-specific proteins, but essentially the process outlined in Figure 9.32 occurs to form a junction between the two chromosomes. By joining together the 3′-OH from the newly synthesized DNAs onto the matching 5′ end, a specific configuration of DNA strands known as a **Holliday structure** is created. Once two regions of homologous DNA are paired in this way, the whole junction can migrate along the DNA strands through the unwinding in front, and rewinding behind, in a process called **branch migration**. In order to resolve the interaction between the two duplexes into a recombination between the two chromosomes, cleavage of all four DNA backbones must occur.

Take a look at the Holliday structure shown in Figure 9.33. This represents the point of interaction of the four DNA strands between two homologous chromosomes after strand invasion and branch migration has occurred. For recombination to occur, this junction is cleaved in a very specific fashion by cellular proteins and each end is then ligated to that of the other chromosome. The resolution of this interaction simply involves cleavage, swapping and rejoining of each strand. For example, for chromosome A (pink), follow the top strand to point 3 and join this end to the lower strand of chromosome B (purple) at point 4. Note that the 5′–3′ strand orientation is maintained. Similarly, the lower strand of chromosome A is joined to the upper strand of chromosome B at the 1–2 cleavage point.

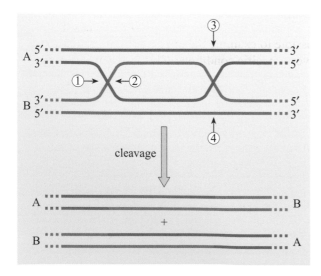

Figure 9.33
Resolution of a meiotic Holliday structure by strand cleavage. The four DNA strands of two chromosomes (A, pink; B, purple) are shown with a Holliday junction formed between two of the strands. In order for recombination to occur between the two chromosomes, the strands are cleaved at four points. This strand cleavage occurs in two areas. Cleavage of chromosome A at 1 and chromosome B at 2 occurs at the left-hand cross-over point. Chromosome A is then joined to B and B to A (note that the strand orientation allows this). Cleavage then occurs at the right-hand cross-over point, at position 3 on chromosome A and at 4 on chromosome B, and the broken strands are joined A to B and B to A as before. The result of these cleavage and rejoining reactions is shown in the lower half of the figure. Note that the outcome of this reaction is a recombination event; that is, chromosome A has been recombined with chromosome B. Note that a small region of overlap exists between the junctions.

Many proteins are involved in meiotic recombination pathways, including the meiosis-specific proteins that create the DSBs and promote strand invasion and branch migration.

9.9.3 Site-specific recombination

The processes outlined above describe how any two sections of DNA within a cell can interact and exchange blocks of genetic material, either through an exchange event or by acting as a template for synthesis. There is another type of recombination event, which allows DNA to be integrated or excised at specific points along a chromosome; this is called **site-specific recombination**.

Many DNA elements that infect cells, such as viruses, encode proteins that catalyse their integration into a recipient cell's genomic DNA. Two such proteins are the cre and flp recombinases. The cre recombinase is encoded by a gene on a bacterial virus, or bacteriophage, called P1. This enzyme acts at a specific DNA sequence called a *loxP* site within the viral genome to promote insertion or excision from the host chromosome. The flp recombinase is encoded on a yeast circular plasmid DNA called the 2 micron plasmid. It specifically recognizes a target site called an *frt* site. Both these enzymes are capable of catalysing a recombination event between two DNA fragments carrying their specific target sites. The two strands of DNA are cleaved and exchanged as in Figure 9.33, in this case allowing insertion or excision of DNA as outlined in Figure 9.34. The cre and flp recombinases are commonly used to manipulate DNA fragments *in vivo* as outlined in Box 9.4.

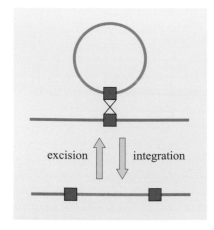

Figure 9.34
Site-specific recombination allows integration and excision at a target site. Site-specific recombination enzymes catalyse the recombination between target sites between DNA elements. These interactions allow the integration of a DNA fragment into a linear chromosome or its excision.

| Box 9.4 | Exploiting site-specific recombination to manipulate DNA *in vivo* |

Site-specific recombinases from several organisms have been exploited that allow DNA to be manipulated or rearranged *in vivo*. The ability to accurately target and repair DNA segments has allowed researchers to study transgenes in a more refined and controlled manner. Such control is important, for example, if the absence of an endogenous gene in a knock-out mouse proves to be lethal during embryonic life or if the investigation requires a study of specific cell types or stages of development. To address the problem of lethality, various strategies have been developed which involve combining transgenic cells expressing either of the site-specific cre or flp recombinase proteins, with expression vectors carrying their target sites. This combination of approaches is regularly used in a wide range of organisms, including mice, *Drosophila* and several plant species.

One common approach is to engineer a transgene with two *loxP* sites flanking an inserted DNA fragment that blocks transcription of the transgene, as shown in Figure 9.35a. When cre recombinase (encoded by the CRE gene) is present in the same cells as this

transgene, a site-specific recombination event results in the removal of the fragment between the *loxP* sites, resulting in transgene transcription. The gene will remain silent in all other cells in which cre is not expressed. In the example shown in Figure 9.35a, cre is present only in neuronal cells and thus the transgene will only be expressed in the mouse brain (Figure 9.35b). Many different transgenic mice have been generated that express cre recombinase in one specific cell type or at different developmental stages. This means that it is possible to examine the effects of gene expression under very specific conditions. This is also the case for *Drosophila* and many plant species.

○ How can this strategy be adopted to make a transgenic mouse with a cell-specific gene knock-out?

● By engineering a transgene that carries the target sites flanking either the gene promoter or perhaps one or more of the transgene's exons. When cre recombinase is present, the gene fragment will be deleted, creating a cell-specific gene knock-out.

Site-specific recombination is also exploited to allow targeting of transgenes to specific chromosomal positions, as shown schematically in Figure 9.35c. In this case, a mammalian cell line carries an integrated *frt* site. When DNA carrying a target site is introduced into these cells in the presence of flp recombinase, the DNA is integrated at the single target site in the chromosomal DNA. This strategy allows insertion of any transgene into a specific chromosomal site each time it is required. The integration site is important, as the expression of transgenes that integrate randomly into chromosomes is heavily influenced by local factors such as chromatin conformation, or the transcriptional activity of genes near the site of integration. For example, integration could occur into DNA that is packaged into highly condensed local chromatin structure, which would result in low levels of expression of the transgene or override promoter elements in the transgene.

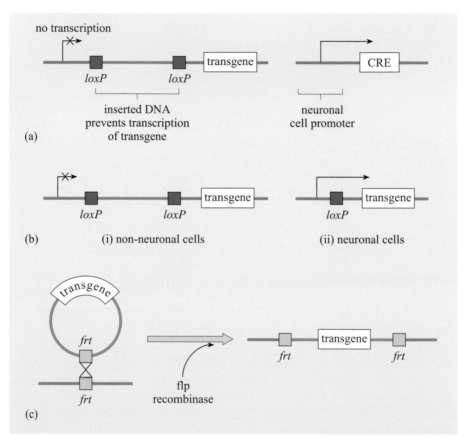

Figure 9.35   Site-specific recombination using cre and flp recombinase in mammalian cells. (a) Maps of two small chromosome segments of a transgenic mouse. In one segment (left) a DNA segment containing a specific transgene has been introduced by homologous recombination in embryonic stem (ES) cells. The transgene is preceded by an inserted fragment of DNA that serves to block its transcription. This DNA fragment is flanked by two *loxP* sites. Inserted into the other chromosome segment (right) is a copy of the cre recombinase gene (CRE), which is controlled by a neuronal-specific promoter. (b) In non-neuronal cells (i), no cre recombinase is produced, and the transgene is not transcribed. In neuronal cells (ii), transcription of cre is activated by neuronal-specific transcription factors, and the action of the recombinase results in the removal of the DNA fragment from the target gene promoter by site-specific recombination. As a consequence, the transgene is expressed. (c) A mammalian chromosome into which DNA fragments will be inserted is shown. Random insertion of DNA into a chromosome can result in interference from the flanking chromatin or gene regulatory elements. Using a cell line grown *in vitro* into which a single *frt* site has been added to a chromosome, DNA can be targeted to this site in any subsequent experiment by inserting an *frt* site into the vector carrying the incoming transgene. When the transgene is introduced into the cells in the transient presence of flp recombinase, it integrates at the same position in each experiment.

Summary of Section 9.9

1   Interactions between DNA strands by recombination are initiated by a DSB and enhanced by proteins such as BRCA1. Strand invasion by a 3′-OH primes DNA synthesis from the recipient duplex.

2   A Holliday structure represents the interaction of four strands of two recombining duplexes; this structure can migrate along each duplex.

3   Resolution of the Holliday junction generates exchanged DNA strands in meiosis.

4   Site-specific recombinase proteins promote targeted recombination to allow insertion and excision of DNA fragments. These have been exploited experimentally through the use of cre/*loxP* and flp/*frt* systems in transgenic organisms.

Reading scientific literature 2

Go to the Study Skills file: *Reading scientific literature 2*, for this activity.

Learning outcomes for Chapter 9

When you have studied this chapter, you should be able to:

9.1 Define and use each of the terms printed in **bold** in the text.

9.2 Understand the applications of the techniques described.

9.3 Discuss the structure of replication origins, their distribution and functional interactions with ORC in relation to cell cycle regulation and discuss the temporal order of replication of eukaryote genomes.

9.4 Discuss and give examples of the roles of polymerases, helicases and topoisomerases in DNA replication, repair and recombination.

9.5 Discuss, with examples, how DNA damage is detected and repaired.

9.6 Outline the mechanism of recombination between homologous DNA sites and discuss examples and applications of site-specific recombination systems.

9.7 Discuss, using examples, the functional conservation of DNA replication, repair and recombination components between *E. coli* and eukaryotes.

9.8 Discuss the relationship between key components of the DNA repair system and the cell cycle.

Questions for Chapter 9

Question 9.1

Outline the principle of pulsed labelling with nucleoside analogues, giving examples and experimental approaches that have been used to study DNA replication.

Question 9.2

How does the newly replicated duplex DNA at the replication fork differ from DNA in the metaphase chromosome?

Question 9.3

How is replication fidelity maintained?

Question 9.4

How are damaged or mispaired DNA bases detected?

Question 9.5

Outline the interactions between components of the eukaryotic cell cycle machinery and components of the replication origin.

References

Beese, L. S., Derbyshire, V. and Steitz, T. A. (1993) Structure of DNA polymerase I Klenow fragment bound to duplex DNA, *Science*, **260**, p. 352.

Blasco, M. A., Lee, H. W., Hande, M. P., Samper, E., Lansdorp, P. M., DePinho, R. A. and Greider, C. W. (1997) Telomere shortening and tumour formation by mouse cells lacking telomerase RNA, *Cell*, **91**, pp. 25–34.

Hansen, R. S., Canfield, T. K., Fjeld, A. D. and Gartler, S. M. (1996) Role of late replication timing in the silencing of X-linked genes, *Human Molecular Genetics*, **9**, pp. 1345–1353.

Hansen, R. S., Canfield, T. K., Fjeld, A. D., Mumm, S., Laird, C. D. and Gartler, S. M. (1997) A variable domain of delayed replication in FRAXA fragile X chromosomes: X inactivation-like spread of late replication, *Proceedings of the National Academy of Sciences, USA*, **94**, pp. 4587–4592.

Raghuraman, M. K., Winzeler, E. A., Collingwood, D., Hunt, S., Wodicka, L., Conway, A., Lockhart, D. J., Davis, R. W., Brewer, B. J. and Fangman, W. L. (2001) Replication dynamics of the yeast genome, *Science*, **294**, pp. 115–121.

Schubeler, D., Scalzo, D., Kooperberg, C., van Steensel, B., Delrow, J. and Groudine, M. (2002) Genome-wide DNA replication profile for *Drosophila melanogaster*: a link between transcription and replication timing, *Nature Genetics*, **32**, pp. 438–442.

Further source

Kunckel, T. A. and Bebenek, K. (2000) DNA replication fidelity, *Annual Review of Biochemistry*, **69**, pp. 497–529.

10 GENE EXPRESSION

10.1 Introduction

With very few exceptions, all the cells of a multicellular organism have identical DNA content. It follows, therefore, that morphological, biochemical and behavioural differences between cells must result from different patterns of gene expression. Recall that, according to the central dogma, genetic information flows from DNA to RNA to protein (Figure 5.2). In this chapter, we shall examine in more detail the stage from the DNA template to mature RNA molecules, focusing primarily on mRNA. The processes by which genes are expressed are subject to control at several stages, notably transcriptional regulation and post-transcriptional modification. The topic of translation – that is, the synthesis of polypeptides from the information contained within mature mRNA molecules (and the regulatory aspects of this process) – will be covered in Chapter 11.

As you have seen in earlier chapters, cellular processes in eukaryotes – in particular, multicellular eukaryotes – are more complex than in prokaryotes. We therefore begin our discussion of gene expression with a description of the structure of prokaryotic genes, and how transcription is regulated in these relatively simple systems. The bulk of this chapter, however, deals with the mechanisms used to control gene expression in eukaryotic cells. Many of the differences in gene expression between prokaryotes and eukaryotes are illustrated in Figure 10.1.

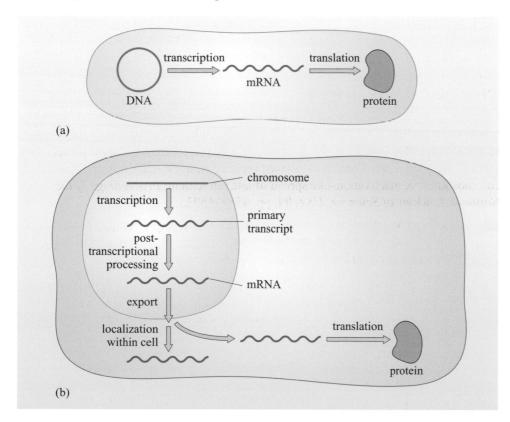

Figure 10.1
Pathways of gene expression in prokaryotes and eukaryotes. (a) In prokaryotes, transcription and translation do not occur in separate compartments within the cell, and translation of mRNA begins before transcription is complete (Chapter 11). (b) In eukaryotic systems, transcription is spatially (and temporally) separated from translation, and occurs within the nucleus. The greater complexity of eukaryotes offers the possibility of control of gene expression at many points in the flow of information from gene to protein.

The study of gene structure in prokaryotic systems (notably *E. coli*) has allowed insight into the molecular processes of transcriptional control. Because of the relative simplicity of prokaryotic genes and the genetic techniques available, many classic genetic experiments have been performed which reveal mechanisms of protein–DNA interaction and transcriptional control. These have illuminated similar processes in the more complex eukaryotic genes. From the examples chosen to illustrate transcriptional processes and their control, it will be apparent that many were first characterized in model organisms such as *C. elegans*, *S. cerevisiae* and *D. melanogaster*. Most of these processes are evolutionarily highly conserved and no doubt occur in many other species.

A generalized view of gene struc ture is that of a linear DNA chain with sequence elements essential for correct transcription lying immediately adjacent to the protein coding region, the **open reading frame (ORF)**, which is flanked by translation start and stop codons. This picture is largely derived from the prokaryotic systems that form the paradigm of gene structure.

Chapter 5 reviewed the salient features of DNA; several features were noted that are relevant to our description of gene transcription at this stage. Firstly, the helical B-form of DNA found in all cells has both major and minor grooves. These two grooves differ in the degree of exposure of the base pairs; in general, it is the major groove that provides greater exposure of the base residues, with which proteins can interact in a sequence-specific manner. Secondly, the B-form helical structure can be deformed when a protein binds to it – typically causing a kink or bend in the DNA helix, which can influence the binding characteristics of other proteins. Finally, DNA is under a helical stress as a result of DNA twisting, and this influences both the 'opening' of the helix and the torsional energy of the flanking helix.

10.2 Transcription of prokaryotic genes

The bacterium *E. coli* contains a cluster of five genes that encode proteins with activities relevant to the synthesis of tryptophan. This cluster, which is called the *trp* **operon**, is shown in Figure 10.2. We shall discuss its regulation in detail shortly.

Operons are collections of genes with related function, which are transcribed from one promoter as a single RNA transcript known as a **polycistronic mRNA**. In the absence of a nucleus, translation occurs on the growing mRNA as transcription occurs.

○ What is the advantage to the prokaryotic cell of clustering genes that encode proteins with functionally related activities into an operon?

● As all the genes in an operon are transcribed as a single polycistronic mRNA, and as translation occurs concurrently, it follows that their proteins will be expressed in a coordinated way rather than independently.

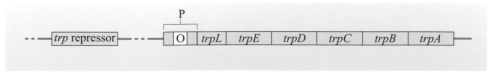

Figure 10.2 A typical prokaryotic gene cluster, the *E. coli trp* operon. *trpA* to *trpE* encode enzymes required for the synthesis of tryptophan. *trpL* is a short open reading frame, with a regulatory role. The elements responsible for regulating transcription – promoter (P) and operator (O) – are found before the site at which transcription starts. The *trp* repressor, which regulates the operon, is encoded elsewhere on the chromosome.

The mechanism by which each ORF is accurately and separately translated will be described in Chapter 11.

10.2.1 RNA polymerase

Transcription in *E. coli*, and in particular the function of RNA polymerase, was extensively discussed in S204, Book 3 *The Core of Life*, Vol. II, Chapter 9.

DNA and RNA are chemically similar, although there are some important differences (Section 5.2). This similarity is reflected in the way in which DNA is used as a template for RNA synthesis – that is, by exploiting the capacity for base pairing between incoming bases and the DNA template. This ensures the accurate transfer of the genetic information encoded in each ORF. The synthesis of RNA on the DNA template is carried out by enzymes known as RNA polymerases, which have been intensively studied in both prokaryotes and eukaryotes. Their catalytic action involves the transfer of a ribonucleoside monophosphate to a 3'-OH terminus of a growing RNA molecule, using the corresponding ribonucleoside triphosphate as a substrate (Figure 10.3).

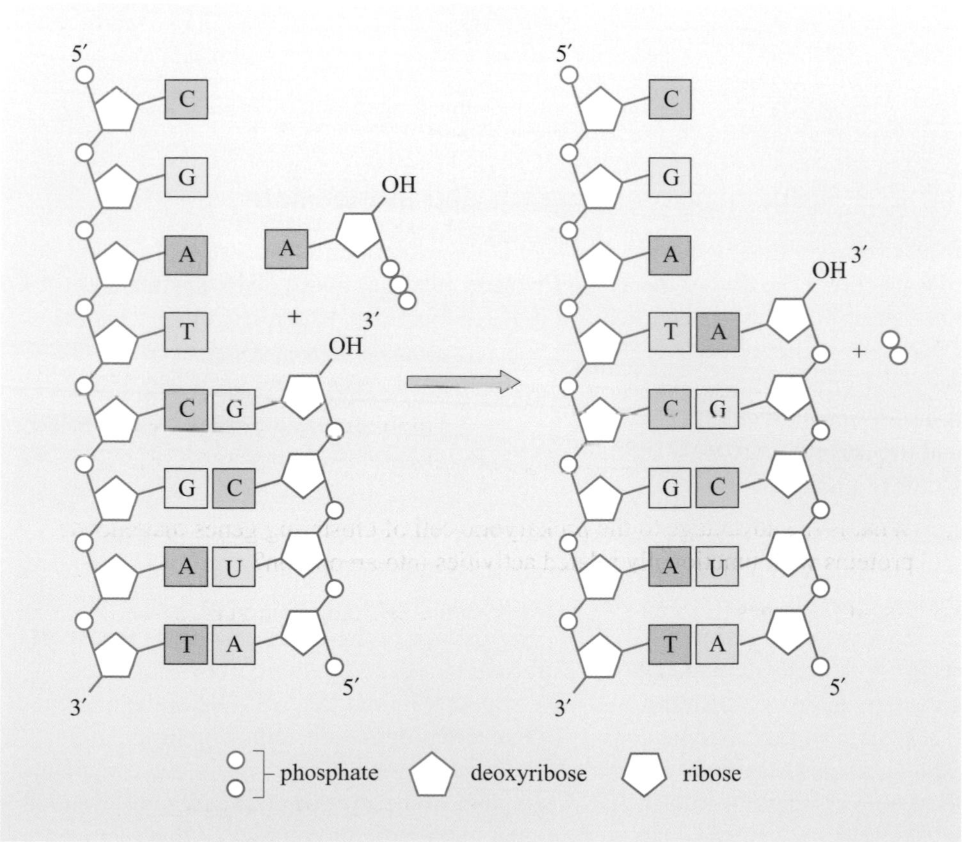

Figure 10.3 Synthesis of RNA. The incoming ribonucleoside monophosphate is added by transfer from a ribonucleoside triphosphate, to the 3'-OH terminus of the nascent RNA chain. This reaction is catalysed by RNA polymerase (not shown). The DNA template strand is shown in pink and the RNA is in orange.

In contrast to DNA polymerases, RNA polymerases do not require a primer to provide a 3′-OH from which to initiate synthesis. Rather, RNA polymerases are recruited to specific sequences of bases within the genome at which to initiate transcription. Prokaryotes, as typified by bacteria such as *E. coli*, use a single RNA polymerase, which is responsible for the synthesis of all RNA classes, including mRNA, tRNA and various structural RNAs. Bacterial RNA polymerase is a multisubunit enzyme; the so-called core polymerase complex consists of four subunits (β, β′ and two α subunits). One additional subunit, the sigma (σ) factor, which is detachable from the core complex, is responsible for the recognition of specific sequences of bases within the helical DNA template at which transcription will initiate. In fact, there are several σ factors (Table 10.1), which recognize different consensus sequences within the promoters of different classes of genes. When the RNA polymerase complex is bound to the σ factor, it can associate weakly with helical DNA, and can 'slide' freely along the double helix.

Table 10.1   Sigma factors and the promoters they recognize.

Sigma factor	Promoters recognized
σ^{70}	most genes
σ^{32}	heat shock induced genes
σ^{28}	genes for motility and chemotaxis
σ^{38}	genes for stationary phase and stress response
σ^{54}	genes for nitrogen metabolism and other functions

10.2.2 Transcription initiation and elongation

Prokaryotic promoters contain two core DNA sequences, which are critical for transcription. The first of these, the **Pribnow box**, lies about 10 bp upstream of the transcriptional start site (hence it is also called the −10 sequence), and has the DNA base sequence TATAATR (where R represents a purine, either G or A). The second sequence, known as the **−35 box**, is located about 35 bp upstream of the transcription start site. These sequences serve to facilitate RNA polymerase binding and transcription complex assembly at the promoter and are bound by the sigma (σ) factor (Figure 10.4).

In order to expose template bases in the DNA, the RNA polymerase must first unwind the DNA helix. In *E. coli*, this process does not require ATP, as it utilizes the torsional energy stored within the negatively supercoiled DNA helix and maintained by DNA gyrase (Section 5.3.2). The consequence of this helix opening is that short regions of single-stranded DNA are created, to which incoming ribonucleotides anneal by hydrogen bonding, and are covalently linked to the 3′-OH of the nascent RNA chain by the catalytic activity of the core polymerase. When approximately 10 nucleotides have been assembled, the σ factor is no longer required to maintain the stable association with the DNA template strand. At this point, the conformation of the RNA polymerase changes from that of an initiator complex to that of an elongation complex. This conformational shift allows the polymerase to proceed rapidly along the template, synthesizing RNA at a rate of approximately 50 nucleotides per second.

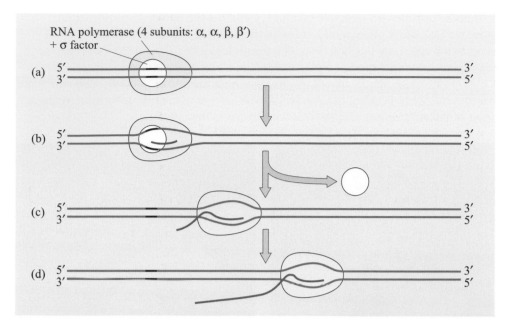

RNA polymerase (4 subunits: α, α, β, β')
+ σ factor

(a) 5'
    3'

(b) 5'
    3'

(c) 5'
    3'

(d) 5'
    3'

Figure 10.4
Prokaryotic RNA polymerase catalyses the synthesis of RNA chains. (a) RNA polymerase consists of five subunits, and assembles at the promoter (black) by binding of the sigma (σ) factor to the region containing the −10 and −35 sequences. (b) RNA polymerase initiates transcription on the template strand of the double helix. (c) Once RNA synthesis has commenced, the σ factor dissociates from the RNA polymerase and synthesis proceeds (d).

☐ As RNA polymerase proceeds along the helical DNA template, how does this affect the helical stresses around the transcription complex?

■ Unwinding of the DNA helix results in a positive DNA twist ahead of the transcription complex and a negative twist behind it (Figure 5.12).

☐ Which enzyme is required to manage helical stress changes ahead of the transcriptional elongation complex?

■ DNA topoisomerase (Section 5.3.2, Figure 5.12).

Transcriptional elongation continues until a termination signal in the template DNA is reached, whereupon the RNA polymerase detaches from both the newly synthesized RNA molecule and the DNA template. The RNA polymerase molecule can then begin the process afresh through association with a σ factor at another promoter. Because the compartmentalization of transcription and translation that is found in eukaryotes is not present in prokaryotes, translation may (and generally does) begin before the transcript is complete. Thus, transcription and translation are intimately associated.

The important mechanistic alteration that occurs within the RNA polymerase during the switch from initiation to elongation has been extensively studied using RNA polymerases encoded by bacteriophages, the viruses that infect bacterial cells.

Bacteriophage T7 RNA polymerase

The RNA polymerase encoded in the T7 bacteriophage genome consists of a single polypeptide, but despite this, it exemplifies many of the features of the multisubunit cellular RNA polymerase. In particular, the enzyme displays the same transition from an initiation state to an elongation state. As the T7 RNA polymerase is a single polypeptide, it has been studied extensively, particularly by X-ray diffraction, complexed with DNA template strands and RNA transcripts. These structural studies have revealed that RNA synthesis is initially limited by steric hindrance within the polymerase–template complex, such that the initiation conformation is rather unstable. Consequently, many of the initiated transcripts are aborted. As soon as the transcript reaches 10 to 12 nucleotides in length, however, the enzyme undergoes a conformational change to form an elongation complex, which is more stable. In this situation, a 'tunnel' is formed within the polypeptide through which the nascent transcript is extruded (Figure 10.5). A second consequence of this structural change is that the promoter binding site of the enzyme is lost.

Figure 10.5
The three-dimensional structure of T7 RNA polymerase. (a) The initiation complex has a small section of RNA (yellow) entirely enclosed within the polypeptide (based on pdb file 1q1n). (b) The elongation complex has a more open structure such that the growing RNA transcript can readily exit the polymerase through a 'tunnel' in the surrounding polypeptide. In this view, the RNA is exiting the elongation complex downwards and towards the viewer. The two DNA strands are shown in grey and white, and the RNA transcript is shown in yellow (based on pdb file 1msw).

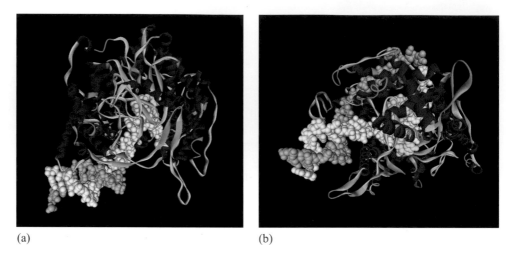

(a)   (b)

10.2.3 Transcriptional termination

In addition to recognizing specific DNA signals to start transcription, RNA polymerase must terminate transcription at an appropriate point. In prokaryotes, there are two mechanisms for terminating transcription, known as **Rho-independent** and **Rho-dependent** termination.

Rho-independent termination relies solely on sequences in the template DNA strand, which when transcribed cause the RNA polymerase to dissociate from the template. These sequences are generally a stretch of G–C-rich DNA, followed by a sequence that is A–T-rich. The G–C-rich section is self-complementary, and can form a stem–loop structure (Figure 10.6) in the nascent RNA transcript. The stem–loop secondary structure adopted by the mRNA causes the RNA polymerase to pause, and the nascent RNA dissociates from the template DNA because of the weakness of A–U base pairing between the A–T-rich template and the transcript.

Rho-dependent termination requires a protein, Rho, which also functions as a helicase (Section 9.2.1). Rho binds to a specific termination sequence, and separates the nascent RNA chain from its template, thereby terminating transcription.

⬭ Why are transcriptional termination signals important?

⬛ Without termination signals, the RNA polymerase would continue to transcribe a gene beyond the end of the ORF.

Failure to properly terminate transcription would be undesirable, both from the point of view of economy (wasted components of new mRNA), and also from the point of view of gene regulation. As most genes are regulated through transcriptional initiation, only genes that are required to be expressed together are not interrupted by termination signals and generate polycistronic mRNAs.

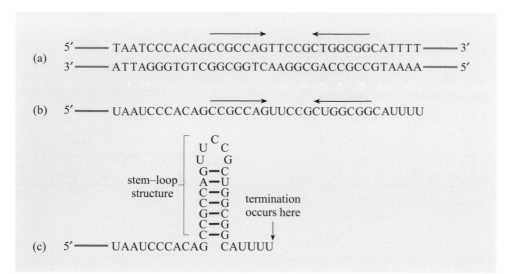

(a)
5′ —— TAATCCCACAGCCGCCAGTTCCGCTGGCGGCATTTT —— 3′
3′ —— ATTAGGGTGTCGGCGGTCAAGGCGACCGCCGTAAAA —— 5′

(b) 5′ —— UAAUCCCACAGCCGCCAGUUCCGCUGGCGGCAUUUU

stem–loop structure

```
           U  C C
           U     G
           G — C
           A — U
           C — G
           C — G       termination
           G — C       occurs here
           C — G
           C — G         ↓
```

(c) 5′ —— UAAUCCCACAG   CAUUUU

Figure 10.6
Rho-independent transcriptional termination in prokaryotes. The termination signal of the *trp* operon of *E. coli* is shown. (a) The DNA sequence in the region of transcriptional termination. Notice that two short sequence stretches, indicated by the arrows, form an interrupted palindrome. (b) This means that the nascent transcript of these sequences has the potential to form a stem–loop structure, as shown in (c). It is the stem–loop structure, followed by the four U residues, that is responsible for the termination of transcription.

10.2.4 Prokaryotic RNA polymerases as a general model for RNA polymerases

Like many prokaryotic polypeptides, the RNA polymerases are very amenable to biochemical and molecular characterization, particularly in well-studied species such as *E. coli* and its bacteriophages. It is possible to reconstitute RNA polymerase from its subunits *in vitro*, and thereby obtain a functional protein. The production of bacteriophage-encoded polymerases has proved particularly useful as both a model and a molecular tool (Box 10.1). Is prokaryotic RNA polymerase valuable as a model for RNA polymerase in eukaryotes, which must cope with several features not present in prokaryotes? Among these are chromatin, a wider range of interacting transcription factors, and interaction with some of the components of the post-transcriptional processing system. The biochemical activity of RNA polymerase is indeed similar in eukaryotes. We shall return to the process of transcription in eukaryotes later in this chapter.

Box 10.1   *In vitro* synthesis of RNA

Many experimental investigations require the *in vitro* synthesis of RNA, for example to provide defined mRNA species for *in vitro* translation, to provide labelled RNA for use as a hybridization probe for *in situ* hybridization (Box 5.1), or to prepare double-stranded RNA. Several methods for the *in vitro* synthesis of RNA are commonly used. Typically, these methods use RNA polymerases derived from *E. coli* bacteriophage such as T3, T7 and SP6. The major advantages of these RNA polymerases is that they are single polypeptides, which can be readily purified from infected *E. coli*. Suitable promoter sequences can easily be introduced into plasmids or fragments of DNA generated by PCR. As RNA polymerases do not require a primer to initiate transcription, these enzymes will initiate synthesis of a large quantity of RNA from their appropriate promoter sequence, even on naked DNA (Figure 10.7).

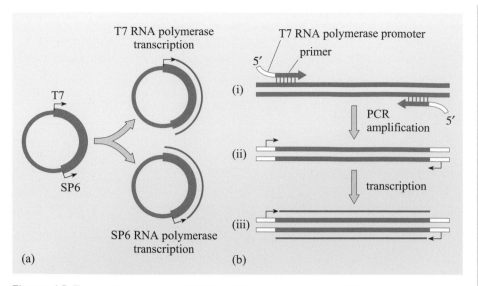

Figure 10.7   *In vitro* synthesis of RNA. (a) Transcription from DNA segments cloned adjacent to RNA polymerase promoters. Note that in this situation, T7 and SP6 RNA polymerases will synthesize complementary RNAs as shown. (b) Transcription from RNA polymerase promoters incorporated in PCR primers. (i) In this example, in addition to priming sequences homologous to the target DNA, each amplification primer has sequences corresponding to the T7 RNA polymerase promoter. (ii) The PCR product generated carries T7 promoter sequences a t each end, which (iii) can be used to generate RNA by incubation with T7 RNA polymerase and ribonucleotides.

Figure 10.7a shows how a segment of DNA that has been inserted into a plasmid, immediately adjacent to RNA polymerase recognition sequences, can be transcribed. Typically, such plasmids contain promoters for two different RNA polymerases. In the case illustrated, recognition sequences specific for the SP6 and T7 RNA polymerases are used. Note that in this configuration, both the DNA strands can be transcribed. This is a useful facility, particularly for the generation of RNAs to serve as experimental controls.

○ Which of the two possible transcripts would be used to detect mRNAs by ISH?

◖ The transcript that is complementary to the target mRNA probe would be used, as it must hybridize to its target (Box 5.1).

As an alternative to cloning DNA segments in an appropriate vector, PCR primers containing the RNA polymerase recognition sequence can be used. When used in PCR reactions, such synthetic primers result in the addition of an RNA polymerase recognition site to one or both termini of the amplified DNA fragment. In the example shown in Figure 10.7b, a T7 recognition site is added to each end.

○ What would be the result of an *in vitro* transcription reaction using T7 polymerase and this PCR product?

◖ Transcription using T7 RNA polymerase would yield two complementary RNA molecules (Figure 10.7b (iii)).

Summary of Section 10.2

1   Prokaryotic genes are compact and often organized as operons, in which several open reading frames are transcribed as a single polycistronic mRNA.

2   Prokaryotes have a single RNA polymerase, consisting of five subunits, including a σ factor, required for initiation (through binding to the −35/−10 regions), but not for elongation. RNA polymerase initiates transcription at specific promoter sequences at the 5′ end of the transcription unit.

3   A conformational change, allowing the growing mRNA chain to exit the RNA polymerase, accompanies the shift from initiation to elongation phases.

4   Transcription termination occurs at specific sites, driven by particular sequences in the DNA and mRNA.

5   The RNA polymerase of bacteriophage T7 consists of a single subunit, but shares many features with bacterial RNA polymerase.

10.3 Transcriptional regulation

Transcription is regulated at many levels within the cell. At the level of a single gene, we shall begin our discussion of gene regulation by discussing the classes of proteins that bind to the regulatory elements of a gene's promoter. Once bound to a gene's promoter, we shall see how regulatory DNA binding proteins act through both activator and repressor activities.

10.3.1 The structure of transcriptional regulatory proteins

We shall discuss four classes of DNA binding proteins that can exert a regulatory effect on transcription. Examples of these classes may be found in both prokaryotic and eukaryotic systems. (A discussion of the thermodynamics of these protein-DNA interactions is given in Book 1, Section 4.6.4 and Figure 4.15.) The common feature of these proteins is that they possess a domain that can recognize and bind to double-stranded DNA in a sequence-specific manner.

We have previously discussed two types of DNA binding protein, and we shall only briefly mention these again here. The first is one of the earliest classes of DNA binding proteins to be identified; proteins containing the helix–turn–helix (HTH) motif have been found in DNA binding proteins from a diverse range of species, both prokaryotic and eukaryotic.

▢   Which HTH protein have you encountered earlier in this course?

◼   Ultrabithorax (Section 5.6.2, Figure 5.22).

Recall that an HTH motif consists of two α helices, linked by a short stretch of amino acid residues comprising the turn.

▢   What term is used to describe the α helix that lies within the major groove?

◼   This helix recognizes specific sequences within the major groove of the DNA double helix, and is known as the recognition helix.

The general mode of action of HTH proteins is to function as a dimer, either as homodimers (two of the same polypeptide) or as heterodimers (a pair of two different polypeptides). A second example of an HTH protein is shown in Figure 10.8, where the *E. coli* catabolite activator protein (CAP) is shown bound to the *lac* promoter.

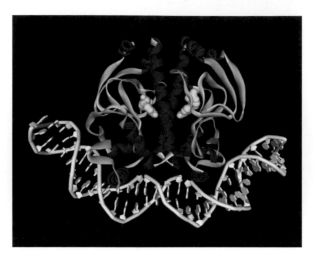

Figure 10.8
The *E. coli* catabolite activator protein (CAP) binds as a dimer to the *lac* promoter. This structure shows a dimer of the CAP protein bound to molecules of cAMP (yellow). These induce a conformational change in the CAP protein which enables it to contact the major groove of the DNA via α helices. The DNA duplex (shown in white) bends when CAP binds (based on pdb file 1cgp).

The second class of DNA binding proteins we discussed earlier is that of the zinc finger proteins. These proteins carry DNA binding domains which bind zinc ions, bound by histidine and cysteine residues (Section 5.6.2, Figure 5.23). Proteins often carry multiple zinc finger motifs, allowing them to target different sequence elements within gene promoters.

○ How many bases does each zinc finger contact within the major groove?

● Three (Section 5.6.2).

In addition to the HTH and zinc finger proteins, two other important types of DNA binding domain are commonly found in transcriptional regulators. These are the proteins that contain leucine zippers and **β sheet DNA binding domains**.

Leucine zipper domains

Leucine zipper domains (Section 3.2.3) consist of two intertwined α helices. This interaction is mediated by amino acid residues with hydrophobic side-chains, frequently leucine. Over 60 leucine zipper proteins have been identified. Although they all function as dimers, some generally form homodimers, whereas others principally form heterodimers. The recognition sequences of homodimeric leucine zipper proteins are in the form of palindromes, whereas those of heterodimers bind a combination of 'half-sites', each corresponding to one of the α helices engaging with the major groove. An example of a leucine zipper DNA binding protein, the mammalian Pap1 protein, is shown in Figure 10.9.

β sheet domains

The above discussion of three classes of DNA binding domain might give the impression that all such domains involve an interaction between α-helical structures and the DNA duplex. Although it is certainly true that most DNA binding proteins do

Figure 10.9
An example of a leucine zipper protein, Pap1, bound to its target DNA. The target DNA duplex is shown in white and grey. The DNA binding structure is formed by the association of two helices, which project into the major groove of the DNA duplex. Only one interacting helix can be seen; the other lies behind the DNA (based on pdb 1gd2).

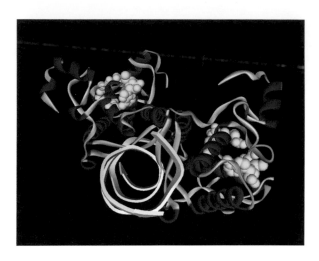

Figure 10.10
An example of a β sheet DNA binding protein, the *E. coli met* operon repressor, in which a section of β sheet interacts with the major groove of the DNA double helix. For clarity, only the backbone of the DNA (white) is shown. Bound methionine is shown in yellow. The view presented is down the axis of the DNA double helix, so that the β sheet region (cyan) of the *met* repressor can be seen localized in the DNA major groove (based on pdb file 1cma).

so via their α helices, some proteins bind DNA with β sheet structures. One such example is the bacterial *met* repressor protein (which represses transcription of the *met* operon in the presence of methionine), in which a β sheet fits into the major groove of the DNA duplex (Figure 10.10).

10.3.2 Target site recognition by DNA binding proteins

It should be apparent from the above overview of DNA binding domains that many operate as dimers. In some cases, fine-tuning of sequence recognition is achieved by heterodimerization between members of the same class of DNA binding proteins.

○ What is the effect on target sequence specificity of the capacity of DNA binding proteins to dimerize?

● Dimerization offers the possibility of extending the repertoire of DNA binding sites within promoters.

As we saw above, leucine zippers allow proteins to form dimers, but dimerization between two proteins is frequently enhanced by other domains within the polypeptides. One example is the **helix–loop helix (HLH)** motif. The polypeptide chain at the HLH motif forms an unstructured loop between two α helices. This region of unstructured chain serves to enhance the dimerization of two proteins carrying the motifs. An example of this is shown in Figure 10.11 for the mammalian Myc and Max proteins. In this example, the HLH motifs within these proteins enhance the leucine zipper interaction between these two proteins. HLH motifs are carried by many DNA binding proteins, not just those with leucine zippers.

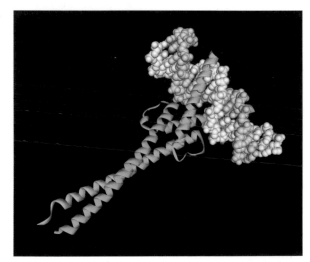

Figure 10.11
Dimerization of Myc and Max leucine zipper proteins is enhanced by HLH motifs. Myc (green) and Max (cyan) are seen in this dimer interacting with a DNA chain. The HLH motifs can be clearly seen as unstructured loops linking the two α helices of each protein (based on pdb file 1nkp).

The examples of DNA binding proteins that we have described in Chapter 5 and in this section illustrate that sequence-specific DNA binding occurs by non-covalent bonding between specific amino acid residue side-chains and the nucleotide bases exposed in the major groove of the double helix.

○ How many potential hydrogen-bonding sites are present in the major groove for each base pair?

■ There is one potential site for each base, and therefore two for each A–T or G–C base pair (Figure 5.9).

The sequence specificity of DNA binding is due to the precise spatial arrangement of these components of the interaction. Although in principle it could be possible to predict from a protein sequence what DNA sequences would be recognized by the protein, in practice this is not the case, as the predictive methods for determining the tertiary and quaternary structures of proteins are not yet accurate enough. (Remember that many DNA binding proteins function as dimers.)

It is experimentally more feasible to address this question in reverse – that is, asking which proteins bind to a specific DNA region, such as a gene promoter. This can be addressed in several ways. The first approach is based on a bioinformatics approach – that is, the use of databases that contain the sequences of known DNA binding sites. These are collated from structural and experimental studies to yield **consensus sequences** for DNA binding proteins – that is, a sequence of bases to which a particular protein preferentially binds. The consensus sequence is a 'best fit' representation of a DNA recognition sequence for a protein. Normally, there is some variation in the sequences that a typical transcription factor can bind. On examination of the sequence of a particular gene's promoter, it is therefore possible to predict possible binding sites, based solely on its DNA sequence. In this case, all such predictions require experimental validation using the techniques outlined in Box 10.2.

Box 10.2   The experimental determination of interactions between DNA and protein

In order to experimentally determine which proteins bind to a DNA fragment, several approaches can be used.

Band shift assays

If a radiolabelled DNA fragment is mixed with a mixture of proteins, such as a whole cell extract or a purified transcription factor, DNA–protein complexes will form under favourable conditions. The DNA–protein complex can then be fractionated by gel electrophoresis, and compared to control samples containing only the DNA fragment. Recall that gel electrophoresis separates DNA molecules on the basis of size: larger molecules migrate through the gel matrix more slowly than small molecules. The final position in the gel matrix can be seen after exposure to X-ray film. If a DNA fragment has bound to a protein, it will migrate more slowly through the gel than naked DNA, and the corresponding band on the autoradiogram will be 'shifted' to an apparently higher molecular mass (Figure 10.12). This technique can be used to confirm the binding of a transcription factor predicted from sequence analysis, or to identify which fragments bind from a complex mixture of fragments.

Affinity chromatography

The technique of affinity chromatography uses a column with a porous matrix to which target DNA is bound. When a mixture of proteins is passed through the column, those that bind the target DNA will be retarded. These proteins are then eluted after the non-binding proteins have been washed from the column and analysed by SDS–PAGE.

DNA footprinting

This technique relies on the fact that DNA to which protein is bound is relatively inaccessible to nucleases or other chemical agents – for example, to chemicals that react with DNA in the major groove. A commonly used experimental approach is to mix together the

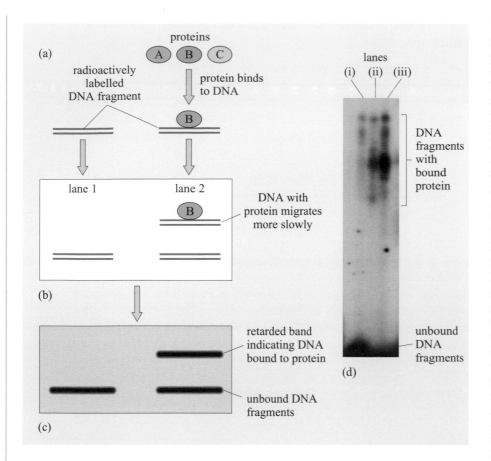

Figure 10.12
Example of a band shift assay for proteins binding to DNA.
(a) A schematic representation on a band shift assay. A DNA fragment is radioactively labelled and mixed with proteins. In this example, protein B binds to a sequence within the labelled DNA fragment, whereas proteins A and C do not. (b) A schematic representation of a polyacrylamide gel on which the labelled DNA and DNA–protein complexes have been separated, with migration from top to bottom. Lane 1 is loaded with labelled DNA only, and lane 2 is loaded with the DNA plus protein mixture. Some DNA molecules have bound protein and consequently migrate through the gel more slowly than unbound DNA. (c) A schematic representation of an autoradiograph of the gel in (b). The gel is exposed to X-ray film, which is darkened over the regions of the gel where the radioactive DNA has migrated. Bands corresponding to the radioactive DNA are revealed. (d) An example of a band shift assay in which the binding of three cell extracts, lanes (i)–(iii), have been mixed with a radiolabelled DNA fragment containing a transcription factor binding site. Several DNA–protein complexes are apparent, particularly in lane (iii).

DNA and protein concerned, and examine the ability of the protein to 'protect' the DNA from chemical or enzymatic attack. Commonly used chemicals include those that lead to guanosine methylation (shown in Table 5.3e). In this way, the pattern of nuclease digestion or chemical attack can be used to determine which areas are 'protected' by the binding of a protein. For example, binding of a transcription factor to a gene promoter will protect sites that are bound to proteins. The protection profile is referred to as a 'footprint', since it was determined by the position of the bound protein on the DNA fragment being investigated. In the above cases, DNA–protein interaction is analysed on naked DNA to which a protein has been added *in vitro*.

◻ Can you recall a method used to analyse DNA–protein interactions in a chromatin context?

◼ Chromatin immunoprecipitation (ChIp) analysis (Box 5.3).

The same approach may be used to identify areas of genomic DNA to which transcription factors bind.

◻ What advantage does this technique have over the others described?

◼ It may better reflect the *in vivo* situation, since the analysis is based on native chromatin with naturally bound factors rather than naked DNA.

As you saw with the use of ChIp across the entire yeast genome, it also allows analysis of very large DNA regions (Section 9.2.3).

10.3.3 How DNA binding proteins function as transcriptional regulators

There are numerous ways in which the binding of regulatory proteins to a gene promoter modifies the level of transcription by RNA polymerase. *In vivo*, where and when a gene is transcribed is the result of numerous regulatory signals, which are integrated to yield a particular pattern of transcription. We shall discuss several specific cases throughout this chapter, but here we provide an overview of how regulation is achieved.

We can consider transcriptional regulators as falling into two general classes, **activators** and **repressors**. Activators produce stimulatory signals for the transcriptional machinery, and repressors produce inhibitory signals. In both cases, these factors can exert their effects on the transcriptional machinery either directly or indirectly. For example, a transcriptional activator could carry a DNA binding domain, which interacts with its target sequence within the gene promoter, and an activator domain, which directly stimulates RNA polymerase activity. This could be achieved by increasing access to the important core sites required for RNA polymerase function, such as the prokaryote –10 and –35 boxes, by helping to recruit RNA polymerase to the promoter in other ways, or by stabilizing the initiator complex such that more rounds of initiation reach the elongation stage. The binding of the transcriptional activator to its target DNA sequence may be prevented or enhanced by binding a ligand, by modifications such as phosphorylation, or through the actions of other proteins already bound.

Repressors can act to counteract activators, for example by competing for regulatory sites, by directly blocking RNA polymerase binding, by destabilizing initiation complexes or by binding activator molecules, thus preventing transcriptional activation. The binding of a ligand or protein modification can be used to regulate this activity.

In many cases, particularly in eukaryotic cells, transcriptional regulators can also influence the accessibility to promoter elements indirectly through the modulation of DNA structure, particularly through chromatin structure. We shall discuss this type of regulation in more detail later.

Transcriptional regulation can best be seen at the level of the genetic switches observed in prokaryotic systems. We will now consider one such example, the *E. coli trp* operon, which was introduced on p.106 (Figure 10.2).

The trp *operon*

The structure of the bacterial *trp* operon is illustrated in Figure 10.13. It consists of five ORFs (*trpA–E*) transcribed as a single polycistronic transcript; all five ORFs are present on a single mRNA molecule, and are translated to produce the five enzymes required for tryptophan biosynthesis. The *trp* promoter is a stretch of DNA overlapping the transcriptional start site; it contains an **operator** sequence to which a protein called the *trp* repressor binds. The *trp* repressor acts by obstructing the promoter, and hence preventing RNA polymerase assembly, by binding to the operator sequence. In order to bind to the operator, the *trp* repressor must undergo a conformational change, which is brought about when it binds tryptophan. The *trp* repressor is therefore only active in the presence of tryptophan, which results in *trp* operon transcription being sensitive to the intracellular tryptophan concentration.

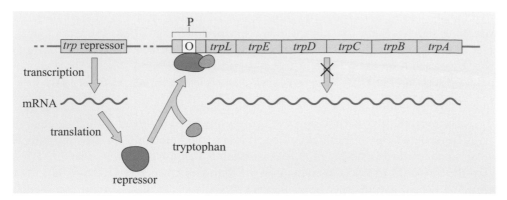

Figure 10.13
The *E. coli trp* operon. The operon contains five ORFs – each encoding a protein with activity relevant to the biosynthesis of tryptophan – which are all transcribed in a single mRNA. A separate transcription unit encodes the *trp* repressor, which is inactive until it binds tryptophan. This binding induces a conformational change that allows it to bind to the *trp* operator, thereby preventing transcription from the *trp* promoter. A further ORF, *trpL*, plays an additional role in transcriptional control.

○ Is transcription of the *trp* operon on or off when tryptophan is abundant?

● Transcription of the *trp* operon does not occur when tryptophan is abundant.

○ What is the advantage to the cell of this response?

● This benefits the cell as it does not waste energy and materials synthesizing the enzymes required for tryptophan biosynthesis when it is already abundant in the cell's environment.

The *trp* repressor is an HTH DNA binding protein that operates as a homodimer. Since its binding site lies within the promoter sequence, RNA synthesis cannot proceed until the repressor is displaced, as it disrupts the binding of σ factor and RNA polymerase. The repressor contains an α-helical projection that makes contact with the major groove, in a sequence-specific manner (Figure 10.14). This interaction only occurs when the repressor binds tryptophan (two molecules per dimer), causing a change in its conformation.

As can be seen from this example, the *trp* operon behaves as a simple switch – *on* in conditions of tryptophan starvation, and *off* in conditions of tryptophan surplus.

In addition to the repressor described above, the *trp* operon possesses a second mechanism of transcriptional control, known as **attenuation**. A short region at the start of the *trp* operon contains what is termed the *trpL* leader sequence. This short ORF, which encodes a peptide of only 14 amino acids, lies between the promoter/operator region and *trpE*, the first of the *trp* ORFs. Within *trpL* are two adjacent

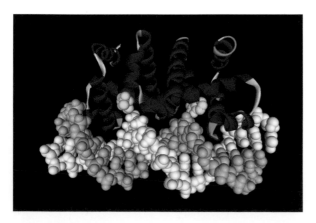

Figure 10.14
The structure of *trp* repressor bound to the *trp* operator. The *trp* repressor is a member of the HTH class of DNA binding proteins. Here, the two strands of the DNA helix are coloured white and grey. The α helices of the repressor dimer can be seen to project into the major groove. The *trp* repressor only binds the operator sequence when it has bound tryptophan: two molecules of tryptophan are shown in yellow (based on pdb file 1tro).

tryptophan codons. RNA transcripts of *trpL* can form different types of secondary structure, and this is key to its function in transcriptional regulation. There are four sections (1–4) within the mRNA spanning this region of the operon that can undergo base pairing to form three different secondary structures (Figure 10.15). These are between sections 1 and 2, between sections 2 and 3, and between sections 3 and 4.

Recall that translation is concurrent with transcription in *E. coli*. As mRNA from the *trp* operon is produced, several possible configurations of secondary structure can arise, dependent upon the progress of the ribosome along the mRNA. This progress is determined by the availability of tRNAs carrying the amino acid tryptophan (Trp-tRNA^{Trp}). When levels of tryptophan are high, the level of Trp-tRNA^{Trp} is abundant; when they are low, the tryptophan tRNA levels in the cell are diminished.

There is a precise nomenclature for the description of a tRNA. Each one has a specific abbreviation. Thus, a tRNA carrying an anticodon that recognizes the tryptophan codon is called tRNA^{Trp}. When charged with its amino acid, it is designated Trp-tRNA^{Trp}.

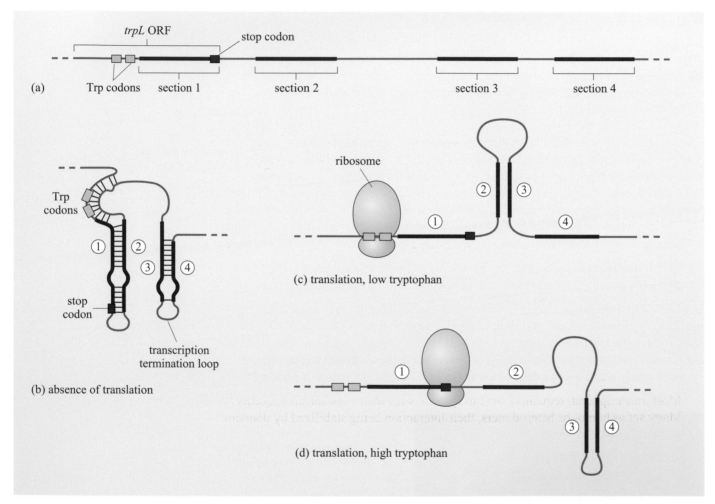

Figure 10.15   RNA structure, translation and attenuation in the control of *trp* operon transcription. (a) *trpL* lies between the promoter and *trpE*, the first ORF of the operon (Figure 10.13). (b) In the absence of concurrent translation of the mRNA, two secondary structures form in the RNA: between sections 1 and 2, and between 3 and 4. As the 3–4 structure serves as a transcriptional terminator, the continuation of RNA polymerase through the rest of the operon (*trpA–E*) is stopped. (c) In a low tryptophan environment, concurrent translation stalls at the two Trp codons, due to the lack of appropriate tRNAs bound to tryptophan. This stalling allows formation of a secondary structure between sections 2 and 3. As a result, the 3–4 transcriptional terminator is not formed and RNA polymerase can continue to synthesize *trp* operon mRNA. (d) In a high tryptophan environment, concurrent translation proceeds past the Trp codons, preventing the formation of the 2–3 section, but allowing formation of the 3–4 transcription termination section. This results in termination of RNA polymerase activity.

In the absence of any translation, secondary structures form in the mRNA between sections 1 and 2 *and* between sections 3 and 4 (Figure 10.15b). The formation of the 3–4 pairing acts as a transcriptional terminator, resulting in the termination of RNA polymerase transcription through the rest of the *trp* operon. In the presence of translation, however, two possible configurations can be observed, each with a different outcome. In an environment low in tryptophan, the cell requires the enzymes encoded by the *trp* operon to synthesize the amino acid. In this situation, as the ribosome translates the mRNA, it stalls at the Trp codons due to a lack of the tryptophan tRNA. Notice that the two consecutive tryptophan-encoding codons lie in section 1 and the stalled ribosome therefore prevents the formation of the 1–2 structure (Figure 10.15c). A secondary structure now preferentially forms between regions 2 and 3 and the transcriptional terminator 3–4 pair is prevented from forming. RNA polymerase continues through the operon to yield mRNA from which the key biosynthetic enzymes are produced.

In an environment that is rich in tryptophan, the ribosome does not stall at the Trp codons and progresses through the end of the *trpL* ORF to the stop codon. In this position, the ribosome prevents the formation of structure 2–3, the structure between sections 3 and 4 forms and transcription is terminated. It is clear from this example that attenuation control of the *trp* operon is a 'fine-tuning' control acting above the simple on/off mode of control used by the *trp* repressor.

◯ Would you expect attenuation control such as this to be found in eukaryotes?

⬤ No, since this form of attenuation control requires simultaneous transcription and translation, which does not occur in eukaryotes.

Summary of Section 10.3

1 Transcriptional regulators contain DNA binding domains that can bind to specific DNA sequences through interactions with bases in the major groove. These domains include HTH, zinc finger, leucine zipper and β sheet domains.

2 Several experimental methods are available to study DNA binding proteins or investigate which factors bind gene promoters: gel shift assays, affinity chromatography, DNA footprinting and ChIp analysis.

3 Transcriptional activity is controlled by DNA binding proteins, which interact with DNA in a sequence-dependent manner and act as activators or repressors.

4 Most transcriptional regulators bind to specific sites with a consensus sequence. Many act as homo- or heterodimers, their interaction being stabilized by domains such as the HLH domain.

5 The activity of both activators and repressors can be modulated by other factors, such as ligand binding, which serves to increase their regulation.

6 An example of a simple genetic switch in prokaryotes is the *trp* operon.

7 Transcription of the *trp* operon is regulated by the *trp* repressor, which represses transcription when it has bound a molecule of tryptophan. Transcription of the *trp* operon is also subject to a second level of control, namely attenuation, which is intimately linked to translation.

10.4 Transcription of eukaryotic genes

In the previous section, we saw the general principles of how prokaryotes regulate gene transcription. We now move on to the corresponding situation in eukaryotes. How similar are the processes in molecular terms, and can the prokaryotic model help us understand eukaryotic transcriptional regulation? In this section, we shall discuss how the eukaryotic RNA polymerases differ from those of prokaryotes, and the ways in which they are similar.

In contrast to the situation seen in prokaryotes, the generation of a mature mRNA suitable for translation in eukaryotic cells is subject to additional regulatory points, both at the level of transcription and during post-transcriptional processing (Figure 10.16).

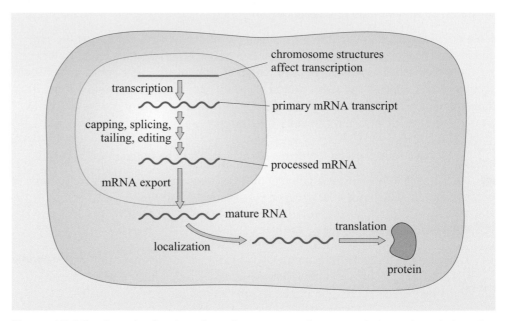

Figure 10.16   Control points for eukaryotic gene expression. Transcription and translation take place in the nucleus and cytosol, respectively. This, together with the complex post-transcriptional processing of mRNA in eukaryotes, permits the control of gene expression at many stages in the flow of information from gene to protein.

The first major difference from prokaryotes is that eukaryotes have distinct cellular compartments in which transcription and translation take place, which offers opportunities for the fine-tuning of transcriptional activity not possible in the simpler prokaryotic cell.

○ What are the cellular compartments in which transcription and translation take place?

● Transcription takes place in the nucleus, whereas translation occurs in the cytosol.

Furthermore, the modification of eukaryotic DNA by cytosine methylation, its packaging into chromatin, and modifications to the histone proteins themselves, add still further to transcriptional complexity.

10.4.1 Eukaryotic gene complexity

A schematic representation of the structure of a typical eukaryotic gene is shown in Figure 10.17. The details of how transcription in eukaryotes is regulated will be discussed later in this chapter, but for now we shall focus on the structure of the eukaryotic gene and its encoded mRNA. In contrast to genes within the *trp* operon discussed in Section 10.3, the ORF of a eukaryotic gene is generally split into sections, known as exons, separated by non-coding sequences, commonly known as introns. Transcription originating within the promoter will generate a primary mRNA transcript from which the introns need to be removed prior to translation. This process is known as **splicing**, and will be discussed in Section 10.6, together with other forms of RNA processing.

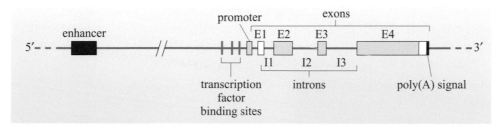

A mature mRNA has two regions at the extreme 5′ and 3′ ends termed **untranslated regions** (**UTRs**). Although these sections of the mRNA do not encode polypeptide sequences, they frequently contain signals required for the promotion of translation, signals for mRNA stability which regulate its degradation, and signals for certain kinds of mRNA modification. Since transcription (and translation) proceeds in a 5′ to 3′ direction, segments of the transcript on the 5′ side of the ORF are referred to as 'upstream sequences', whereas those on the 3′ side are referred to as 'downstream sequences'.

Finally, the terms 'sense' and 'antisense' are often applied to describe the two DNA strands comprising a gene. These terms are often misunderstood. The DNA strand complementary to the mRNA is referred to as the **template** strand; this is the strand to which incoming ribonucleotides bind during transcription. The DNA strand complementary to the template strand has the same sequence as the transcribed RNA (but with T replacing U), and is therefore known as the **sense** or + strand. Thus, the template strand may also be referred to as the antisense strand. The use of all these terms is clarified by Figure 10.18.

Figure 10.17
The structure of a typical eukaryotic gene is organized with a promoter near the transcriptional start point. In this example, the region transcribed contains four exons (E1–E4) and three intervening sequences, or introns (I1–I3), which are non-coding, and which are removed post-transcriptionally. White sections of the exons represent untranslated regions. The activity of the promoter is governed by enhancer elements, which may lie upstream or downstream of the promoter, and even within the gene itself. The sites to which transcription factors bind are indicated by pink bars. Transcription ends next to the polyadenylation signal.

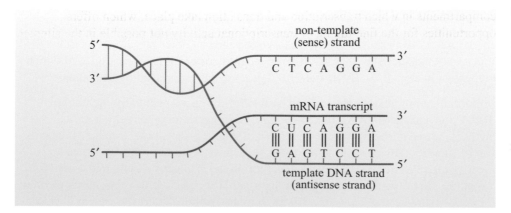

Figure 10.18
DNA and RNA strands in transcription. It is necessary to discriminate between the two DNA strands because only one acts as the template for transcription. The RNA transcript has the same sequence of bases as the non-template (or sense) DNA strand, except for the substitution of U for T. RNA is synthesized in the 5′ to 3′ direction, reading DNA in the 3′ to 5′ direction.

10.4.2 Eukaryotic RNA polymerases

Whereas prokaryotes have a single RNA polymerase, the general situation in eukaryotes is that there are three RNA polymerases, termed RNA polymerase I, II and III; each of these enzymes transcribes a different group of genes. In this chapter, we shall mostly be concerned with the transcription of protein-coding genes into mRNA, which is carried out by RNA polymerase II. This polymerase is also responsible for the transcription of small nuclear RNAs (snRNA), which form part of the components of the splicing mechanism. Most of the ribosomal RNA genes (rRNA) are transcribed by RNA polymerase I, whereas RNA polymerase III transcribes the 5 S ribosomal RNA, some other small RNA species, and transfer RNA (tRNA) genes.

RNA polymerases I, II and III differ in their sensitivity to α-amanitin, a potent inhibitor of RNA synthesis. Experimentally, this drug can therefore be used to distinguish these activities: generally, RNA polymerase II is the most sensitive to α-amanitin, and RNA polymerase I the least sensitive.

In our discussion of eukaryotic RNA polymerase structure and function, we shall principally be examining those occurring in the budding yeast *S. cerevisiae*. The structure of the key components of the transcriptional process are evolutionarily highly conserved from yeast to mammals; in fact, the structure of yeast RNA polymerases can be seen as an excellent model for those of other eukaryotes. In particular, we shall consider the structure and function of RNA polymerase II.

Eukaryotic RNA polymerase II is more complex than prokaryotic RNA polymerase, consisting of 12 subunits. Figure 10.19 is a diagrammatic representation showing this increased complexity. The bacterial RNA polymerase subunits are well defined and are all required for full catalytic activity. In contrast, some of the components of eukaryotic RNA polymerase are merely identified as being a part of the active polymerase complex, their exact roles being uncertain. Despite these differences in composition, the purified RNA polymerases from yeast show many similarities with that from *E. coli*.

The 12 yeast RNA polymerase II subunit polypeptides are named RPB1 to RPB12 (Figure 10.20). The RPB1 and RPB2 subunits have functional correspondence to the prokaryotic β and β′ subunits, whereas the RPB3 and RPB11 subunits correspond to the α subunits of prokaryotic RNA polymerase. The structure of the yeast RNA polymerase II is shown in Figure 10.21.

Initiation and elongation in RNA polymerase II transcription

As in prokaryotic genes, a typical eukaryotic gene promoter lies close to the transcriptional start site. It contains various regulatory elements, examples of which are shown in Figure 10.22 for the *Hsp70* gene, which is induced by heat stress.

Important common elements utilized by the transcription machinery include the **TATA box** and the **CCAAT box**. However, both these and other cell-specific elements are required for the correct expression of a gene. These sequence elements can be identified by comparing the DNA sequences upstream of many genes to identify the presence of consensus sites. Within the *Hsp* gene shown in Figure 10.22, a specific factor called the heat shock factor, or HSF, binds to the heat shock element (HSE), which lies about 100 bases from the transcriptional start site on the 5′ side. The HSE is found in all genes regulated by HSF.

α-Amanitin is a potent inhibitor of RNA synthesis. It is extracted from poisonous mushrooms such as the death cap. It is only one of the toxins that make this species so toxic by ingestion.

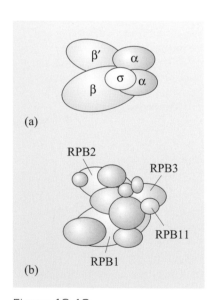

Figure 10.19
(a) Prokaryotic and (b) eukaryotic RNA polymerases. Eukaryotic RNA polymerases are larger and more complex than those of prokaryotes. They possess a greater number of subunits, some of which are common to all three polymerases found in eukaryotes.

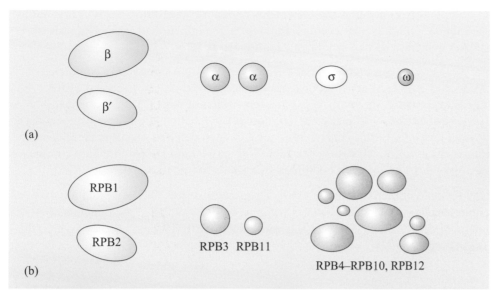

Figure 10.20
Conservation between (a) prokaryotic and (b) eukaryotic RNA polymerases. Some of the subunits of a typical eukaryotic RNA polymerase have direct counterparts in the prokaryotic enzyme, whereas others do not. The ω (omega) subunit is also associated with the enzyme, but its function is not fully understood. It is known to interact physically with β′. Unlike the β, β′ and α subunits, ω is not absolutely required for catalytic activity.

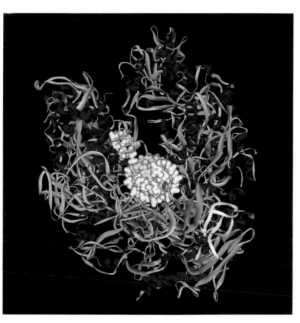

Figure 10.21
Structure of RNA polymerase II bound to a DNA template. Here, the DNA template and the nascent RNA are shown in white and yellow, respectively. Notice how the template and RNA lie in a deep groove or furrow within the RNA polymerase (based on pdb file 1i6h).

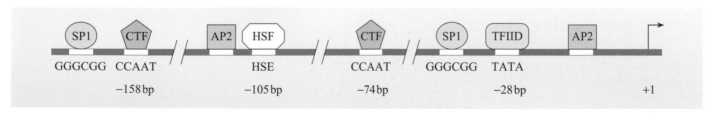

Figure 10.22 Transcriptional control elements of the eukaryotic *Hsp70* gene. A number of consensus sequence elements are found, which are the binding targets of a variety of transcription factor proteins; some are general transcription factors (SP1, AP2, TFIID and CTF), whereas others are function-specific (HSF). The numbers indicates the distance from the transcriptional start site (at +1).

In order to understand how these elements regulate transcription, we will first outline the sequence of molecular events leading up to the initiation of RNA synthesis by RNA polymerase II. This is illustrated in Figure 10.23.

As you can see from Figure 10.23, assembly of the RNA polymerase complex involves a number of general transcription factors or complexes (named TFIIA, TFIIB, etc.) which are involved in the transcription of most RNA polymerase II-transcribed genes. A detailed description of the function of all these components is beyond the scope of this course; however, it is reasonable to state that these general transcription factors play roles in establishing most transcription initiation complexes by aiding RNA polymerase binding or by stimulating its enzymatic activity.

One factor is of particular importance. The process of transcription initiation commences when TFIID associates with the TATA box. One of the component polypeptides of TFIID is responsible for binding the TATA box, and is known as the TATA binding protein, or TBP.

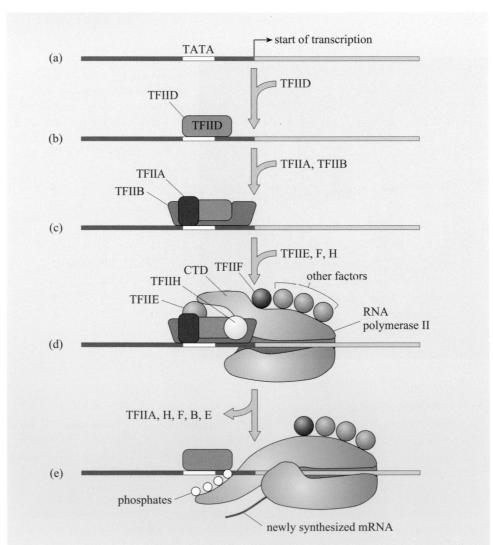

Figure 10.23
Initiation of RNA polymerase II transcription in eukaryotes. The TATA box (a), lying immediately upstream from the transcription start site, is recognized and bound by TFIID (b). TFIIA and B then join the complex (c), and finally other factors and RNA polymerase II itself are recruited (d). Initiation of mRNA synthesis occurs, and if conditions are permissive, the transition to the elongation conf iguration occurs, followed by loss of many of the factors that bound earlier (e). The switch to the elongation stage is associated with phosphorylation of amino acid residues in the C-terminal domains (CTD) of the RPB1 and RPB2 subunits of RNA polymerase II.

○ Can you recall what is unusual about the interaction between TBP and the DNA helix?

● TBP binds through interactions in the minor groove (Section 5.6.4, Figure 5.24).

○ Based on what you know about the effect of TBP binding on DNA conformation, what can you say about the representation of TFIID and transcription initiation shown in Figure 10.23?

● Recall that TBP induces a bend within the DNA helix at its binding site (Section 5.6.4). Therefore, you would predict that *in vivo* the promoter region will not be linear, but will have a bend within it.

As we shall see in the following section, the arrangement of a typical eukaryotic promoter does contain DNA bends; these configurations bring both local and distant transcriptional regulators into the proximity of the RNA polymerase.

Once TFIID has bound to a promoter, other factors such as TFIIA and TFIIB are recruited to the promoter, followed by the RNA polymerase itself and further general transcription factors. TFIIB plays an important role in the location of the transcription start site. It achieves this by directly binding TBP and positioning the RNA polymerase catalytic site at the initiation site. In contrast to the prokaryotic RNA polymerase, eukaryotic RNA polymerase II requires the action of a helicase to open the duplex DNA at the transcription start site. This helicase activity is provided by a component of TFIIH. Once assembled, a short initiator RNA chain between 9 and 11 ribonucleotides in length is synthesized. At this point, RNA polymerase II undergoes a change in conformation, similar to that described earlier for T7 RNA polymerase (Section 10.2.2), the transcription factors dissociate and the polymerase is released from the promoter region, leaving TBP bound to the TATA box.

The transition from initiation to elongation is marked by the phosphorylation of several amino acids that lie within the C-terminal domains of the RPB1 and RPB2 subunits of RNA polymerase II, by a component of the TFIIH complex. These domains play an essential role in the process of transcription, and carry several stretches of a repetitive amino acid motif rich in tyrosine, serine and threonine residues, all of which are target sites for various cellular kinases. Most of the proteins that interact with RNA polymerase II during transcription do so by interacting with and phosphorylating amino acid residues within these C-terminal domains. These include the components of the splicing, capping and polyadenylation machinery, which we will discuss later in Section 10.6.

As we saw with prokaryote RNA polymerases, many initial mRNA chains are never extended, and the initiation to elongation transition is a critical regulatory point influenced by many transcription factors. In many cases, transcription factors bound to the promoter region act by enhancing the kinase activity of TFIIH, or by activating other kinases to phosphorylate the C-terminal domains, enhancing the transition to the elongation phase.

Once in the elongation phase, the eukaryotic RNA polymerase II-catalysed RNA synthesis progresses at approximately 25 nucleotides per second *in vivo*, which is considerably slower than the elongation rate for bacterial polymerases. The relatively slow rate of eukaryotic transcription is mainly due to the fact that RNA polymerase II is required to extend through nucleosomal DNA. This raises the question as to how this occurs. The answer lies with an ancillary complex called

FACT, which forms part of the transcription elongation complex. Components of FACT are responsible for the remodelling of chromatin ahead of the transcription complex – that is, the release of the DNA template from its nucleosomal location, and its reassembly behind it. The exact mechanism through which this process occurs is unclear.

Finally, one component of the RNA polymerase complex also has a role to play in DNA repair. A component of the TFIIH complex provides a link between the transcription machinery and DNA repair. Two of the polypeptides within this complex are the XPB and XPD proteins, which are involved in nucleotide excision repair (NER; Section 9.8.2 and Table 9.4). These polypeptides, as part of TFIIH, recognize RNA polymerase complexes that have stalled at sites of DNA damage, wherein they bind to the polymerase, recruiting other proteins involved in the transcription-coupled repair pathways (Section 9.8.5), such as CS proteins (Table 9.4), to bring about repair of the damage.

10.4.3 Transcriptional regulators serve to activate or repress transcription

As discussed earlier, most transcriptional regulators can be considered as activators or repressors of transcription, carrying both DNA binding domains and a separate regulatory domain. Figure 10.24 shows a schematic representation of a typical promoter with various regulatory DNA sequences and bound to various transcriptional regulators.

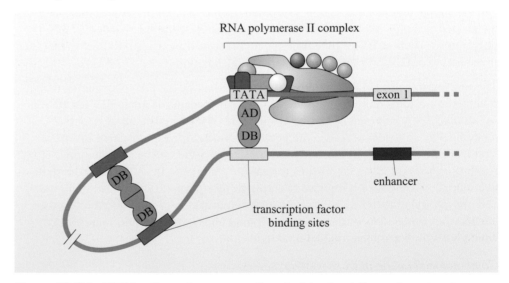

Figure 10.24   DNA bending at the promoter allows both local and distant elements to interact with the transcriptional machinery. A schematic representation of TBP-induced DNA bending within a promoter, allowing local transcriptional regulators to interact with the assembling RNA polymerase complex. Both local and distant elements bind to activator or repressor proteins. These proteins interact with the assembling polymerase complex at the promoter when the DNA loops back to bring them close to the promoter. In this schematic, a transcription factor (dark blue), is shown bound to its recognition sequence by its DNA binding domain (DB) and with its activation domain (AD) interacting with the RNA polymerase II complex. Two other transcription factors are shown interacting with each other (red) to stabilize the promoter configuration. The bend at the promoter allows an enhancer to be brought into close proximity of the RNA polymerase.

The bending of the DNA within the promoter allows many activators or repressors to directly influence the assembly of the polymerase complex on the promoter. In addition, some transcriptional regulators increase the rate of initiation, whereas others stimulate the transition between initiation and elongation. As is shown in Figure 10.24, bending of DNA within the promoter can be stabilized by interactions between transcription factors bound within the promoter, and by interactions with elements more distant from the promoter. Figure 10.24 also illustrates interactions with elements more distant from the promoter. Evidence for such long-range interactions comes from observations that the RNA polymerase II transcription complex found on such a promoter contains not only the local accessory proteins and general transcription factors, but also the transcription factors bound to these distant sites. Such elements can lie from several hundred bases to several tens of kilobases away from the actual promoter, interacting with it through looping of the DNA duplex back on itself. Examples of two such elements are **enhancers** and **silencers**.

An enhancer element is defined as a DNA element that acts to increase the transcription level of a gene, and can act in a manner that is independent of both position and orientation; that is to say, an enhancer can stimulate transcription whether it is located upstream or downstream of the gene it controls, and irrespective of its orientation with respect to the gene. In fact, an enhancer may lie to the 5′ side or the 3′ side of a gene, or even within an intron. Enhancer elements may function in specific cell or tissue types or in particular developmental stages. For example, the promoters of two of the genes coding for *Drosophila* yolk protein lie very close to each other, and these genes are transcribed in opposite directions away from each other. Two enhancer elements that control the expression of these genes lie in the intergenic space between the promoters of the two genes. One enhancer drives expression of both genes in the fat body (an energy storage organ), whereas the other drives expression in ovaries. Silencers have similar properties, except that they cause transcriptional repression.

It should be appreciated from this definition of enhancers and silencers that some mechanism must exist to prevent their inappropriate action over a distance that could result in unwanted patterns of gene expression. After all, if one of the main characteristics of enhancer sequences is that they increase transcriptional activity of a gene irrespective of their location or orientation relative to the gene's promoter, what prevents an enhancer, or a silencer, from acting on 'the wrong gene'? The answer is that particular DNA sequences interfere with the enhancer's function. Before we discuss how transcription is influenced by these sequences, we shall consider several examples of how complex regulation of gene expression can be achieved.

Combinatorial action of transcription factors

Many genes have a very complex pattern of expression, both in the sense of *when* transcription occurs, and *where* it occurs. Such expression patterns are generally the result of the cumulative action of many transcription factors acting in combination. As we have seen, some of these transcription factors are repressors of transcription, whereas others are activators, and the resultant level of mRNA produced within any one cell will depend upon which transcription factors are present and upon the relative strength of their stimulation or repression of RNA polymerase. The combinatorial effect of the many factors bound to any one promoter serves to determine the overall activity of the promoter in terms of how many mRNA molecules are synthesized.

An excellent example of combinatorial action of transcription factors is the even-skipped (*eve*) gene which encodes a protein important in the establishment of the segmental organization of the *Drosophila* embryo. The combinatorial effects of many transcription factors bound to the *eve* promoter results in the gene being transcribed in a striped pattern in the *Drosophila* embryo. This was discussed in detail in S204 Book 3 *The Core of Life*, Vol. II, Section 10.2.1.

The roles of individual transcription factors in establishing such complex expression patterns may be investigated experimentally in several ways. Regions of DNA to which individual transcription factors bind can be identified using the approaches outlined in Box 10.2. Additionally, reporter genes can then be used to visualize transcriptional activity, as described in Box 10.3.

Box 10.3   The use of reporter genes

A reporter gene (Section 3.8.2) is a gene whose product can be monitored for expression, either quantitatively or by its distribution in a cell, tissue, or organism. Typical reporter genes encode enzymes for which a colorimetric assay exists, or a protein that can be identified immunologically or by some intrinsic characteristic. Examples include: the *E. coli* gene *lacZ*, which can be detected by a simple staining reaction; any protein not present in the system being studied, and for which a good antibody is available; and the green fluorescent protein (GFP), which is derived from a jellyfish. GFP fluoresces when exposed to ultraviolet radiation.

The expression pattern of reporter genes can also be monitored at the mRNA level, by Northern blot hybridization, or by ISH to cells or fixed tissue sections. Gene promoter regions can be analysed by generating fusions with a reporter gene, and introducing the construct to the experimental system, for example by introducing cloned promoters adjacent to reporter genes into cultured cells, or (as in the case of *Drosophila*) by generating strains transgenic for the reporter construct. In this case, expression of the reporter gene is driven by the promoter.

Complex expression control: mammalian globins

Eukaryotes have a greater requirement for transcriptional control than prokaryotes, since their cells are compartmentalized. Multicellular organisms have a still greater array of transcriptional control mechanisms, as genes must be expressed not only in response to specific stimuli, but in the correct cells/tissues, and at the correct developmental times. One example of this is in the expression of the mammalian globin genes. Mature haemoglobin contains two α- and two β-type globin polypeptides. In humans, the genes encoding the β-globin proteins are arranged in a cluster on chromosome 11. The arrangement of the β-globin genes within the cluster can be seen in Figure 10.25.

The genes in the β-globin cluster are regulated such that different genes are transcribed at different developmental stages, a process that requires well-regulated control to ensure that at each stage the appropriate β-globin genes are transcribed.

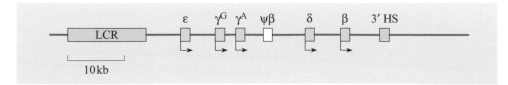

Figure 10.25
The organization of the β-globin gene cluster on chromosome 11 in humans. Genes are indicated by blue boxes, and the regulatory regions – locus control region (LCR) and 3′ hypersensitive site (3′ HS) – by pink boxes. The ψβ pseudogene is shown as a white box. Direction of transcription is indicated by the small black arrows.

The α-globin genes are similarly regulated to ensure that the correct amounts of the globin proteins are synthesized to form the mature quaternary haemoglobin (Table 10.2). Additionally, during mammalian development the site of erythrocyte formation changes from the yolk sac to the liver and finally the bone marrow, requiring additional regulation (Table 10.2). This, therefore, represents a case of spatial as well as temporal control of gene expression.

Table 10.2 Globin gene expression in development.

Developmental stage	Tissue	β-type globins	α-type globins
early embryo	yolk sac	ε	ζ, α2, α1
fetus	liver	γ^G, γ^A	α2, α1
neonate, adult	bone marrow	β (and some δ)	α2, α1

The β-globin genes have been the subject of much molecular analysis; on the one hand, because as abundantly expressed genes they were relatively easy to clone and study in the early days of molecular biology (they were among the first eukaryotic genes to be cloned), and, on the other, because defects in globin gene expression (due to either regulatory or structural mutation) frequently lead to human diseases involving defective haemoglobins, such as sickle cell anaemia and thalassaemia.

○ What techniques could be used to study the proteins bound to the globin gene promoter?

● You could have thought of DNA footprinting, affinity chromatography and gel shift assays (Box 10.2), ChIp (Box 5.3) or DNAase hypersensitivity site mapping (Figure 5.33).

The individual genes within the β-globin cluster appear to have arisen through gene duplication; in this process, one copy has lost its function and is referred to as a **pseudogene** (ψβ; Figure 10.25). Transcription of each gene within the cluster is orientated in the same direction, as indicated in Figure 10.25.

As you might expect with such a highly regulated gene, transcriptional control is complex. How is this achieved? It appears not to be at the level of the individual gene, as the local promoter regions of genes within the β-globin cluster are all very similar, containing consensus binding sequences such as TATA and CCAAT elements, and also containing sites for the binding of an erythrocyte-specific factor called GATA-1. Rather, β-globin expression appears to be controlled by the regulatory region upstream called the β-globin locus control region (LCR), which contains several DNAase I hypersensitive sites (Figure 5.33). In comparisons of β-globin cluster sequences between many different species, these sites appear to be evolutionarily well conserved, indicating their biological importance. It also carries an additional hypersensitive site called the 3′ HS.

○ What does a DNAase hypersensitive site indicate about the chromatin structure in this region?

● It suggests that the chromatin is not tightly packed, allowing access to the enzyme. You saw examples of this in Chapter 5 (Figures 5.31 and 5.33).

The β-globin cluster LCR sites correspond to the binding sites of various transcriptional regulators, including both erythroid-specific and general transcription factors. The LCR serves as an enhancer for the β-globin gene cluster. Studies have suggested that each gene within the cluster interacts individually with the LCR at the time of its expression, suggesting that the LCR functions through a looping mechanism selectively with the appropriate gene for the particular developmental phase. The precise mechanism by which this is achieved is still unknown, but involves factors that bind both the local promoter and the LCR. The 3′ HS element is also important in regulating β-globin gene expression but we will not discuss its role further here.

10.4.4 Insulator elements protect genes from inappropriate regulation

We saw earlier how the activity of eukaryotic promoters is governed by specific enhancer elements, which can be located upstream, downstream, or even within the gene itself. In particular, the observation that an enhancer may influence the activity of a gene promoter some tens or hundreds of kilobases distant raises the question of why an enhancer does not activate inappropriate genes. The answer lies in a DNA sequence element known as an **insulator element**. Insulators have three characteristic properties, shown schematically in Figure 10.26.

Firstly, insulator elements are position-dependent: in order to disrupt the regulatory interaction between an enhancer and a promoter, the insulator must lie between an enhancer and the promoter affected by the enhancer. Secondly, insulator elements act by impeding enhancer–promoter communication; neither element is inactivated. Finally, insulators have no inherent enhancer activity of their own.

Insulator elements are not well understood at the molecular level, but may share some features with particular structural elements of the chromosome. If you recall that regulatory elements that act at a distance from a promoter must contact their targets through DNA looping (Figure 10.24), it is clear that the ability to loop will be somewhat dependent on the structural configuration of the chromosome in the

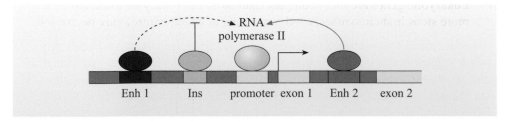

Figure 10.26   Insulator elements buffer chromosome areas from the influence of transcriptional repressors and enhancers. The promoter region of a hypothetical gene is shown with two enhancers (Enh 1 and Enh 2) lying nearby; Enh 2 within the intron between exons 1 and 2, Enh 1 upstream of the gene promoter. The insulator element (Ins) in the interval between Enh 1 and the promoter inhibits transcriptional regulators bound to the enhancer from influencing gene transcription from the promoter (dashed arrow). Enh 2, however, continues to modulate transcriptional activity (full arrow).

region. Recall from Chapter 5 that chromosomal DNA is organized as loops of about 20–200 kb fastened to the chromosome scaffold (Section 5.8.1), and that alterations in loop length arise as DNA is condensed or decondensed (Figure 5.40). It would seem reasonable that the relative position of the promoter and enhancer concerned within an individual loop could influence this interaction, and that interactions between loops are restricted or regulated in some way.

The points of attachment of the chromatin to the supporting scaffold are known as **scaffold attachment regions (SARs)**, and are generally A–T-rich sequences.

○ Which class of enzymes is present at a site of attachment to the chromosome scaffold?

● DNA topoisomerases (Section 5.8.1).

Where it has been possible to analyse a chromosome loop in detail for promoter activity and enhancer function, it appears that some SARs, but not all, appear to act as insulator elements.

10.4.5 Are there operons in eukaryotes?

One of the benefits deriving from the completion of several eukaryotic genome projects is the acquisition of a considerable body of information concerning the structure and distribution of genes within the genomes of these organisms. One observation made following the analysis of the *C. elegans* genome was that many genes are clustered as operons in the genome. This feature of its transcriptional behaviour remains unique, at least among those genomes that have been fully sequenced, but in the case of *Drosophila melanogaster* there appears to be clustering of genes with similar spatiotemporal expression patterns into domains along the chromosomes. It is increasingly clear that greater insights into the regulation of gene expression in eukaryotes will continue to be gained as the genomes of further species are sequenced, and their analysis perfected.

A further compounding factor in understanding gene regulation is that eukaryotic genes frequently overlap other genes, or even lie entirely within an intron of another gene. A particular gene may have a very large number of elements controlling its expression.

Summary of Section 10.4

1   Eukaryotic genes are more complex than those of prokaryotes, and have many more steps in their synthesis and processing at which control may be exerted.

2   Three RNA polymerases, I, II and III, operate in eukaryotes. RNA polymerase II is responsible for the transcription of most protein-coding genes, whereas RNA polymerase I transcribes most of the rRNA, and RNA polymerase III transcribes the tRNAs, the 5 S rRNA, and several species of small RNA.

3   Most promoters have a number of local binding sites for general and specific transcriptional regulators, which play a role in the assembly of the RNA polymerase II complex at the promoter. The establishment of transcriptionally active promoters involves DNA bending, which allows upstream regulatory elements within the promoter region to regulate transcription.

4   Regulatory elements at some distance away from the promoter form part of the transcriptionally active promoter through DNA looping. These include enhancer or suppressor elements, which may lie some distance from the gene promoter. An enhancer may be on the 5′ or 3′ side of a gene; they may also occur within a gene.

5   Transcription regulators (activators and repressors) act in combination to specify the precise timing of gene expression, both temporally and spatially.

6   Insulator elements serve to protect genes from inappropriate regulation from distant elements. Chromosome structure may influence insulator function at the level of attachment to the chromosome scaffold.

10.5 Chromatin structure and transcription

Recall that eukaryotic DNA is packaged within chromatin, and all nuclear processes, including transcription, must occur within this context. Considerable levels of complexity are seen in the chromosomal architecture of eukaryotes. Chromatin components play several important roles in gene regulation by influencing access to target sites within genomic DNA, both at the local promoter level and more indirectly through global changes. As an example of control at the local level, consider zinc-finger binding proteins.

◻ How do these proteins interact with DNA?

◼ The zinc fingers interact with critical bases within the major groove of the DNA helix.

◻ How could the position of DNA on the nucleosome influence this binding?

◼ The rotational positioning of the DNA on the nucleosome could result in the recognition site within the major groove being face-out and therefore accessible, or face-in and inaccessible (Figure 5.30).

This rotational positioning can be influenced by a twist in the DNA of only five base pairs, highlighting the subtlety of how nucleosome positioning can influence transcriptional regulator binding. Note that binding of one factor upstream or downstream could exert a rotational effect on other factors and thereby exclude them from binding. Local chromatin modifications can also effect the establishment of RNA polymerase II initiation complexes at a promoter by, for example, influencing the binding of TBP, or through modulating phosphorylation of the RNA polymerase C-terminal domain (CTD).

More globally, the different degrees of chromosome compaction, histone modifications and DNA methylation all play important roles in transcriptional regulation. An indication that chromatin structure plays an important role in the regulation of gene activity initially came from observations that chromatin could be divided into two forms: **euchromatin**, the portion of the chromatin that contains most of the gene complement, and **heterochromatin**, which is more densely condensed and contains few genes. Heterochromatin is found in many areas of genomes, including structurally important regions such as centromeres.

Studies on the giant polytene chromosomes of certain insects, notably the midge *Chironomus* and the fruit-fly *Drosophila melanogaster*, revealed that activation of genes is accompanied by a lessening of chromatin compaction. An example is given in Figure 10.27, which shows the response of a section of *Drosophila* polytene chromosome to exposure of the cells to the moulting hormone β-ecdysone over a period of 12 hours. Polytene chromosomes have reproducible banding patterns which represent local variation in chromatin condensation.

As can be seen from Figure 10.27, a series of changes to the polytene chromosome structure is observed after treatment of the cells with β-ecdysone. In each case, the structure of the chromosome is loosened and the chromosome swells to form a 'puff', in a process known as 'puffing'. Puffing reflects the loosening of the chromatin structure as transcription takes place, and, not surprisingly, the puffs formed in response to β-ecdysone correspond to the chromosomal locations of the genes known to be responsive to the hormone. Within 0.25 hours, the genes located at 75B and 74EF show signs of transcription, whereas those within the puff located at 78D and 71CD occur only later (4–8 hours).

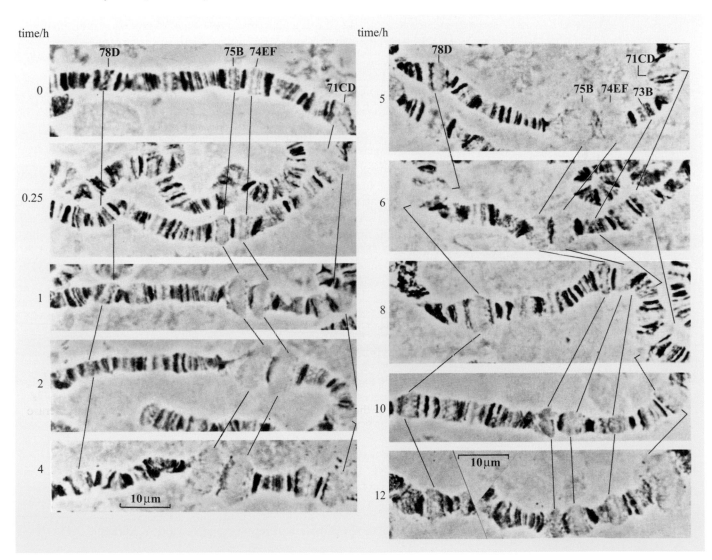

Figure 10.27   The response of *Drosophila* polytene chromosomes to treatment with β-ecdysone. The alignment of the chromosome region shown in each panel is indicated by lines. The locations of the regions at which puffs occur in response to β-ecdysone can be seen at 78D, 75B, 74EF and 71CD. Each panel corresponds to a successively longer incubation with the hormone, as indicated in hours. Note that some puffs occur before others; notably, early puffs appear at 75B and 74EF (at 0.25 hours).

Heterochromatin remains in a more condensed condition through interphase than euchromatin, and this affects transcription of genes located within it. The inhibitory effects of heterochromatin can be seen under certain experimental circumstances, and provided the first evidence that the local state of chromatin structure can influence gene expression. We shall examine several examples of how studies of gene silencing have provided insights into our understanding of chromatin and gene regulation.

10.5.1 Position-effect variegation in *Drosophila*

An example of the effects of heterochromatin on gene expression is seen when a chromosome inversion brings the *Drosophila white* gene into proximity with heterochromatin. This causes inactivation of the *white* gene, through the spreading of the inactive heterochromatin structure across the *white* gene promoter, an effect known as **position-effect variegation (PEV)**.

The *Drosophila white* gene encodes a protein responsible for importing the reddish-brown eye pigments into the eye. Loss of the *white* gene product therefore leads to a white eye phenotype.

The silenced heterochromatin that forms in PEV has characteristic features, including hypoacetylated histones (i.e. those with a low level of acetyl groups in their histone tails), H3-K9 methylation and a more condensed structure.

○ Which enzymes are responsible for the removal of acetyl groups from histones?

● Histone deacetylases (HDAC; Section 5.7.2).

Genetic screens have been used to identify genes encoding proteins that enhance PEV. Molecular characterization of these genes identified two classes of protein. The first are proteins that act as histone methytransferases (HMTs), and, in particular, methylate the H3-K9 residue (Book 1, p. 237). The second are a group of proteins called HP1 proteins (heterochromatin protein 1), which bind specifically to H3-K9-Me via a so-called 'chromodomain'. Members of the HP1 family of proteins appear to be essential for the maintenance of transcriptionally inert heterochromatin and appear to link the histone tail modification to its transcription silencing effect. Similar proteins are found in all eukaryotes, highlighting the importance of H3-K9 methylation in this process.

10.5.2 Mating-type loci in yeast

Several loci in the budding yeast *S. cerevisiae* are known to be subject to transcriptional silencing mediated by changes in the chromatin state. Several examples include the mating-type loci HMR and HML and the regions immediately adjacent to the telomeres. The HMR and HML loci are flanked by what are termed 'silencer elements' (Figure 10.28), which contain specific DNA sequences to which a number of proteins may bind.

The crucial step in the adoption of a silenced state is the recruitment of the DNA binding proteins Rap1, Abf1 and ORC.

○ What role does ORC normally play in cells?

● It serves to regulate the initiation of replication (Sections 8.3.5 and 9.2.1).

An additional protein called Sir1 binds via an interaction with ORC, which enables it to recruit additional proteins (Sir2, Sir3 and Sir4). The chromatin region becomes locally hypoacetylated, leading to the binding of additional Sir proteins, which

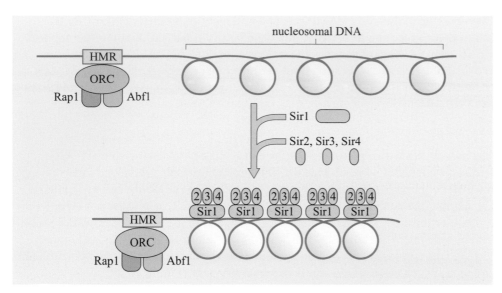

Figure 10.28
Stepwise illustration of chromatin inactivation at the yeast HMR locus. The silencing element HMR is bound by a complex of ORC, Rap1 and Abf1 proteins. These proteins recruit Sir1 protein to the HMR locus, which in turn recruits Sir2–Sir4, spreading across the locus. Nucleosomal DNA is shown forming a more condensed structure.

spread along the chromosome, binding to the deacetylated histones, and establishing a more condensed silenced chromatin structure.

The examples of both PEV and HML/HMR silencing highlight the importance of histone modification, both deacetylation and methylation, in modulating chromatin structure. In both cases, alterations in histone modification lead to the recruitment of proteins that serve to maintain the condensed state. This condensed state serves to exclude the transcription machinery.

10.5.3 DNA methylation in eukaryotes

Although the DNA of some eukaryotes, including *S. pombe*, *S. cerevisiae* and *D. melanogaster*, is known not to be methylated, methylation is known to play an important role in gene regulation in general.

○ What particular base methylation is found in most eukaryotes?

● 5-Methylcytosine (Figure 5.4 and Section 9.4).

In vertebrates, DNA methylation is typically associated with transcriptionally inactive regions, such as the inactivated X chromosome, and also with areas of heterochromatin such as centromeres.

How does methylation alter gene transcription? In some cases, localized variations in methylation can directly affect the binding of a transcriptional regulator to its binding site. This could occur only when a 5′-CG base grouping is present within their consensus binding site.

○ How might methylation of cytosine residues alter transcription regulator binding?

● Recall that the methyl group lies within the major groove of helical DNA, which is where most DNA binding proteins interact with their target DNA sequences. Methylation may alter or interfere with these interactions.

One example of this is the cAMP-responsive transcription factor called CREB. Methylation at the single 5′-CG within the CREB's consensus binding site prevents CREB from binding. In contrast, the transcriptional regulator SP1, whose target site contains several 5′-CG sites, binds irrespective of its methylation status. Most transcription regulators are not affected by methylation in this way, so how does methylation lead to silencing?

Methyl-DNA binding proteins induce chromatin changes

The answer lies with a group of proteins that bind to DNA methylated at 5′-CG sites, an example of which is MeCP2. This protein binds in a sequence-independent manner, targeting just the presence of the methylated 5′-CG, although its binding is most likely modulated by other nearby proteins. MeCP2 acts to recruit other proteins to these sites, including HDAC, which lead to localized deacetylation, and also histone methyltransferases, which methylate amino acid residues within the histone tails such as H3-K9. These alterations lead to a localized change in chromatin structure, which can exclude access to regulatory sites (Figure 10.29).

MeCP2 therefore acts as a transcriptional repressor, inducing transcriptional silencing, not by directly interacting with RNA polymerase or other components of the transcriptional complex, but by inducing localized modifications in chromatin structure, which causes a promoter to become inaccessible.

Recall that the pattern of methylation in genomic DNA is restored in newly synthesized DNA immediately after DNA replication (Section 9.4). Local chromatin structure also undergoes a maturation following the distribution of 'old' nucleosomes and the incorporation of newly acetylated nucleosomes (Figure 9.19).

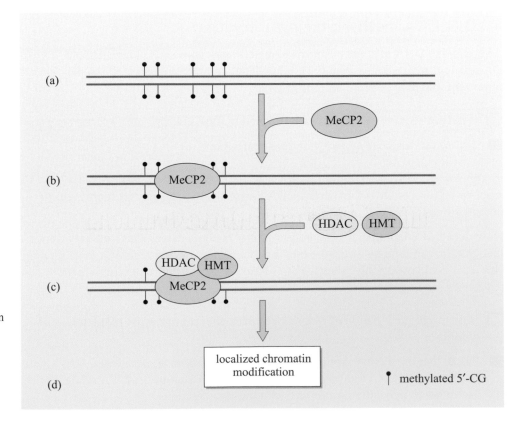

Figure 10.29
DNA methylation and MeCP2 binding lead to localized chromatin modifications. Regions of eukaryotic DNA containing methylated 5′-CG (a) are recognized and bound by the protein MeCP2 (b). This recruits a complex of other proteins, including both HDAC and HMT proteins (c), which together modulate local chromatin structure (d) to a transcriptionally inert configuration.

As chromatin matures, it is locally modified such that the modifications on the original chromosome are stably inherited. Although this is certainly influenced by the distributed 'old' nucleosomes, we can now also attribute some of this maintenance role to DNA methylation on the genomic DNA by proteins such as MeCP2. Methylation therefore serves as a marker to aid the inheritance of stable chromatin states.

Gene reactivation

During mammalian development, DNA methylation and chromatin modification are the primary methods for establishing stable gene expression patterns within specializing and differentiated cell types. This ensures that developmentally silenced genes are effectively 'locked out' from engagement with any of the transcriptional machinery. How this is achieved across a genome is unclear, but most likely it involves developmentally regulated factors that target specific genes, inducing their silencing and localized methylation.

There are situations, however, where genes that have been silenced by a developmental program are required to be activated. In this case, transcriptional activators are capable of accessing their binding sites by interfering with local chromatin structure or by localized remodelling of nucleosome positioning (Figure 10.30). Such transcriptional activators function by recruiting histone acetyltransferases (HATs; Section 5.7.2) to remodel the local chromatin, which causes it to become less compact and allows access to the transcription machinery.

○ What would be the consequences of global defects in methylation in a differentiated cell?

■ It would result in the reactivation of genes that had been silenced as part of the cell's differentiation pathway.

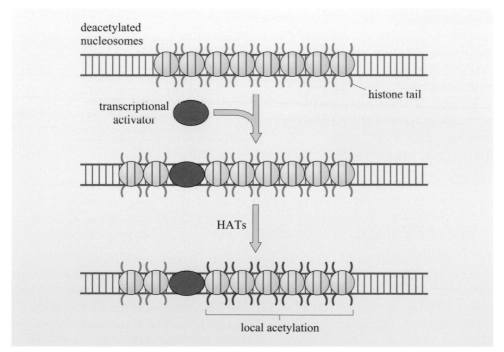

Figure 10.30
Reactivation of genes by chromatin remodelling. A region of chromatin is shown containing nucleosomes with deacetylated histone tails (blue). Binding of a transcription activator can both alter nucleosome position (left) and lead to the recruitment of HAT proteins (right). These acetylate local chromatin components, leading to decondensation and allowing transcriptional activity to occur.

Such changes are common in cells within tumours, and most likely contribute to the tumorigenic cell phenotype. We shall return to this subject when we discuss tumorigenesis in Chapter 19.

The role of methylation in the maintenance of developmentally programmed gene expression in mammals raises the interesting question as to how this is achieved robustly in organisms such as *Drosophila,* whose DNA does not undergo base methylation.

10.5.4 Persistent chromatin remodelling in the absence of methylation

Transcriptional regulation plays a central role in *Drosophila* development. As development continues, many genes must be activated or repressed in specific cell lineages, and this transcriptional state of the genes must be 'remembered' by the cells for one or more cell divisions. We saw earlier that in the specific case of heterochromatin, silencing is maintained by the binding of proteins such as HP1. An example of how this is achieved at specific genes within euchromatin is seen for the case of an important class of developmentally regulated genes called the **homeotic genes**. Although these genes were originally identified in *Drosophila*, homologous genes have been identified in all animals studied so far, including mammals such as mice and humans.

As development proceeds, the anterior–posterior and dorsal–ventral axes, and the subsequent segmentation pattern of the embryo, are determined. The segmental identity is specified by the spectrum of homeotic genes expressed in any given segment. The homeotic genes then act as important developmental switches, influencing a multitude of downstream genes. The maintenance of appropriate homeotic gene expression through each cell division is therefore critical. This is achieved through the establishment of what is called **persistent chromatin remodelling**, wherein a regulatory protein remains bound to a region of DNA to maintain local chromatin structure. Two classes of protein appear to be involved, namely the polycomb group (PcG) and the trithorax group (TrxG) proteins. The PcG and TrxG proteins form complexes that maintain the stable inherited expression of the homoeotic genes. Generally, PcG complexes act to repress transcription of homeotic genes in a specific lineage, and TrxG complexes act to maintain the transcriptional activity of homeotic genes.

10.5.5 Mediation of X chromosome inactivation

The inactive X chromosome (Xi) in female mammals is visible in the interphase nucleus as a compact area known as a **Barr body**. The Barr body is condensed in a heterochromatin-like state, which persists after its establishment, about 72 hours following the onset of cell differentiation. But how is an X chromosome inactivated?

The key factor in the establishment of the inactive state is a region of the X chromosome known as the **X inactivation centre** (**XIC**). This functions as a regulatory element, which is required to initiate the inactive chromatin state. The XIC contains a transcription unit known as *Xist*; *Xist* RNA remains in the nucleus and so is not translated. The transcripts are found to coat the inactive X chromosome and the *Xist* RNA chains appear to play a role in initiating the silent state of the inactivated chromosome. Once the chromosome is inactivated, however, *Xist* RNA is no longer required for its maintenance.

The inactivated X chromosome contains various modified or specialized chromatin components, some of which are listed in Table 10.3.

Table 10.3 Enriched or depleted histone forms in the inactivated X chromosome, relative to the active X chromosome in mammals.

Histone	Enriched/depleted in Xi
macroH2A1	enriched
macroH2A2	enriched
H3-K9-CH$_3$	enriched
H3-Ac	depleted
H4-Ac	depleted
H3-K4-CH$_3$	depleted

As can be seen from Table 10.3 (and also Section 5.7), the inactivated X chromosome is enriched in modified histones associated with silent chromosomes (e.g. H3-K9-Me) and depleted of acetylated histones. In addition, it contains specific forms of H2A, and its DNA is highly methylated at 5'-CG sites.

How is the presence of the *Xist* RNA linked to the establishment of this altered chromatin state? While the X-inactive state is being initiated, it is believed that *Xist* RNA recruits histone deacetylases and histone methyltransferases to the chromosome. This silencing establishment complex modifies the chromatin structure, thereby preventing transcription. Subsequently, on cell development and differentiation, the genomic DNA becomes methylated *de novo* through the action of DNA methylases, which methylate cytosine residues at unmethylated 5'-CG sites (Figure 10.31). The action of these enzymes is in contrast to other DNA methylases, which act on hemi-methylated DNA (Section 9.4).

○ What will be the effect of the methylation of this chromosome on its subsequent activity?

● Once methylated at 5'-CG sites, this inactivated chromosome will be bound by methyl-DNA binding proteins such as MeCP2, which will further recruit HDACs and histone methyltransferases.

In turn, this serves as a method of maintaining the X-inactive state through all subsequent cell divisions, explaining why *Xist* RNA is not required for its maintenance. It is of interest to note that in human Rett's syndrome, mutations within the MeCP2 gene mean that the MeCP2 protein is defective, leading to a global deregulation of gene expression, particularly from the X chromosome.

10.5.6 Transcriptional regulation at the genome level

The detailed genetic analyses possible with some model organisms, especially *Drosophila*, have revealed a basis for a genomic level of chromosomal organization in the control of gene expression. Interphase chromatin is not homogeneous: the nucleus is not simply a bag of chromatin with an essentially random distribution of

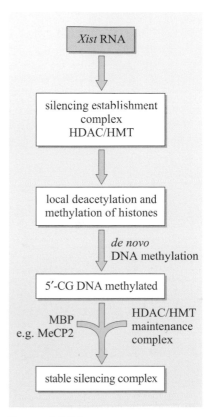

Figure 10.31
Possible mechanism of X inactivation. *Xist* RNA coats the X chromosome and is believed to recruit a silencing establishment complex containing histone deacetylases (HDAC) and histone methyltransferases (HMT). This leads to localized changes in chromatin modification. Subsequently, *de novo* methylation occurs and the methylated DNA now binds to methyl-DNA binding proteins (MBP) such as MeCP2. Methylation and MeCP2 binding serve to maintain the chromatin state through an HDAC/HMT complex, as shown in Figure 10.29, leading to a stable silencing complex.

chromosome arms. By looking carefully at Figure 5.42, you can see that each chromosome arm occupies a specific region within the nucleus. In this case, the two copies of human chromosome 5 lie on opposite sides of the interphase nucleus.

It is not clear as to whether this is representative of all eukaryotes, as genetic evidence from *Drosophila* suggests strongly that in this species homologous chromosomes actually remain closely associated with each other through interphase. This is known as **somatic pairing**, which has some interesting consequences on the regulation of gene control through an effect known as **transvection**. Transvection reflects the ability of transcriptional activators bound to a regulatory sequence on one chromosome homologue to influence the transcriptional activity of the other homologue ('cross-talk'). If you recall that regulators acting at a distance can interact with promoters via DNA loops (Figure 10.24), it is possible to see how these loops can also extend from the homologous chromosome if the two chromosomes are held together by somatic pairing (Figure 10.32).

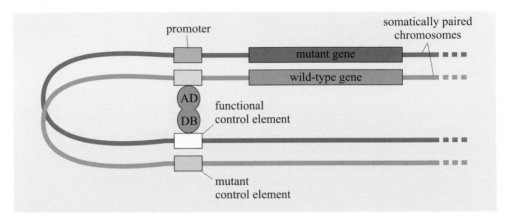

Figure 10.32 Cross-talk between homologous chromosomes (transvection). Regulatory elements present on one chromosome homologue may, in some circumstances, be seen to exert a regulatory influence on the other homologue. In this example, a pair of somatically paired *Drosophila* chromosomes are shown. One chromosome carries a mutant gene (encoding a non-functional protein) and a functional control element. The other chromosome carries a wild-type gene and a mutant, non-functional control element. Due to somatic pairing, the functional control element is able to direct transcription of the wild-type gene on the homologous chromosome, leading to the production of a functional polypeptide.

Monitoring global gene expression

From the mid-1990s, molecular biological techniques for the determination of DNA sequences reached levels of efficiency that enabled the very large genomes typically found in eukaryotes to be sequenced in their entirety. These projects made available very large collections of data: not only were the DNA sequences of these organisms elucidated, but a combination of computer-based and laboratory-based analytical techniques permitted the identification of most of the genes contained in each genome. This information makes it possible to monitor the level of transcription for every gene in a genome, for example throughout development, between disease and normal states, or in response to certain experimental treatments (Box 10.4).

Box 10.4 Microarrays and the assessment of global levels of transcription

In microarray analysis, a collection of DNA molecules with sequences corresponding to some or all of the predicted transcription units of a genome are first spotted on a glass slide in a tightly packed microarray. In a typical experiment, mRNA from appropriate cells is incubated with reverse transcriptase, which produces a single-stranded DNA copy of the mRNA called complementary DNA (cDNA). This DNA is labelled with a fluorescent dye and then incubated with the microarray, enabling cDNAs to hybridize to their complementary DNA chains (Box 5.1).

○ cDNA is synthesized using an mRNA as a template. If the cDNA strand sequence is compared with the DNA sequence of the gene encoding the mRNA, does the cDNA strand have the same sequence as the template or the non-template strand?

■ It has the same sequence as the template strand, as its sequence is complementary to the mRNA sequence.

After hybridization, the amount of cDNA hybridized to each spot on the microarray is detected by measuring the amount of fluorescent tag. The combined signal detected for every transcription unit will therefore quantitatively reflect the full diversity of mRNA species in the original RNA sample. Frequently, two states are compared. An example of microarray data obtaining using this approach is shown in Figure 10.33.

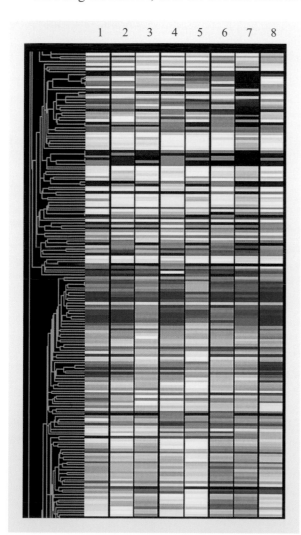

Figure 10.33

A representation of microarray data. This figure shows an example of a real microarray analysis of mRNA extracted from two groups of *Drosophila*. One group of flies was treated with a chemical that induced oxidative stress, while the other group was untreated. Fluorescently tagged cDNA was synthesized from the two mRNA samples. Both probes were hybridized simultaneously to each slide: one probe was tagged with a red fluorescent tag, the other with a green fluorescent tag. Each of the columns, 1–8, represents an independent hybridization to a microarray slide. Within a column, each horizontal bar represents one gene, and its colour shows the relative balance between red and green fluorescence. This indicates the relative abundance of the mRNA corresponding to that particular gene in the comparison of the two mRNA populations. The relative strength of fluorescence of the green and red dyes for each gene is shown as a scale of blue to red. To control for variation of fluorescence due to different levels of incorporation of the fluorescent tags into the probes, a 'dye swap' is performed: the probes prepared from the treated and untreated samples are tagged with the red and green dyes respectively in one hybridization, and with the green and red tags respectively in the second hybridization. Columns 3, 6 and 7 correspond to the 'dye swap' hybridizations – note how the coloration of the bars is the inverse of the corresponding bars in the other columns. The coloration of each bar is remarkably consistent across each of the eight hybridizations shown. The green tree structure to the left of the panel shows how the computer has grouped the genes according to their hybridization patterns.

Analysis of global mRNA changes using microarrays allows a rapid screening of cells to identify critical genes that might be components of particular pathways of interest. In most cases, the genes will be those showing dramatic increases or decreases in levels between, for example, normal and diseased cells. A first stage in confirming data from microarray experiments such as that shown in Figure 10.33, is to examine the levels of mRNA within cells by more quantitative techniques.

It is possible to monitor levels of mRNA present within cells using Northern blotting, but more sensitive techniques are being commonly used. These include **quantitative PCR**, in which fluorescent dyes are incorporated into the PCR product and the fluorescence measured after every cycle of the reaction. This technique provides a real time measurement of amplification and is therefore commonly referred to as **real time PCR**.

Summary of Section 10.5

1   The complexity in the packaging and structure of eukaryotic genomes affords many opportunities for regulatory interactions.

2   Chromatin components are modified in all eukaryotes, although the mechanisms by which they are maintained and persist through cell division differ. In many eukaryotes, DNA methylation is used as a mechanism to establish chromatin changes through methyl-DNA binding proteins. In other organisms without methylation, specific proteins are utilized to maintain heterochromatin or maintain stable inherited patterns of chromatin modification.

3   The methylation of DNA, the acetylation of histones and persistent remodelling of chromatin all have the potential to influence the activity of genes, or indeed entire chromosomes or chromosomal domains.

4   Chromosomes lie within nuclear domains. In some cases, it is known that there is regulatory cross-talk between homologous chromosomes, made possible by the close proximity between homologues in the interphase nucleus.

Molecular modelling 6

Go to the Study Skills file: *Molecular modelling 6*. This activity will provide you with an opportunity to examine nucleic acid structure and to investigate DNA–protein interactions using ViewerLite™.

10.6 Post-transcriptional events in eukaryotes

Many of the post-transcriptional modifications of eukaryotic mRNAs are closely tied to transcription itself, and in many cases these occur as transcription proceeds. Many of the protein complexes effecting these processing events interact with the C-terminal domains of RNA polymerase II, altering its phosphorylation as the mRNA is processed. The modifications we shall discuss occur progressively as the mRNA is produced. First, as the 5′ end of the mRNA is produced, it becomes 'capped' with a specific modified base. As synthesis continues, the immature mRNA is spliced and finally tailed with a stretch of adenine residues. We shall complete this section by discussing the control of mRNA export from the nucleus, and the chemical modification that occurs in some RNAs.

10.6.1 mRNA modification

mRNA capping

One of the characteristics of eukaryotic mRNAs that distinguishes them from those of prokaryotes is the presence of what is termed the **5′ cap** or **m⁷G cap**. The formation of the 5′ cap is the first modification to be made following transcription. It is the addition of a 7-methylguanosine residue (m⁷G) via three phosphate groups to the 5′ terminus of the **pre-mRNA** (the primary mRNA transcript) in an unusual 5′ to 5′ linkage (Figure 10.34a).

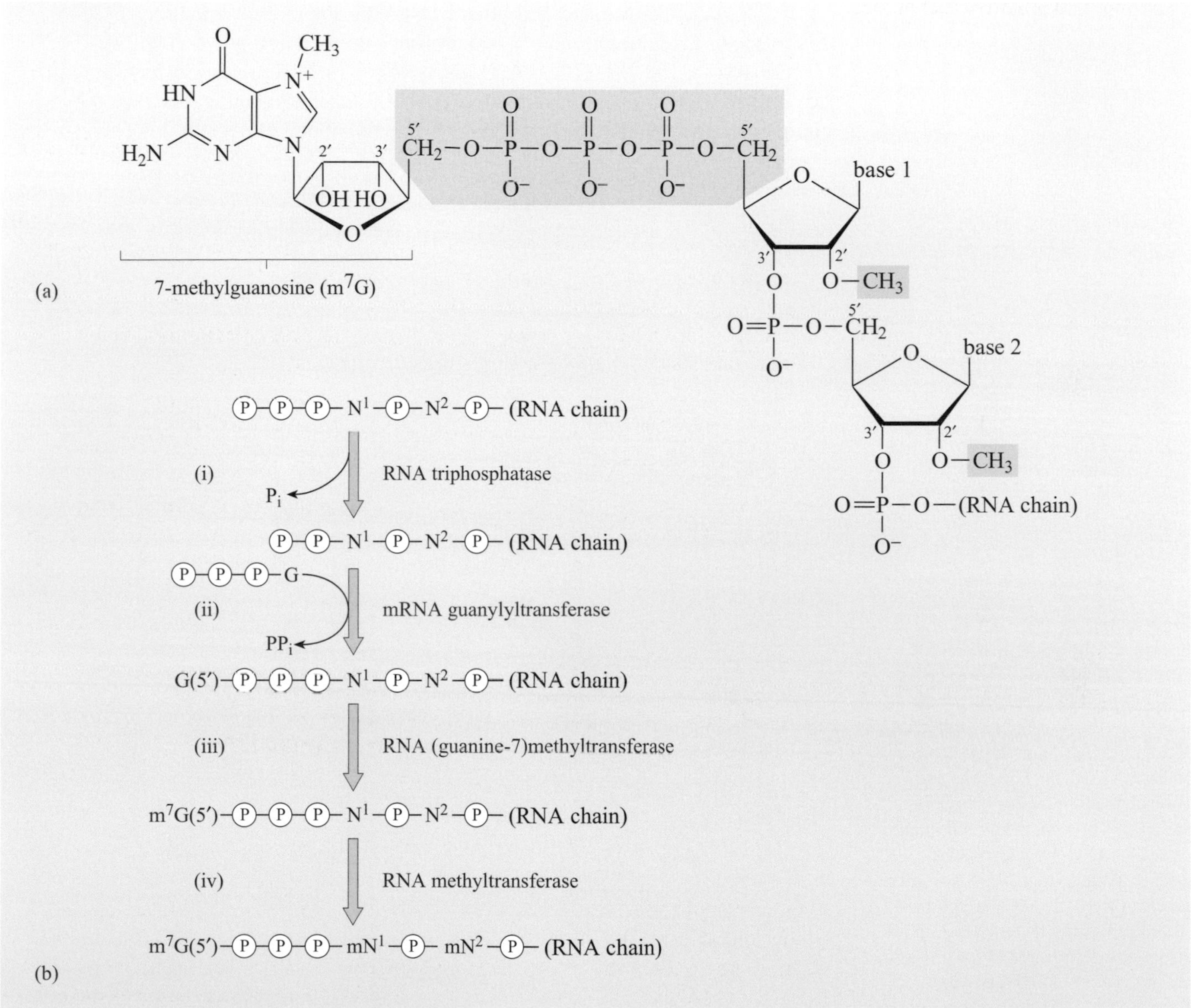

Figure 10.34 (a) The 5′ cap structure of eukaryotic mRNA. Base 1 and base 2 are the first two bases of the mRNA. The unusual 5′–5′ linkage and the 2′-O-linked methyl group are highlighted in lilac and blue respectively. (b) The four-step process leading to the addition of the 5′-m⁷G cap to an mRNA, where N^1 and N^2 represent the two most 5′ nucleotides of the chain. The most 5′ phosphate group is removed (i), a guanosine monophosphate is added to this end (ii) and subsequently methylated (iii). Finally, the 2′-OH of the ribose sugar of each of nucleotides 1 and 2 is methylated (iv).

Cap addition requires the sequential activity of four enzymes; firstly, RNA triphosphatase removes the terminal phosphate group; secondly, mRNA guanylyltransferase transfers a guanosine monophosphate, a methyltransferase modifies the guanosine by addition of a methyl group to the 7 position and finally, an RNA methyltransferase adds a methyl group to the 2′-OH on the ribose of each of the end bases (Figure 10.34). The presence of the m^{7}G cap at the 5′ end of mRNAs is required for export through the nuclear pores and for efficient translation (Chapter 11), and protects the mRNA from degradation of the 5′ end by cellular nucleases.

mRNA tailing

Most eukaryotic mRNAs are modified by the addition of approximately 250 adenosine residues at their 3′ end in what is known as a poly(A) tail (Figure 10.35). The 3′ UTR of the majority of pre-mRNA molecules have at least one **polyadenylation signal sequence**, AAUAAA. This signal is recognized by a complex of proteins that cleaves the RNA at a site about 20 nucleotides downstream,

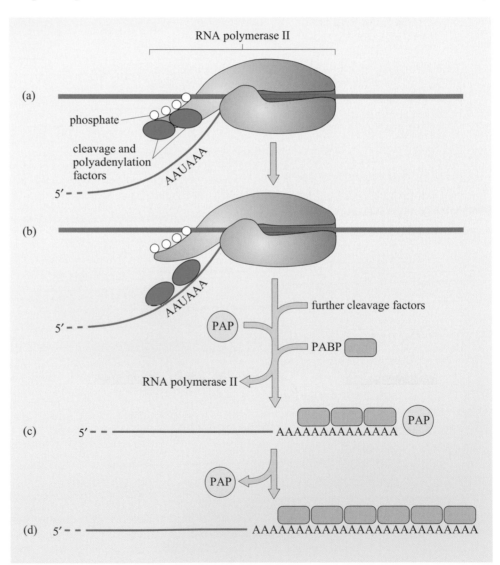

Figure 10.35
Polyadenylation tailing of mRNA.
(a) Polyadenylation of pre-mRNAs begins when RNA polymerase II, bound to cleavage and polyadenylation factors, reaches the poly(A) addition signal. (b) Cleavage and polyadenylation factors recognize the mRNA polyadenylation sequence (AAUAAA) and transfer to the mRNA. At this stage, RNA polymerase detaches from the DNA template. (c and d) Further factors required for cleavage are recruited to the mRNA and the nascent mRNA is separated from the DNA. The enzyme poly(A) polymerase (PAP) adds successive adenosine residues, and poly(A) binding protein (PABP) binds to the resulting poly(A) tail.

where an enzyme, called poly(A) polymerase (PAP) adds a series of adenine residues to the new 3′ end. This adenylation stage serves to terminate transcription and RNA polymerase II detaches from its DNA template, releasing the mRNA. The RNA polymerase C-terminal domain undergoes a series of dephosphorylation reactions and is recycled into another round of transcription initiation.

The function of the 3′ poly A tail appears to be to protect the 3′ end of the mature mRNA from exonuclease degradation, although it should be noted that some mRNAs, notably those encoding histones, lack poly(A) tails. A gene may possess more than one polyadenylation signal sequence, and the particular one used may depend on the exact pattern of intron processing. The genomes of animal mitochondria are extremely compact, with genes closely abutted, and in some cases overlapping. In fact, some mitochondrial genes have incomplete stop codons, which are completed by the addition of a poly(A) tail.

The poly(A) tail is the site of binding of a protein called **poly(A) binding protein (PABP)**, which, as we shall see later, plays an important role in both the regulation of translation and in mRNA degradation.

mRNA splicing

Virtually all genes in eukaryotes have their coding regions broken into intron–exon structures; some genes in higher eukaryotes can have surprisingly large numbers of exons. The removal of introns from a primary transcript is performed sequentially, each being removed, one by one, by a protein complex known as the **spliceosome**. An outline of the process is shown in Figure 10.36. It consists of two sequential reactions, resulting in the excision of the intron as a lariat-shaped molecule. Each splice reaction requires several molecules of ATP. Note that this pathway is distinct from that seen in self-splicing ribozymes (Section 5.4.4) which has no cofactor requirement.

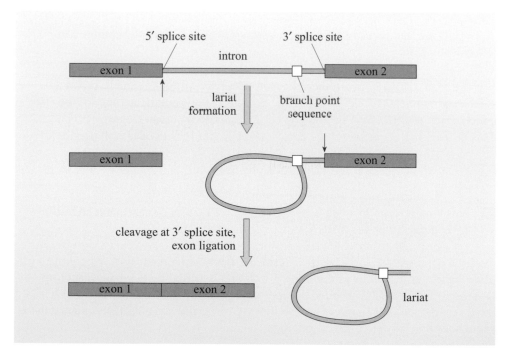

Figure 10.36
Splicing of eukaryotic pre-mRNA. This two-stage process is catalysed by the spliceosome (not shown), a complex of over 50 proteins and five RNA molecules. Firstly, the 5′ splice site of the intron is cleaved and attached to a base within the branch point sequence, leading to the formation of the lariat. Secondly, the 3′ splice site is cleaved and the 5′ end of exon 2 is joined to the 3′ end of exon 1.

The spliceosome is a complex of over 50 proteins and five RNA molecules. It is obviously vital that splicing events are carried out accurately, which is presumably why the spliceosome is so complex. The RNA components of the spliceosome are all **small nuclear RNAs (snRNAs)**, which are less than 200 nucleotides in length. Those involved in splicing are the U1, U2, U4, U5 and U6 snRNAs. The roles of U2, U5 and U6 snRNAs are indicated in Figure 10.37. These RNAs are complexed with proteins to form ribonucleoproteins (RNPs), and are known as small nuclear RNPs (snRNPs).

Why are RNA molecules crucial to the spliceosome's function? The answer lies in the mechanism the cell uses to recognize the intron/exon boundaries. Examination of DNA sequences around these boundaries reveals the presence of conserved sequences, one at the 5′ side of the intron, the other at the 3′ side. These **splice site consensus sequences** are recognized by hybridization between snRNAs in the spliceosome and the target mRNA, and are a major factor is determining where the splice occurs. In addition to the 5′ and 3′ splice site consensus sequences, a third sequence, the branch point sequence, is essential. The splice site consensus sequences are shown in Table 10.4.

Table 10.4 Splice site consensus sequences within primary mRNA molecules.

Location	Consensus sequence
5′ splice site	5′-AGGUAAGU-3′
3′ splice site	5′-YYYYYYYNCAG-3′
branch point sequence (10–40 bases upstream of 3′ splice site)	5′-CURAY-3′(vertebrates) 5′-UACUAAC-3′(yeast)

A, G, C, U are four standard RNA bases, Y = pyrimidine (U or C), R = purine (A or G) and N = any base.

It is the base pairing between the splice site sequence within the mRNA, and the snRNA components of the spliceosome, that direct the catalytic activity of the spliceosome to the correct position along the pre-mRNA chain (Figure 10.37). This positioning is crucial for the correct synthesis of the encoded polypeptide.

☐ What would be the consequence of a one-base shift in a splice site within an ORF?

◼ This would result in a one-base shift in the ORF, with a subsequent alteration to the codons within the mRNA, downstream of the splice site.

Such an error would lead to what is termed a **frameshift mutation**, where the three-base reading frame of the mRNA is altered (shifted by one base), leading to a major effect on the encoded polypeptide. Aberrant splicing can obviously have severe effects, and many human diseases arise due to mutations in consensus sequences that prevent correct splicing.

It is immediately apparent that mRNA splicing has the potential to add further control to gene expression: not only may a gene be transcribed in specific tissues or at specific times, but slight variants of the gene product may be produced in specific spatiotemporal patterns by splicing different combinations of exons.

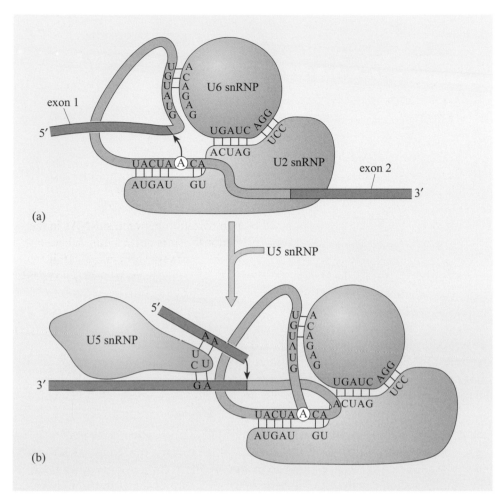

Figure 10.37
The relationship between some of the spliceosome RNP components and consensus mRNA sequences involved in the splicing reaction. The intron to be removed is shown in light orange and exons are in dark orange. (a) The RNA components of the U6 and U2 snRNPs anneal with complementary consensus sequences within the intron of the target mRNA. This configuration brings the branch point sequence close to the 5′ splice site. A reaction between the A residue within the branch point sequence and the 5′ splice site results in lariat formation. (b) Binding of the U5 snRNP to exons 1 and 2 brings the 3′ end of exon 1 into proximity of the 5′ end of exon 2, wherein a reaction between them generates the exon–exon linkage, releasing the intron.

Alternative splicing – generation of several proteins from one gene

One obvious corollary from the existence of introns is that several distinct, but related, polypeptides may be synthesized from the information held by a single gene. This may be achieved by **alternative splicing** (or **differential splicing**). In alternative splicing, several distinct mRNA species may be derived by splicing from a single pre-mRNA. Figure 10.38 illustrates how alternative splicing can generate different transcripts that encode distinct, but related, polypeptides.

Firstly, different combinations of exons can be spliced together (Figure 10.38a). Similarly, alternative translational start or stop sites may be determined by particular combinations of exons. Different splice sites within an exon can be selected (Figure 10.38b). Alternative spliced exons need not be protein coding; for example, Figure 10.38c shows two splice products with different non-coding products at the 5′ end.

⬭ Will the polypeptides encoded by the two splicing products of Figure 10.38c be the same or different?

⬛ They will be the same as they contain the same ORF.

Finally, alternative splicing products may result from an intron being excised or not (Figure 10.38d).

Figure 10.38
Alternative splicing yields different mature mRNAs. Primary transcripts are shown on the left, with alternative splicing possibilities for exons A–D indicated above (i) and below (ii). The corresponding products of alternative splicing are shown on the right.
(a) Different combinations of exons;
(b) different splice sites within exons;
(c) alternative splicing yields alternative UTRs (white boxes); (d) note that one of the two products contains an intron that has been removed from the other splice variant.

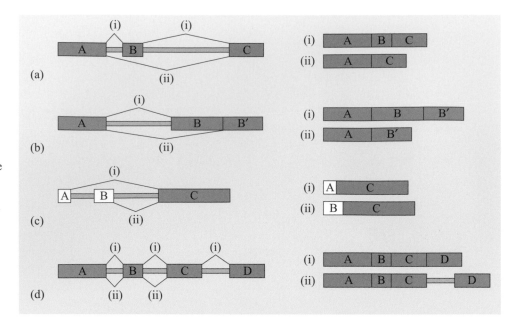

For typical mammalian systems, in which a gene may have many tens or even hundreds of introns, the number of distinct mature mRNAs may be very large. In some cases, the theoretical number of alternatively spliced forms may be in the thousands, although it is unlikely that this many would ever be used. It is estimated that 60% of human genes have alternative splice variants.

One example that illustrates the critical role that alternative splicing can play is in the sex determination pathway in *Drosophila*. In this species, the males are XY, and females are XX. However, in contrast to mammals, the Y chromosome is not male-determining; rather, it is the ratio of the number of X chromosomes to the number of complete autosome sets (X : A) that is the primary sex-determining signal. In females, which have two X chromosomes and two sets of autosomes, this ratio is 1 : 1 and this initiates female development. In males, with only a single X chromosome this ratio is 1 : 2 and this initiates male development. The sex determination step occurs early in development, and splicing pathways are an integral part of this process, as shown in Figure 10.39.

The primary sex determination signal affects the expression and splicing of a gene called *Sex-lethal* (*Sxl*). If the X : A ratio is 1 : 1 (i.e. female) expression of *Sxl* occurs early in embryogenesis. This early transcript leads to the production of a specific form of the SXL protein called SXL^E (early) (Figure 10.39, left). The SXL^E protein regulates splicing of the *Sxl* mRNA, preventing the inclusion of a male-specific exon in the *Sxl* mRNA, and ensuring a female-specific splice event. This establishes the production of more SXL protein, as SXL acts on its own transcript to ensure its synthesis. This ensures that the sex-specific expression of SXL and the downstream genes is permanently maintained. When the X : A ratio is 1 : 2 (i.e. male) the *Sxl* mRNA is still produced, but the male-specific splice pattern produces an mRNA that does not yield a viable protein.

SXL further regulates the splicing of several downstream target genes which effect the somatic differentiation of female cells. The *transformer* (*tra*) mRNA only encodes a functional protein when a male-specific splicing event is suppressed by SXL. TRA protein itself also directs sex-specific splicing of two other genes: *doublesex*

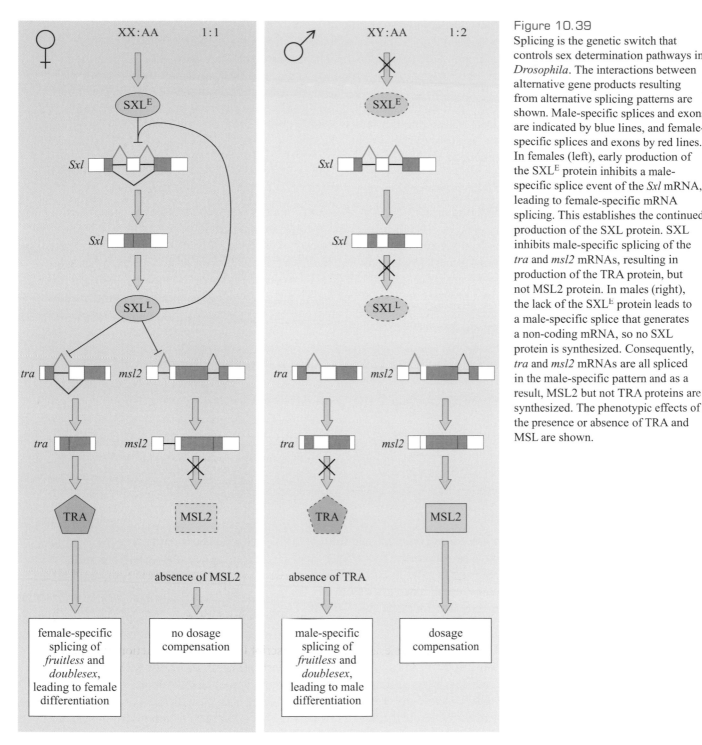

Figure 10.39
Splicing is the genetic switch that controls sex determination pathways in *Drosophila*. The interactions between alternative gene products resulting from alternative splicing patterns are shown. Male-specific splices and exons are indicated by blue lines, and female-specific splices and exons by red lines. In females (left), early production of the SXL^E protein inhibits a male-specific splice event of the *Sxl* mRNA, leading to female-specific mRNA splicing. This establishes the continued production of the SXL protein. SXL inhibits male-specific splicing of the *tra* and *msl2* mRNAs, resulting in production of the TRA protein, but not MSL2 protein. In males (right), the lack of the SXL^E protein leads to a male-specific splice that generates a non-coding mRNA, so no SXL protein is synthesized. Consequently, *tra* and *msl2* mRNAs are all spliced in the male-specific pattern and as a result, MSL2 but not TRA proteins are synthesized. The phenotypic effects of the presence or absence of TRA and MSL are shown.

(*dsx*), leading to sex-specific differentiation, and *fruitless* (*fru*), which influences sex-specific behaviour. In addition, SXL also regulates the establishment of dosage compensation, the process by which male and female *Drosophila* equalize the expression levels of X chromosomal genes to take account of the fact that males have one X, whereas the females have two. When SXL is absent (i.e. in males), the splicing of a downstream gene called *msl2* is affected; the first intron is removed and MSL protein is produced, which directs the process of dosage compensation. In females, the presence of SXL inhibits the splicing of the first intron and no MSL protein is produced.

The evolutionary origin of splicing

Splicing of mRNA is not ubiquitous: not only do some transcripts encoded within the genome of a given species lack introns, but introns do not occur in prokaryotes, and indeed are rare in some eukaryotes. For example, only approximately 3% of budding yeast genes have introns. The question therefore arises as to whether splicing arose in the ancestral state or whether it was acquired during evolution. In other words, have prokaryotes *lost* introns and splicing mechanisms, whereas eukaryotes have maintained them during the course of evolution, or have eukaryotes *acquired* them? The generally accepted view is that introns, and the associated systems of splicing, have been acquired by eukaryotes. You may have noted the similarity between the splicing mechanism outlined earlier and that utilized by self-splicing ribozymes (Figure 5.20). These self-splicing ribozymes have been suggested to be the evolutionary origin of eukaryotic introns.

> The evolutionary role of introns in exon shuffling, in which exons are switched between genes, was discussed in S204 Book 3 *The Core of Life*, Vol. II, Section 8.6.

RNA editing

RNA editing is an unusual form of RNA post-transcriptional processing in which bases are inserted into a primary transcript, or are chemically altered. It was first reported in 1986 in mitochondrial transcripts of certain protoctist species. In these cases, uracil bases not encoded in the mitochondrial genome were found in the mature mRNA molecules. The non-edited transcripts did not encode functional polypeptides; in other words, correct insertion of U bases was a requirement for correct gene expression.

The discovery of two forms of RNA editing in mammalian systems soon followed. Both concern post-transcriptional base modification. For example, in the *apoB* gene (which encodes the apolipoprotein B protein), a single cytidine (C) is changed to a uridine (U). Note that this is different from the insertion of bases seen in the protoctists described above; here the net result is base substitution rather than base insertion. In another case, adenosine residues are changed to inosine (I; see Figure 5.4b) residues within mRNAs encoding receptor components of glutamate-gated ion channels.

RNA editing in trypanosome mitochondria involves a second RNA molecule, the guide RNA (gRNA), which has a sequence substantially complementary to its target mRNA (Figure 10.40). On annealing to the mRNA, the sites to be edited are mismatched. The guide RNA has a poly(U) tail, which provides a source of U residues to be inserted into the mRNA.

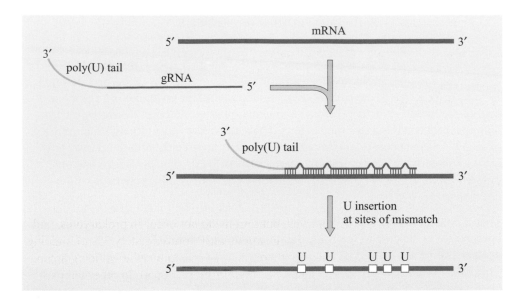

Figure 10.40
A mechanism for RNA editing that is found in trypanosome mitochondria. The editing of mRNAs is a complex procedure, and involves the hybridization of a guide RNA (gRNA) with the target mRNA. At the positions of mismatched bases, the bases within the mRNA chain are converted to U. The gRNA provides the U nucleotides from its own 3′-poly(U) tail.

Many RNAs are now known to undergo RNA editing as part of their normal post-transcriptional processing. Some examples are listed in Table 10.5. In some cases, RNA editing occurs in a process similar to that shown in Figure 10.40. In others, however, the editing occurs via sequence-directed base modification.

Table 10.5 Examples of eukaryotic and viral genes known to undergo RNA editing.

Gene	Edit	Effect
mammalian ApoB	C → U	introduces premature stop codon; alternative protein synthesized
mammalian GluR-B	A → I	amino acid substitution: affects properties of glutamate-gated ion channels in brain
mammalian serotonin 2C receptor	A → I	several codon changes: alternative proteins with different signalling properties
trypanosome mitochondrial RNAs	U insertion	introduction of start and stop codons, and the removal of frameshifts
P. polycephalum (a slime mould) cytochrome *c* oxidase I	C → U C insertion	removal of frameshifts
plant organelle RNAs	C → U	creation of start and stop codons, and multiple codon changes
paramyxovirus P mRNA	G insertion	generation of a frameshift; new mRNA encodes a related protein
hepatitis delta virus	A → I	removal of stop codon; synthesis of an alternative protein
ebola virus G protein	A insertion	removal of stop codon; synthesis of an alternative protein

10.6.2 Export of mRNA from the nucleus

One of the defining characteristics of eukaryotes is that transcription and translation occur in distinct subcellular compartments. It follows, therefore, that mRNA molecules, and other RNA species vital for translation (such as tRNA and rRNA), must be transported to the cytosol. Recall that the nuclear envelope is a complex double-membrane structure, pierced by nuclear pore complexes, through which biomolecules enter and exit the nucleus. These pores are large structures, composed of many protein subunits and linked to the nuclear lamina, the structural protein network underlying the nuclear envelope (Section 8.2.2). Transport into and out of the nucleus is highly regulated, and involves various signal sequences within polypeptides.

Most RNAs in the nucleus are associated with proteins in ribonucleoprotein (RNP) complexes. In the case of mRNAs, the protein component of RNPs destined for nuclear export has both RNA binding activity and a **nuclear export signal (NES)**. This RNP complex is bound by a shuttling receptor protein that is then bound by a G protein called Ran in its GTP-bound form (Ran(GTP)). As a single unit, this is then exported via the nuclear pore complex, as shown in Figure 10.41. Once in the cytosol, Ran(GTP) undergoes hydrolysis to Ran(GDP) after stimulation by a GTPase activating protein (GAP; Book 1, p. 123) called Ran(GAP). The RNP and shuttling receptor protein are released and recycled back into the nucleus. The mRNA is now ready for translation.

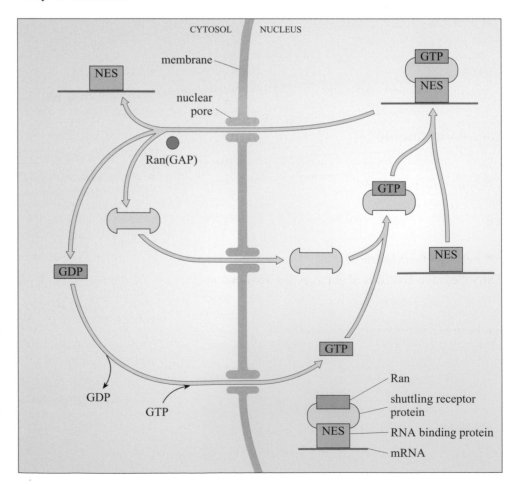

Figure 10.41
Pathway for mRNA export from the nucleus. Nuclear mRNA for export associates with proteins with RNA binding activity and a nuclear export signal (NES). These RNPs associate with Ran(GTP) via a shuttling receptor protein and exit the nucleus via the nuclear pore complex. In the cytosol, Ran-bound GTP is hydrolysed after interacting with Ran(GAP), releasing the RNP and shuttling receptor protein. GDP is lost from Ran and replaced with GTP and both Ran(GTP) and the shuttling receptor protein are recycled back into the nucleus.

RNAs other than mRNAs have slightly different systems for export. rRNA molecules are exported as partially assembled pre-ribosomal subunits. Some snRNAs are first exported to the cytosol, where they associate with a **nuclear localization signal** (**NLS**)-containing protein to form snRNPs, which are then targeted for import back into the nucleus, where they function in processes such as splicing. The nature of the NLS and the mechanism of nuclear transport will be discussed further in Chapter 11.

10.6.3 RNA localization

Many RNA species have been found to occupy spatially restricted areas within cells. This may be necessary for a variety of reasons. Firstly, the protein encoded by an RNA may have properties that mean it is undesirable for the RNA to be translated throughout the entire cell. Secondly, the specific biological activity of the encoded mRNA might be required only in particular regions of the cell, or in response to highly localized signals. Thirdly, there may be a requirement to distinguish between mother and daughter cells. We shall now consider examples of some of these.

In ascidian (sea squirt) embryos, actin mRNA is specifically localized at sites where actin assembly is required. Thus, actin is only synthesized in locations where microfilaments are needed. In yeast, the mRNA of a gene called *Ash1* is localized within the daughter cell (Figure 10.42a), allowing localized translation of its encoded protein, which prevents switching of the mating type of the daughter cell. Similarly, highly localized mRNA for the *Vg1* gene (which encodes an embryonic growth factor) is seen in *Xenopus* oocytes (Figure 10.42b). The polarity of *Xenopus* oocytes and embryos is described in terms of the animal and vegetal poles; *Vg1* is localized to the vegetal pole.

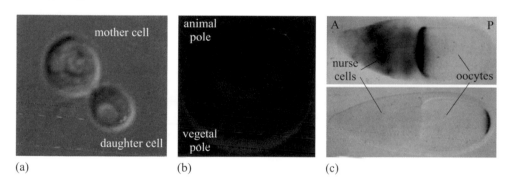

(a)   (b)   (c)

Figure 10.42 Some examples of localized mRNA. These photographs show *in situ* hybridization of probes complementary to mRNA to whole mounted cells. (a) Localization of *Ash1* mRNA (red) to the daughter cell in budding yeast. (b) *Vg1* mRNA (red) localizes to one side of the *Xenopus* oocyte, termed the vegetal pole. (c) mRNA localization in *Drosophila* oocytes, relative to the anterior pole (A) and posterior pole (P) is shown: upper picture shows *bicoid* mRNA localization within cells at the anterior pole; lower picture shows *oskar* localization at the posterior pole.

Embryonic mRNA sequestration

Early cleavage divisions of embryos are asymmetric in terms of cytoplasmic partition between the daughter cells, the location of the cleavage being determined by the mitotic spindle and cytoskeletal factors. Development of the *Drosophila* embryo has been extensively studied and has many examples of partitioned mRNA. One of the transcription factors important in establishing correct expression patterns of genes in the *Drosophila* embryo is the product of *bicoid* (*bcd*). *bcd* encodes a transcription factor with an important role in establishing the anterior–posterior axis of the embryo. The *bcd* mRNA present in the oocyte is deposited from the maternal cells as an RNP, so no new transcription of the embryonic *bicoid* gene occurs in early embryogenesis.

Drosophila oocytes develop in a cluster of 16 cells. Fifteen of these cells function as supporting nurse cells, providing material to the developing oocyte;

eventually their entire cytosol is transferred into the oocyte. The remaining cell undergoes meiosis to form the oocyte. The 16 cells are connected by cytoplasmic bridges, through which proteins and other materials are transferred to the oocyte. One of these components is the *bcd* RNP, which is transported into the oocyte and becomes restricted to its anterior pole (Figure 10.42c). As the *bcd* mRNA is translated, the Bcd protein diffuses across the oocyte, causing a gradient of the transcription factor. Similarly, the *oskar* (*osk*) mRNA is partitioned within the oocyte, initially at the anterior pole, and later becoming relocated to the posterior pole.

A considerable understanding of components required for the localization of mRNAs has been gained by mutational analysis of partitioned mRNAs themselves. From such studies, the factors that influence mRNA localization can be classed into two groups: *cis*-acting signals (i.e. sequences or structures present on the mRNA itself) and *trans*-acting factors (i.e. the protein components of RNP particles). *Cis*-acting elements are generally found in the 3′ untranslated region (3′ UTR) of the mRNA. In the case of *bcd* mRNA, correct localization depends on a stretch of 625 nucleotides, which forms a complex secondary structure involving three stem–loop structures. An example of an RNP component is the staufen protein. Oocytes that are deficient in the staufen protein have defective mRNA localization in the oocyte. For example, *osk* mRNA is not transported to the posterior pole, and *bcd* mRNA loses its correct partitioning soon after fertilization.

10.6.4 mRNA stability

Throughout this chapter we have seen many mechanisms that ensure genes are transcribed at the correct time, in the correct tissues, and in response to appropriate stimuli. However, transcriptional control that relies on altering the amounts of mRNA within the cell will be also influenced by the rate at which the mRNA is degraded.

○ Why must mRNA molecules have to be prevented from persisting indefinitely within the cell?

■ Many of the systems controlling gene activity act at the transcriptional level. If mRNA were very stable at levels that could persist indefinitely, it would be impossible to turn off or modulate levels of gene expression.

To switch off a gene at the transcriptional level therefore requires that there is also a means by which the cell can eliminate previously synthesized mRNA. For example, the human *c-myc* mRNA, which is synthesized transiently in response to mitosis-inducing and differentiation signals, has a typical half-life within cells of 15–30 minutes. This allows for a rapid production of mRNA, which is quickly removed from the cell. Generally speaking, the processes governing mRNA stability in multicellular organisms are complex, and are correspondingly less well understood than those in prokaryotes.

mRNA turnover in prokaryotes depends on its secondary structure

In bacteria, control of gene expression is often at the level of the operon. Generally, there is a correlation between mRNA half-life and the duration of the cell cycle, mRNA stability being lengthened or shortened according to need. The signals that determine mRNA half-life in bacteria are generally located in the 5′ and 3′ UTRs of the mRNAs. These signals influence the susceptibility of the RNA to the action of nucleases, including a protein called ribonuclease III (RNAase III), which is a key regulator of mRNA stability in *E. coli*. RNAase III cleaves target sites formed in duplex areas of mRNA and rRNA molecules. Interestingly, the RNAase III mRNA contains just such a sequence in its own 5′ UTR, making it subject to autoregulation: overproduction of RNAase III protein leads to destruction of its own mRNA by cleavage.

mRNA turnover in eukaryotes

Eukaryotic mRNAs are protected from degradation by the presence of the 5′-m^{7}G cap and the 3′-poly(A) tail. In yeast cells, two general pathways of mRNA degradation exist. The first stage in deg radation appears to be the deadenylation of the mRNA.

◯   Which protein binds to the poly(A) tail of eukaryotic mRNA?

⬤   Poly(A) tail binding protein (PABP; Section 10.6.1).

Binding of PABP serves to protect the mRNA from degradation. When the poly(A) tail becomes shortened, it eventually becomes too short to bind to PABP. At this point, the exposed 3′ end of the mRNA becomes susceptible to a complex of 3′ to 5′ exonucleases called the **exosome**. These proceed to degrade the mRNA sequentially from its 3′ end (Figure 10.43).

A second consequence of losing PABP is that it makes the mRNA vulnerable to decapping enzymes, which remove the 5′-m^{7}G cap from the mRNA, allowing the exposed mRNA chain to be sequentially degraded by 5′ to 3′ exonucleases. When both these degradation pathways are mutated in yeast, mRNAs are very stable and the cells die. This highlights the crucial role of controlled RNA degradation. Both the deadenylation and decapping pathways also exist within mammalian cells.

The principal signals that appear to determine mRNA stability are usually found in the 3′ UTR of the mRNA, although the exact means by which they regulate susceptibility to the degradation pathways is uncertain. In most cases, binding of specific proteins to these regulatory sites is believed to alter the structure of the RNP complex, making it susceptible to degradation.

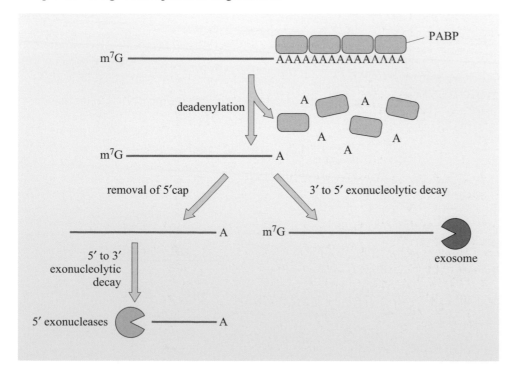

Figure 10.43
Generalized pathways of mRNA degradation in yeast. Deadenylation of mRNAs result in the loss of PABP from the 3′ end of mRNAs. This has two consequences including 5′ decapping (which allows 5′ to 3′ degradation by 5′ exonucleases) and 3′ to 5′ degradation by the exosome.

157

In several cases, mRNA stability is also regulated by the presence of its encoded polypeptide, allowing for an autoregulatory negative feedback link directly from translation. For example, the stability of the human β-tubulin mRNA is regulated by the level of free β-tubulin units in the cell. When these increase in concentration, β-tubulin mRNA becomes destabilized and is degraded rapidly. A similar situation is seen with the stability of the *c-myc* mRNA, where production of the c-Myc protein induces destabilization of the mRNA.

Micro-RNA and gene regulation

Micro-RNAs (miRNAs) are a class of short RNA molecules found within the cell, that play key regulatory roles including the control of mRNA stability and mRNA translation (Section 5.4.3). Here we shall discuss the role of miRNAs in the control of mRNA destruction; the role of miRNAs in regulating translation will be discussed in Section 11.4.5.

The list of examples in which miRNAs are known to play a role in the regulation of gene expression is constantly growing. Some of the earliest examples of small RNA molecules mediating changes to mRNA stability came from the study of mechanisms used by plants to resist viral infection, in which antisense RNA anneals to the viral RNA genome, and brings about its destruction by cellular systems that target double-stranded RNA molecules for degradation. More recently, miRNAs have been shown to play an important role in regulating mRNA levels in *C. elegans* and *Drosophila*. It is likely that it will play an equally important role in other systems, such as vertebrates.

The role of hairpin RNA structures, and their processing to yield miRNAs was discussed in Chapter 5 (Figure 5.19). The pathway by which these miRNA molecules are believed to interact with their target mRNAs is shown in Figure 10.44.

This biological activity is central to a technique of **RNA interference (RNAi)**. Essentially, RNAi takes advantage of an intrinsic cellular system, normally directed towards the processing of miRNA molecules to direct the elimination of specific

Figure 10.44
The action of miRNA in the control of mRNA stability. miRNAs are encoded by genes with an inverted repeat, and form hairpin or stem–loop structures (Section 10.2.3), which are exported to the cytosol. There, the dicer complex cleaves the double-stranded RNA into short molecules about 21 bp in length, which are processed to short miRNAs. These interact with the RISC protein complex to bring about cleavage of the target mRNA and its degradation. The short double-stranded RNAs can also exert an effect on chromatin structure, after re-entering the nucleus. Finally, a dicer-related enzyme known as dicer-like (not shown) may function within the nucleus to generate miRNAs, which also exert effects on chromatin.

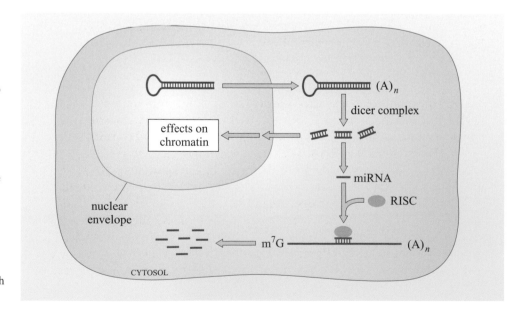

mRNA species. Through the introduction into cells relating to a specific RNA, this intrinsic pathway can be exploited to target destruction of any mRNA within the cell. The experimental applications of this technique are described in Box 10.5.

This pathway has also been shown to be exploited to target chromosomal DNA. For example, transcriptional silencing at the *S. pombe* centromere shown in Figure 5.37 is initiated through the production of a miRNA from within the CEN region. The short RNAs generated from this miRNA are believed to target silencing components to the CEN region wherein they modulate local chromatin structure.

Box 10.5　RNA interference

Many of the model systems that have been used to elucidate basic biological processes possess the advantage of easily manipulated genetic systems. However, many systems are not amenable to genetic analyses, including most systems of cultured cells, and organisms with highly complex genomes, or life cycles of long duration. It is not surprising therefore, that this technique, termed RNA interference (RNAi) has been adopted so widely.

RNAi in cultured cells

For most *in vitro* cell culture systems, RNAi is carried out by introducing into cells a short double-stranded RNA molecule with the same sequence as the target gene. Once within the cell, the double-stranded RNA is a source of single-stranded miRNA, which is taken up by the cellular RISC protein complex to target destruction of that specific mRNA. Removal of the specific mRNA results in decreased production of the corresponding protein. Inactivation of the target gene mRNA sequences (known as 'knockdown') is best monitored by using an antibody specific to the protein encoded by the target mRNA, or, less suitably, by PCR amplification of cDNA synthesized from the target mRNA. Variations in the experimental approach used include the introduction of longer double-stranded RNA chains, of up to 500 bp in length (*Drosophila*), or the production of double-stranded RNAs within cells after introduction of DNA vectors in which the target DNA sequences have been cloned in such a way that double-stranded RNA will be produced.

RNAi in whole organisms

The RNAi technique is also useful in studies of intact organisms, most notably the nematode worm *C. elegans*, which is cultured on a medium in which bacteria such as *E. coli* grow: the bacteria are the food source for the worms. Double-stranded RNA may be administered to the worms in several ways. Firstly, the double-stranded RNA will be taken up directly by the worms if added to the medium. Secondly, if the bacteria have been genetically modified to express the double-stranded RNA, then ingestion of the bacteria has the same effect. Finally, double-stranded RNA can be directly injected into cells. For *Drosophila*, double-stranded RNA may be injected into the embryo if early, transient effects are expected, or expressed from a transgene incorporated in the chromosomes. Similarly, transgenic approaches are used in plants such as *Arabidopsis*.

Summary of Section 10.6

1   Eukaryotic transcripts are extensively processed prior to translation.

2   Processing affords the opportunity of controlling gene expression at a variety of stages.

3   Addition of $5'$-m^7G caps and $3'$-poly(A) tails stabilizes mRNAs.

4   The removal of introns, or splicing, permits a variety of related proteins to be encoded by a single gene.

5   Signals in the $5'$ and $3'$ untranslated regions of an mRNA can direct highly specific localization within a cell.

6   Levels of an mRNA within the cell are in part controlled by factors that influence its stability.

7   Degradation of eukaryotic mRNAs is regulated by proteins within the RNP, and serves to regulate deadenylation.

8   Loss of the poly(A) tail results in $3'$ to $5'$ degradation by the exosome, decapping and further degradation from the $5'$ end.

9   mRNA levels can be experimentally adjusted in many eukaryotes using the technique of RNAi.

10.7 Transcription and processing of non-coding RNAs

Our discussion of transcription and RNA processing in eukaryotes has primarily focused on protein-coding mRNAs synthesized by RNA polymerase II. However, as discussed earlier (Section 10.4.2), there are other eukaryotic RNA polymerases with specialized roles: RNA polymerase I transcribes the 5.8 S, 18 S and 28 S ribosomal RNA genes, whereas RNA polymerase III is responsible for the transcription of tRNA genes, the 5 S ribosomal RNA genes, some snRNAs, and a variety of other small RNA species. Compared with RNA polymcrase II-mediated transcription, there are a number of differences in the transcription of these non-coding RNA molecules.

10.7.1 Structure and transcription of rDNA

Multiple rounds of transcription of a typical protein-coding gene in eukaryotes yield many mRNA molecules, each of which is translated many times, resulting in amplification in the level of its expression, i.e. a large number of protein molecules can be produced from a single gene. This is not the case for structural RNAs such as rRNAs. To ensure that rRNA production is sufficient for the cell, the genes encoding ribosomal RNAs are present in most organisms as long arrays of tandem repeats within a cluster, known as the **rDNA cluster**. These rDNA gene clusters are found to be localized to a specialized structural region of the nucleus called the nucleolus. The nucleolus is not a membrane-bound organelle, but is a large conglomeration of molecules, including the rDNA, and the cellular machinery associated with its transcription and processing. Assembly of rRNAs into the ribosomal subunits also begins in the nucleolus.

RNA polymerase I is found only within the nucleolus, where the rDNA gene clusters are localized. Transcription initiation requires five transcription initiation factors, termed TIFIA, TIFIB, TIFIC, TIFIE and UBF (an upstream binding factor), many of which are specific factors involved in RNA polymerase I transcription. TIFIB contains TBP, and binds to the rDNA promoter. The synthesis of rRNA is regulated at the transcriptional level through the concentration of TIFIA. When cells require synthesis of new proteins in response to growth-promoting signals, the concentration of TIFIA rises accordingly, leading to the synthesis of new ribosomal subunits available for translation. RNA polymerase I transcription termination requires a specific termination factor, which is a DNA binding protein that binds to a DNA sequence downstream of the transcription unit. This is in contrast to the Rho-dependent termination seen in prokaryotes, in which Rho binds to specific RNA structures.

Each 45 S rRNA primary transcript contains the 5.8 S, 18 S and 28 S rRNAs, which are separated by regions called spacers. As shown in Figure 10.45b, the 5′ and 3′ spacers are called the external transcribed spacers (ETS) and internal transcribed spacers (ITS). Processing of the primary transcript to release the mature rRNA molecules occurs in two stages. In the first, the 45 S RNA is chemically modified by 2′-OH methylation of about 100 bases, and isomerization of a similar number of uridine bases to pseudouridine (Figure 5.4b). These chemical modifications are thought to play a role in the structural function of the rRNAs in the mature ribosome, and are made by RNA-modifying proteins, whose specificity is determined by small guide RNAs; the changes are targeted by base pairing between the guide RNAs and the rRNA precursor. In the second stage, the primary rRNA transcript is processed by cleavage to remove the ETS and ITS to yield the mature rRNA molecules (Figure 10.45). This stage is dependent on cleavage proteins targeted by guide RNAs in a similar manner to the targeting of chemical modifications.

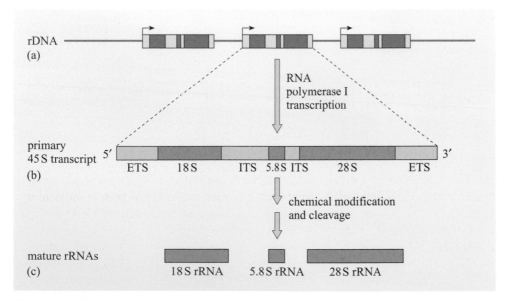

Figure 10.45 rRNA transcription. (a) The rRNA genes are present as long tandem repeats (three are shown here) called rDNA. (b) The primary 45 S transcript contains the 5.8 S, 18 S and 28 S rRNAs interspersed with external (ETS) and internal spacer regions (ITS). (c) This primary transcript undergoes chemical modification before being cleaved to the three mature rRNA molecules.

10.7.2 Transcription of tRNA genes

Transfer RNA molecules are synthesized by transcription of a cluster of tRNA genes by RNA polymerase III. tRNA genes are present in multiple copies in eukaryotic genomes (as for rRNA, this reflects a requirement for large quantities of each tRNA). RNA polymerase III initiation is less complex than that of RNA polymerase II. It requires only a few general transcription factors, including TFIIIB and TFIIIC. TFIIIB contains TBP, binds DNA strongly and is responsible for recruiting RNA polymerase III to the promoter. The termination mechanism of RNA polymerase III transcription resembles Rho-independent termination in prokaryotes: polymerization terminates when RNA polymerase III reaches a series of 4–6 U residues in the transcribed tRNA, corresponding to a sequence of 4–6 T residues in the tDNA gene. In contrast to Rho-independent termination, however, there is no requirement for a specific secondary structure in the RNA.

The tRNA sections within the pre-tRNAs adopt the characteristic cloverleaf secondary structure (Section 5.4.1), and are processed to yield mature tRNAs (Figure 10.46). In many cases, the pre-tRNAs contain several tRNAs, which are released by cleavage at their 5′ and 3′ ends by ribonucleases. Many eukaryotic pre-tRNAs contain a short intron, which is removed by splicing. Further post-transcriptional processing includes chemical modifications.

○ Which modifications are found within tRNA primary transcripts?

● Modifications include ribose methylation, and conversion of uridine to pseudouridine (Figure 5.4b).

The final stages of tRNA processing will be described in Chapter 11.

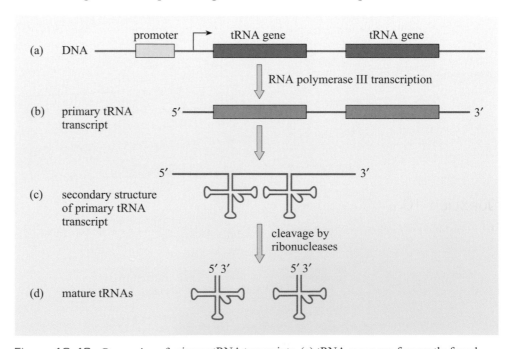

Figure 10.46 Processing of primary tRNA transcripts. (a) tRNA genes are frequently found in small gene clusters, which are transcribed to yield a primary tRNA transcript (b) that contains more than one tRNA chain. (c) The tRNA transcript adopts the characteristic cloverleaf secondary structure and is finally cleaved by ribonucleases (d) to yield individual tRNA molecules.

Summary of Section 10.7

1   Most rRNA genes are transcribed by RNA polymerase I, whereas tRNAs are transcribed by RNA polymerase III.

2   Both pre-rRNA and pre-tRNA molecules are extensively processed.

3   In some mitochondria, gRNA is utilized to direct mRNA editing.

4   rRNA and tRNA molecules are extensively modified, examples being ribose methylation and conversion of uridine to pseudouridine.

Learning outcomes for Chapter 10

When you have studied this chapter, you should be able to:

10.1 Define and use each of the terms printed in **bold** in the text.

10.2 Describe the structural features of DNA and of genes relevant to the control of gene expression, using examples as necessary.

10.3 Describe how the machinery of transcription is assembled, and which of the components enable transcription initiation and/or levels of expression to be controlled, giving examples as necessary.

10.4 Describe how the processing and stability of RNA contribute to the regulation of gene expression.

10.5 Understand how model systems are used to elucidate how various classes of transcription factor function at a molecular level, giving examples as appropriate.

10.6 Be able to discuss the evolutionary conservation of transcriptional mechanisms.

Questions for Chapter 10

Question 10.1

Describe how the structure of bacteriophage T7 RNA polymerase changes as RNA synthesis is initiated.

Question 10.2

What is the significance of the observation that many DNA binding proteins function as heterodimers or homodimers?

Question 10.3

Describe the structure and regulation of the tryptophan operon of *E. coli*.

Question 10.4

How does eukaryotic RNA polymerase compare to that of prokaryotes?

Question 10.5

What are the characteristic features of enhancers and silencers? What role might insulator sequences play in the function of enhancers and silencers?

Question 10.6

How does chromatin modification influence X chromosome function in mammals? Outline how this process is regulated.

Question 10.7

What is a microarray, and how is it used experimentally?

Question 10.8

What are the four main modifications that mRNA molecules undergo in eukaryotes?

Question 10.9

Outline the pathways by which miRNA molecules target specific mRNAs for degradation.

Question 10.10

In which cellular structure does synthesis of rRNA occur in eukaryotes? Briefly outline the synthesis and processing of the major rRNA molecules.

Further sources

Bushnell, D. A., Westover, K. D., Davis, R. E. and Kornberg, R. D. (2004) Structural basis of transcription: an RNA polymerase II-TFIIB cocrystal at 4.5 ångstroms, *Science*, **303**, pp. 983–988.

Palancade, B. and Bensaude, O. (2003) Investigating RNA polymerase II carboxyl-terminal domain (CTD) phosphorylation, *European Journal of Biochemistry*, **270**, pp. 3859–3870.

Westover, K. D., Bushnell, D. A. and Kornberg, R. D. (2004) Structural basis of transcription: separation of RNA from DNA by RNA polymerase II, *Science*, **303**, pp. 1014–1016.

11 TRANSLATION AND PROTEIN TURNOVER

11.1 Introduction

Most key functional roles within the cell are performed by proteins; they serve as the major components of a cell's structure, provide most of the catalytic activities, act as transporters, and serve as regulators of many cellular processes such as the cell cycle, DNA replication and transcription. In this chapter, we shall take a closer look at how proteins are synthesized within the cell, how their tertiary structures are formed during synthesis, and how the cell regulates their levels and localization. Of course, translation is a large subject area to discuss, and though we cannot examine every aspect of it, we shall focus on key components and processes, and consider their role in the dynamic cell. An overview of the scope of this chapter is given in Figure 11.1.

We shall start by examining key RNA types. Having emphasized the central catalytic role of proteins in cellular metabolism, perhaps it seems rather surprising that their synthesis is facilitated by the catalytic activity of a type of nucleic acid, a family called the ribosomal RNAs (or rRNAs). RNA plays other central roles, firstly in the form of the template from which proteins are synthesized (messenger RNA or mRNA), and secondly in the machinery (transfer RNA or tRNA) that translates the stored information into the corresponding amino acid sequence. The genes encoding the ribosomal RNAs and tRNAs are among some of the most highly conserved genes known, reflecting both the central role for RNA during the evolution of life on Earth, and their importance in the process of translation. You saw in Chapter 10 that rDNA is retained within its own nuclear region called the nucleolus, that rRNA is synthesized by its own RNA polymerase and that about 80% of a cell's RNA is in the form of rRNA.

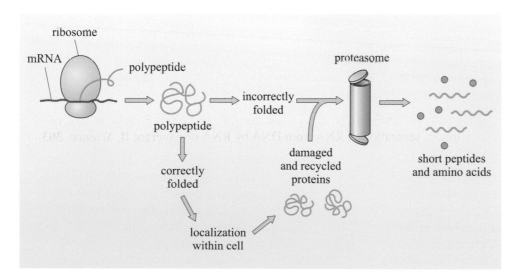

Figure 11.1   An overview of the flow of genetic information from mRNA to protein, the pathways of protein processing and turnover.

The key to the function of these RNA chains is their tertiary structure, which forms through base pairing (as described in Section 5.4), and which is intricate and highly evolutionarily conserved. Rather than being driven by the function of the encoded protein, gene conservation in the ribosomal and tRNA genes appears to be driven by the requirement to maintain the tertiary structure of the encoded RNA itself. As you will see in this chapter, higher-order RNA structure plays an important role in most of the processes central to translation.

The linear sequence of bases in mRNA is used to direct tRNAs to place amino acids into a catalytic site on the ribosome where the growing polypeptide chain is formed. The interaction between the tRNA anticodon and mRNA codon bases at the tRNA–mRNA interface plays a crucial role in determining which amino acid is incorporated, and initiates structural changes that result in peptide bond formation between the incoming amino acid and the nascent polypeptide on the ribosome. In this way, the 'decoding' event is directly linked to the synthesis event. The code itself is read as a series of three-base codons, each codon encoding a specific amino acid; it is non-overlapping, uninterrupted, has extensive degeneracy (with several different codons for the same amino acid), and also carries sequences that code for the start and termination of translation.

Our understanding of how the base sequence in mRNA relates to amino acid order in proteins has come from a number of classic experiments performed by researchers in the 1960s. These experiments are described in Box 11.1. Our current understanding of translation and the localization and turnover of proteins in the cell will be examined in some detail in this chapter.

It was originally thought that the ribosome played only a structural role in translation – in other words, that it provided a framework on which translation occurred, but did not play a catalytic role. Structural studies have now shown that the ribosomal RNA chains provide the structures that form the catalytic site within which peptide bond formation occurs. As we shall see, other structural aspects of ribosomal RNA underlie the recognition of regulatory elements within the mRNA, as well as the interaction with protein assembly cofactors and localization machinery.

Box 11.1   Deciphering the genetic code

The relationship between the order of bases in mRNA and the polypeptide that it encodes was achieved using a variety of methods. In the simplest case, artificial mRNA chains containing only one base were synthesized, and added to extracts of bacteria from which all other mRNAs had been removed, so that only the synthetic mRNA could be used as a template for translation. The resultant peptides were then analysed biochemically for their content (see Figure 11.2). This provided information about certain amino acids, but it did not directly show how many bases code for each amino acid or whether the code was overlapping. It wasn't until mRNAs comprising mixtures of nucleotides were used that the three-base, non-overlapping rule was confirmed.

In the case of an mRNA made to carry alternating C and U bases within the ORF, you could obtain peptides with differing amino acid orders depending on how this is read (as two bases, three bases or overlapping). This mRNA actually gave rise to a peptide with alternating leucine and serine residues (Figure 11.2b), indicating that CUC coded for leucine and UCU coded for serine, and suggesting that the code was non-overlapping (Figure 11.2c and d). This was confirmed when RNA chains were made representing $(CUC)_n$ and $(UCU)_n$, which were translated into homopolymers. Combinations of all bases were used to determine the complete universal code shown in Table 11.1. Only a few slight variants from this code have been found, mostly in mitochondria.

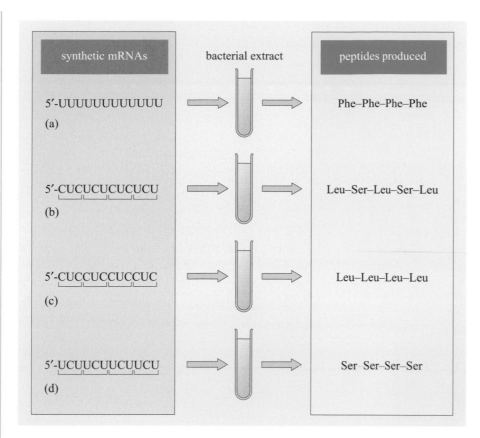

Figure 11.2
Deciphering the genetic code.
Bacterial extracts suitable for translation were used to examine the relationship between mRNA base order and amino acid incorporation into peptides. Synthetic mRNAs of known composition were introduced into such extracts, and the resulting peptides isolated and analysed. To illustrate the principle of these studies, four examples are shown. The simple poly-U mRNA chain (a) leads to synthesis of a peptide containing only phenylalanine. This indicates that the codon for phenylalanine contains only U bases, but gives no indication of whether the codon is U, UU or UUU, etc. This was clarified by using an mRNA with alternating C and U bases (b), which gave rise to a peptide containing alternating leucine and serine residues, suggesting that three-base non-overlapping codons are involved, with CUC encoding leucine and UCU encoding serine. This was confirmed with synthetic chains containing only these two codons (c) and (d).

Table 11.1   The universal genetic code. Locate the first base of the codon (5′ end), and then read the second and third bases. Of the 64 possible combinations, 61 are used to code for amino acids, and three encode stop signals. Some variants to this universal code exist, notably CUG, which encodes threonine in yeast mitochondria, and UGA, which encodes tryptophan in the mitochondria of many other species.

First position 5′end	Second position				Third position 3′end
	U	C	A	G	
U	Phe	Ser	Tyr	Cys	U
	Phe	Ser	Tyr	Cys	C
	Leu	Ser	Stop	Stop	A
	Leu	Ser	Stop	Trp	G
C	Leu	Pro	His	Arg	U
	Leu	Pro	His	Arg	C
	Leu	Pro	Gln	Arg	A
	Leu	Pro	Gln	Arg	G
A	Ile	Thr	Asn	Ser	U
	Ile	Thr	Asn	Ser	C
	Ile	Thr	Lys	Arg	A
	Met (Start)	Thr	Lys	Arg	G
G	Val	Ala	Asp	Gly	U
	Val	Ala	Asp	Gly	C
	Val	Ala	Glu	Gly	A
	Val	Ala	Glu	Gly	G

The timing and location of mRNA translation affects many cellular processes, particularly in multicellular eukaryotes.

After discussing the production of proteins within the cell, in Section 11.7 we shall look at how the cell removes the proteins no longer required, or those that have been damaged or misfolded. We shall examine how these pathways are exploited to regulate protein levels in the cell, and how the accumulation of breakdown products can be toxic to the cell.

11.2 The role of tRNA in translation

Transfer RNA chains are between 70 and 80 nucleotides in length and, as we saw in Section 5.4.2, they form very specific structures which allow them to both base pair with mRNA, and to carry and deliver a specific amino acid to the catalytic site within the ribosome.

◯ How and when are secondary and tertiary structures of a typical tRNA formed?

◼ Their secondary structure is formed through interactions that maximize base-pairing and base-stacking interactions. Tertiary structures are achieved through additional hydrogen bonding (Section 5.4). Structure is also influenced by the modification of various bases as was shown in Figure 5.4c. The structures form in the immature transcript (Section 10.7.2, Figure 10.46).

Several features can be seen in the structure of tRNAs which are important in our discussion of their role in translation. The first is that their tertiary structure (shown in Figure 11.3a) results in the positioning of the three-base anticodon sequence at the opposite end of the structure to the acceptor arm. The point at which the amino acid is covalently joined to the tRNA at the acceptor arm is the 3′ end of the RNA chain (highlighted in yellow in Figure 11.3b), which has the sequence 5′-CCA-3′. In eubacteria, most tRNA genes carry this sequence already, but those of eukaryotes and archaebacteria do not, and the three bases are added post-transcriptionally after each tRNA has been cleaved from the immature transcript. The enzymes responsible for the addition of these three bases are related to DNA polymerases, and are highly conserved through evolution. They contain a specialized nucleotide-binding pocket, within which the CCA is added to the 3′ end of the tRNA. Transfer RNAs are considerably more stable than most other RNAs in the cell, partly due to their compact structure, which protects them from cellular nucleases, but also to the presence of modified bases as detailed in Figure 5.4c.

11.2.1 Amino acid specificity of tRNAs

Each tRNA molecule is joined to a specific amino acid in a process known as **tRNA charging**. In order for the genetic code to be translated accurately, this amino acid must, of course, match the anticodon of the tRNA. This is obviously a critical point, as errors would result in the eventual incorporation of the wrong amino acid into the growing polypeptide chain. The enzymes responsible for the process of tRNA charging are termed **aminoacyl synthases**, and there is one such enzyme for each of the 20 amino acids incorporated into proteins. The specificity by which a tRNA is charged with the correct amino acid is mediated by structural interactions between the tRNA and the synthase (Figure 11.4).

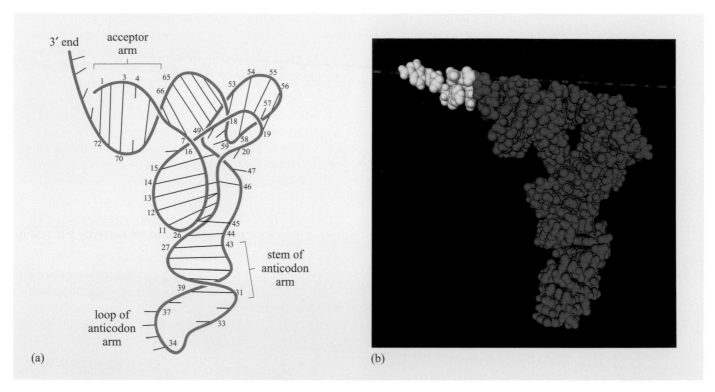

(a)

(b)

Figure 11.3 The tertiary structure of tRNA molecules are crucial in their function. (a) The tertiary structure of a typical tRNA, showing base pairing and hydrogen-bonding interactions (taken from Figure 5.18c). (b) A space-filling representation of yeast phenylalanine-encoding tRNA with the 3′-CCA acceptor, which forms residues 74–76 of the tRNA at the 3′ end, highlighted in yellow. The anticodon region lies at the opposite end of the molecule (based on pdb file 1ehz).

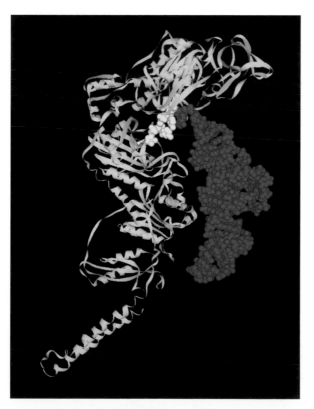

Figure 11.4

The recognition step between a tRNA and its aminoacyl synthase is dependent on the tertiary structure of both molecules. A tRNA molecule is shown (right: blue, CCA acceptor highlighted in yellow) in space-filling format, complexed with its aminoacyl transferase in ribbon format (left, cyan). As can be seen, the acceptor arm lies within a cleft within the synthase. Interactions occur along the interface between the entire length of the two molecules, and especially near the anticodon arm, which interacts with specific amino acids in the synthase (based on pdb file 1eiy).

The shapes of the tRNA and synthase molecules are highly complementary, and, although the tertiary structures of tRNAs are all very similar, each specific synthase protein recognizes and charges only its specific partner tRNA. Key interaction points with the synthase lie throughout the whole tRNA chain, but critical points of discrimination are found primarily in the acceptor arm stem and, not surprisingly, in the anticodon arm. The cell contains 20 tRNA species – one for each amino acid – used in translation, and 20 synthases to charge them. Linkage of the amino acid to the tRNA occurs at the CCA motif, with a covalent bond forming between the 3′ hydroxyl group of the adenine residue and the COOH terminus of the amino acid (see Figure 11.5(iii)). This two-stage process utilizes ATP; the high-energy bond formed between the tRNA and the amino acid provides the energy to drive peptide bond formation on the ribosome.

In addition, cells contain a specialized tRNA known as an **initiator tRNA (tRNA$_i$)**. This tRNA has several base differences to other tRNAs, but its tertiary structure is only slightly altered. Initiator tRNAs in both prokaryotes and eukaryotes are charged with the amino acid methionine by the aminoacyl synthase that charges the methionine tRNA (tRNA^{Met}). In prokaryotes, and in eukaryotic mitochondria, an additional modification occurs to the methionine, in which it is converted into formylmethionine (fMet). The role of these specialized initiator tRNAs will be discussed further in Section 11.4.1.

It is apparent that mRNA containing the four bases A, C, G and U can contain up to 64 possible three-base codons. As noted in Box 11.1, 61 codons are used for amino acid coding. We have just seen, however, that the cell only uses 20 tRNAs, charged by 20 aminoacyl synthases. In 1966, Francis Crick suggested that this disparity could be accounted for by what he called a **wobble** in the normal stringency of the Watson–Crick pairing at the codon–anticodon interface, where the tRNA and mRNA interact. He suggested that the pairing between the third base of the codon (which pairs with the first base of the anticodon) is degenerate.

☐ Look back at Table 11.1. Which codons encode phenylalanine?

■ 5′-UUU and 5′-UUC.

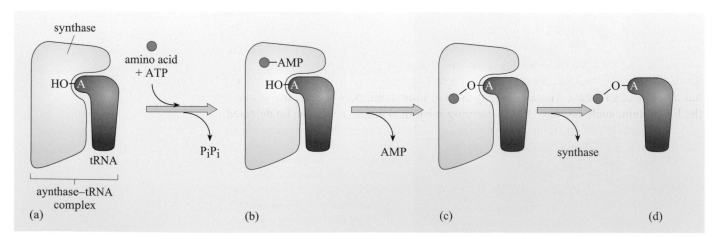

Figure 11.5   Addition of the appropriate amino acid onto the 3′ end of the tRNA chain occurs through a two-stage process. (a) The appropriately paired synthase–tRNA is positioned such that the 3′ OH of the terminal adenine from the CCA motif lies within the acceptor site of the aminoacyl synthase. (b) The incoming amino acid is activated through linkage via its carboxyl group to AMP, with the utilization of two high-energy bonds to drive the reaction and release PP_i. (c) The activated amino acid is then linked to the 3′ hydroxyl group of the tRNA, and (d) the charged tRNA released.

Both these codons are recognized by a single tRNA, which carries the anticodon 5′-GAA.

◯ If these phenylalanine mRNA codons are aligned with their tRNA anticodons, what can you say about the base pairing?

⬤ You should have seen that they align as below (note that the strands run in opposite or antiparallel directions, as do all double-stranded nucleic acids).

The pairing between the third base in the codon and its pair in the anticodon can occur by normal Watson–Crick base-pairing between the C and G bases, but U–G appears to be a mispair.

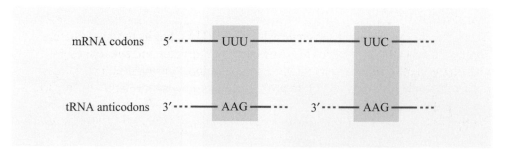

This is an example of the degeneracy or wobble, which is seen in the base pairing in this third base position in the codon. If you look back to Figure 5.5b, you will see that the U–G pairing allows for the formation of several hydrogen bonds. In this third base position, pairing is still restricted to a pair between a purine and a pyrimidine, but pairing between the codon third base U or C to an anticodon G (as above), and also the codon third base A or G to an anticodon U are tolerated. From Table 11.1 you can see that this wobble is common. We shall discuss the molecular basis for this wobble in the next section.

11.2.2 Interaction of charged tRNAs with the ribosome

Before interacting with the mRNA and ribosome, each charged tRNA pairs with an ancillary protein. In the case of the initiation tRNAs, this involves a specific initiation factor, and will be discussed further shortly. For all other tRNAs, it is called an **elongation factor (EF)**. This factor is called EF-Tu in prokaryotes and EF1 in eukaryotes. Elongation factors are G proteins, regulated by the binding of GTP, as discussed in Section 3.6.2. As can be seen from Figure 11.6, the tRNA–EF complex has a compact structure. There are many sites of interaction between the tRNA and the EF protein, such that any tRNAs carrying misjoined amino acids can be detected and are rejected. You should also note that within this complex, the amino acid is effectively 'masked' by the EF protein domains, but the anticodon arm is exposed, as would be expected, to allow it to interact with the mRNA codon.

When the EF–tRNA has successfully base-paired with the mRNA by the anticodon–codon interaction, GTP hydrolysis in the EF results in conformational change in the EF protein such that the domains surrounding the amino acid shift to expose it. You can see this conformational change by comparing the structures of the GTP- and GDP-bound versions of an EF protein shown in Figure 11.6b and c. Once this step has occurred, the interaction between the EF and the tRNA is disrupted and the EF is released from the ribosome, leaving the tRNA bound. We shall see how this step fits within the translation process as a whole later. The elongation factors EF-Tu and EF1 do not interact with charged tRNA$_i$ molecules.

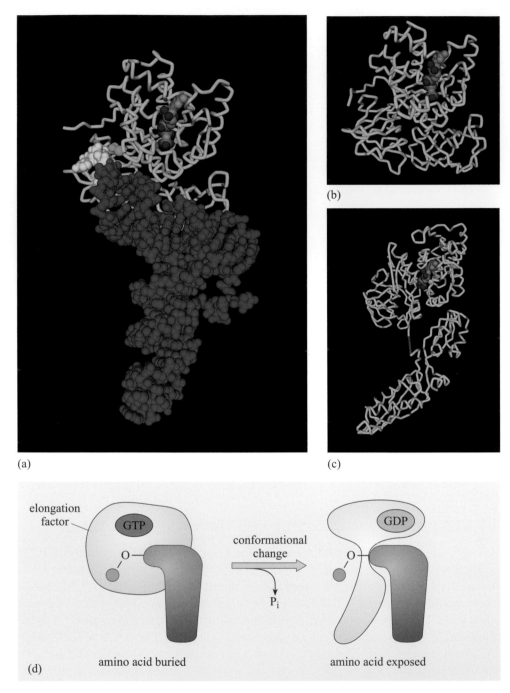

(a)

(b)

(c)

(d)

elongation factor

GTP

O

conformational change

P_i

amino acid buried

GDP

O

amino acid exposed

Figure 11.6   Elongation factor (EF)–tRNA interactions with mRNA trigger a conformational change to expose the amino acid. (a) The structure of an *E. coli* EF-Tu–tRNA complex is shown with the EF-Tu protein in tubes format (cyan), and the tRNA molecule in space-filling format (blue), with the CCA highlighted in yellow (pbd file 1b23). The amino acid cysteine (green) is buried within the EF domain. The location of the GTP molecule within the EF protein is also shown (red and purple). On pairing between the tRNA anticodon and the mRNA codon, GTP hydrolysis results in a conformational change in EF-Tu structure, which reveals the amino acid. Structures of GTP/GDP-bound EF-Tu proteins are shown for comparison: (b) GTP-bound and (c) GDP-bound (based on pdb files 1eft and 1efg). Note that on GTP hydrolysis, a major conformational change is induced within the EF-Tu protein. (d) Schematic depiction of the conformational change, emphasizing how the amino acid is revealed.

Summary of Section 11.2

1   Each of the 20 amino acids is covalently linked to a tRNA by specific aminoacyl synthases via a high-energy bond. Specialized initiator tRNAs are linked to methionine, which is formylated in prokaryotes and in eukaryotic mitochondria.

2   61 codons are able to be decoded by just 20 tRNAs because of degeneracy of the third base-pairing between codon and anticodon.

3   Charged tRNAs interact with a G protein elongation factor. Appropriate pairing between tRNA and mRNA results in activation of the GTPase activity, which triggers a conformational change in the EF, and dissociation of the complex.

11.3 Ribosome structure and mRNA interactions

Ribosomes consist of several component ribosomal RNA chains, complexed with over 50 proteins, which make up approximately 30% of their mass (Figure 11.7). The ribosome can be considered as being composed of two major structural subunits, termed the large and small ribosomal subunits. Each of these is composed of various rRNA chains and ancillary proteins. The lengths of the respective RNA chains are included in Figure 11.7, but note that the sizes of these and the ribosomal units are usually referred to in Svedberg (S) units, and we shall describe them as such from now on.

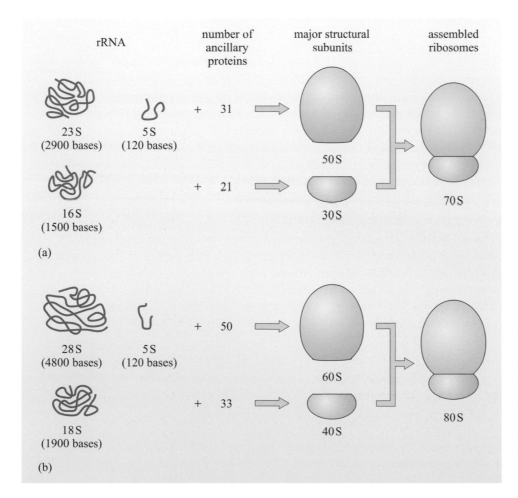

Figure 11.7
The composition of (a) prokaryotic and (b) eukaryotic ribosomes. The fully assembled prokaryotic 70 S ribosome and eukaryotic 80 S ribosomes are both composed of a large and a small subunit. These subunits are formed from ribosomal chains and many ancillary proteins. Note that, although differing in length, the numbers of rRNA chains are the same.

The individual components of ribosomes differ slightly between prokaryotes and eukaryotes, but functionally and structurally they are very similar. Thus, each large subunit contains two rRNA chains, whereas the small subunit has one chain. The large and small subunits come together to form the ribosome itself, 70 S in prokaryotes, 80 S in eukaryotes. Most of the critical interactions between mRNA, tRNA and the catalytic formation of the peptide bond occur within the core of the ribosome structure. We shall discuss these in detail shortly, but first we shall describe the relationships between the important functional sites on the ribosome (Figure 11.8).

Figure 11.8
An overview of the critical ribosomal functional sites involved in translation. The mRNA chain is shown entering and exiting the prokaryotic ribosome through the 30 S small subunit. Lying at the interface with the 50 S large subunit are three sites that will be occupied by tRNA chains. These are abbreviated as the acceptor (A), peptide linkage (P) and exit (E) sites. The newly synthesized nascent peptide chain is shown exiting the P site via a tunnel. Based partially on structures discussed by Sachs and Geballe (2002), and Nissen *et al.* (2000).

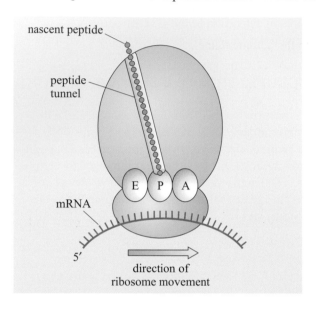

Together, the large and small subunits shape the sites into which tRNAs will be localized, and the catalytic area in which tRNA–EF and peptide interact (A, P and E sites). The major subunit also contains the tunnel through and in which the growing peptide chain is channelled. These structures are formed almost exclusively from the rRNA chains, as most of the ancillary proteins lie on the surface of the ribosome. The molecular events that occur at each of these sites will be discussed in detail shortly. Many of the functions of ribosomes have been analysed by inhibiting ribosome activity using antibiotics, as discussed in Box 11.2.

Each ribosomal subunit has a specialist role in translation; the small subunit is involved in mRNA binding and tRNA recognition, whereas the large subunit contributes to the formation of the peptide linkage and the channel through which the growing peptide chain is released. During peptide synthesis, tRNAs are progressively passed through the acceptor (A), peptide linkage (P) and exit (E) sites. An incoming tRNA, bound to an EF protein, enters the A site, and the EF is released when tRNA–mRNA pairing occurs.

○ What molecular change occurs to the EF–tRNA complex on appropriate tRNA–mRNA pairing?

● The hydrolysis of GTP on the EF protein leads to a conformational change in its structure, exposing the amino acid (Figure 11.6d).

The amino acid is exposed and becomes positioned into the peptide linkage site, and is joined to the growing peptide chain. The tRNA in the A site is now transferred to the P site, displacing the discharged tRNA through the E site.

Box 11.2 The use of antibiotics to study ribosome function in bacteria

Many naturally occurring antibiotics have been utilized to study prokaryotic ribosome structure and function, as many of these agents owe their antibacterial effects as inhibitors of protein synthesis in bacteria to these interactions. They include:

▶ *chloramphenicol*: binds to the peptide linkage (P) site and inhibits peptide synthesis;

▶ *erythromycin*: interferes with the peptide tunnel;

▶ *paromomycin*: interferes with codon–anticodon recognition;

▶ *tetracycline*: interferes with tRNA binding to the acceptor A site.

Some antibiotics also inhibit ribosomal function in eukaryotic cells, including:

▶ *cycloheximide*: blocks translocation of tRNAs between sites during peptide synthesis;

▶ *anisomycin*: inhibits peptide bond formation activity.

Before we describe the process of peptide synthesis in more detail, we can now return to discuss the role of the ribosome in ensuring that the appropriate tRNA–EF complex (that is, one that has an appropriately paired codon–anticodon) enters the A site. Studies of the bacterial 30 S subunit in the presence of the antibiotic paromomycin found that the antibacterial effect of this antibiotic results from the incorporation of the wrong amino acid into growing peptide chains. The binding site for paromomycin was found to be within the 30 S subunit, at a site near where the tRNA anticodon will lie on pairing with the mRNA. Also in this region is a sequence of three nucleotides from the small 16 S subunit rRNA chain, which acts as the 'sensor' for testing the accuracy of the pairing between the codon and anticodon.

A short segment of duplex RNA is formed when tRNA–mRNA pairing occurs. Although the exact nature of how the 'sensor' is able to discriminate mispaired bases within this duplex is not fully understood, it is known to involve an interaction between the three bases within the 16 S subunit and the minor groove formed between the three paired mRNA codon–tRNA anticodon bases. This 'sensor' acts stringently in the case of the first two base pairs, but is far less stringent at the third, tolerating pairs such as G–U as discussed earlier. This observation appears to provide a molecular basis for the tolerated non-Watson–Crick pairing at the third base position. Bound paromomycin alters the location of the three-base 'sensor' RNA portion of the small subunit, and decreases its ability to interact with the minor groove of the codon–anticodon region. This allows more extensive mispairing to occur, and leads to the incorporation of wrong amino acids into peptides. The discriminatory ability provided by the small ribosomal subunit contributes to maintaining the error rate of translation at less than one misincorporated amino acid in 10^3–10^4 peptide linkages.

Summary of Section 11.3

1   The structure and composition of ribosome subunits is highly conserved, with ribosomal RNAs forming the core structure.

2   Three sites (A, P and E) for tRNA positioning lie at the interface of the large and small subunits.

3 Many naturally occurring antibiotics interfere with ribosome function, and have been used as tools to study translation.

4 Appropriate base pairing is detected by a sensor lying within the small ribosomal subunit. This tolerates mispairings in the third base position of the codon.

11.4 Translation as a dynamic process

Having examined the key components and molecular interactions that are a prerequisite for translation, we shall now turn our attention to how these come together in peptide chain formation. As a process, we shall consider it in three stages – initiation, elongation and termination. Although both subunits of the ribosome contribute to these stages through the formation of the key sites of activity, the role of the small subunit is primarily in mRNA–tRNA recognition, whereas the large subunit is where the peptide synthesis actually occurs. Despite the slight differences in ribosome subunit components, translation is mechanistically very similar in prokaryotes and eukaryotes. One important difference occurs during the initiation stage, in which the small ribosomal subunit locates the position of the first codon at the 5′ end of the mRNA. The second important difference is in the timing of translation. In prokaryotes, translation is concerted with transcription; in contrast, translation in eukaryotes only occurs after mRNA export from the nucleus to the cytoplasm.

11.4.1 Initiation factors' recognition of mRNA sequences

The first codon in virtually all mRNAs is coded in the DNA as an ATG codon, positioned at the start of the open reading frame (ORF). The AUG within the mRNA is recognized by a specific initiator complex carrying the charged $tRNA_i$.

○ What amino acid is carried by the prokaryotic initiator $tRNA_i$?

● Formylmethionine, fMet (Section 11.2.1).

In prokaryotes, the early stages of translation involve the 30 S subunit. Two initiation factors, IF1 and IF3, bind to a free 30 S subunit, and in doing so block its association with the 50 S subunit. A third initiation factor, IF2, binds to the formylmethionine–$tRNA_i$ complex ($fMet–tRNA_i^{fMet}$). IF2 contains a tRNA-binding domain very similar to that found in EF-Tu, and is also a GTP-binding protein. This IF(GTP)–fMet–$tRNA_i^{fMet}$ complex can only bind to the P site of the ribosome.

The establishment of translation, and recognition of the initiator AUG, is guided by a short stretch of 3–10 nucleotides within the 3′ end of the 30 S ribosomal subunit. These nucleotides are complementary to a short stretch of nucleotides called the **Shine–Dalgarno (SD) sequence** within the 5′ untranslated region (5′ UTR) of the mRNA (Figure 11.9a (ii), p. 178). Base pairing occurs between the SD sequence and the 16 S rRNA chain in the 30 S subunit. Directed by the SD sequence, the 30 S small subunit bound by IF1, IF3 and an IF2(GTP)–fMet–$tRNA_i f^{Met}$ complex, binds to the mRNA, with the tRNA molecule paired with the mRNA AUG initiator codon (Figure 11.9a (iii)). At this stage, the area of the 30 S subunit that will form part of the ribosomal A site is bound by IF1, preventing a second tRNA from binding. Once the initiator complex is formed, IF1 and IF3 are released (Figure 11.9a (iv)).

Loss of IF1 allows the large 50 S subunit to bind. As the ribosome assembles, IF2(GTP) hydrolysis occurs, followed by the release of IF2(GDP), and then fMet–tRNA$_i^{fMet}$ is positioned into the completed ribosome P site (Figure 11.9a (iv)). Formylmethionine is now positioned for covalent linkage to the next amino acid to be positioned into the A site.

Initiation in eukaryotes involves essentially similar components as in prokaryotes, but as many as 10 initiator factors are involved. The methionine-charged initiator tRNA (Met–tRNA$_i^{Met}$) is bound to eukaryotic IF2 (eIF2) bound to GTP. The major difference from prokaryotes, however, is that the initiator components do not assemble directly at the AUG site. With the majority of mRNAs, a pre-initiation complex forms between the small 40 S ribosomal subunit, eIF2(GTP)-Met-tRNA$_i^{Met}$ and other IFs. In order for initiation to occur, this complex must now combine with the 5′ end of the mRNA.

○ What modification is found at the 5′ end of a eukaryotic mRNA?

● The addition of an m^{7}G cap (Figure 10.34).

Assembly of this complex then takes place on the m^{7}G cap of the mRNA, as shown in Figure 11.9b. Note that IF4 binds directly to the m^{7}G mRNA cap (not shown), which explains why the cap is required on mRNAs which are to be translated. Once assembled, this initiator complex translocates along the mRNA in a 5′ to 3′ direction, until it detects the position of the AUG codon, a process called **scanning**. It is assisted in this by a short stretch of bases termed the **Kozak sequence**, a region of eight nucleotides, frequently found upstream of the initiator AUG site in eukaryotic mRNA. In contrast to prokaryotic translation, no base pairing takes place. In some eukaryotic mRNAs, initiation complexes form within the mRNA, at a site called an **internal ribosome entry site (IRES)**, wherein the initiator complex translocates to an internal AUG initiator codon. In both cases, once the appropriate initiator AUG codon is recognized, the large 60 S subunit binds, triggering GTP hydrolysis, eIF2–tRNA separation, and tRNA$_i^{Met}$ is positioned in the ribosomal P site.

The difference between the mechanics of prokaryotic and eukaryotic initiation, almost certainly reflect the differing structural and translational requirements of these cells. The prokaryotic system, where the initiator complex is directly assembled at the AUG site, could allow more rapid translation to occur, as translation takes place on mRNA while transcription is still occurring.

○ What feature of prokaryotic mRNAs make this type of assembly necessary?

● Polycistronic mRNAs (Section 10.2).

Direct assembly at SD sequences at the beginning of the open reading frame (as opposed to the 5′ end of the mRNA) allows for the simultaneous translation of several individual ORFs from within a polycistronic mRNA, again maximizing protein production and possibly simplifying regulation.

In eukaryotes, mRNA is processed extensively by splicing as we saw in Chapter 10, and translation occurs outside the nucleus. Thus, each polypeptide is synthesized from a single mRNA. One important exception to this occurs when an IRES sequence is present within a eukaryotic mRNA, an arrangement which can result in the production of two polypeptides from a single mRNA chain.

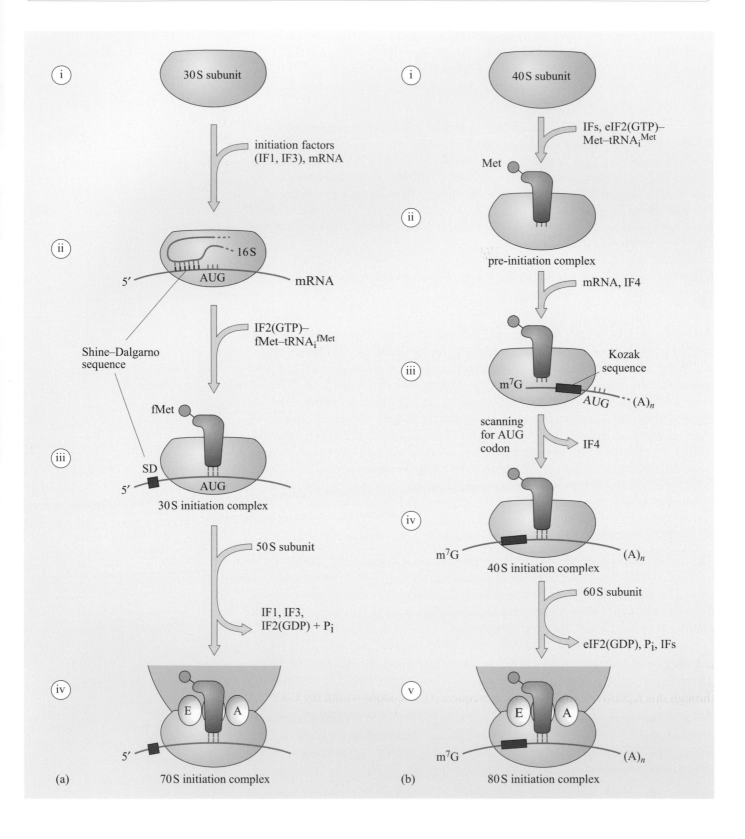

Figure 11.9   Initiation of translation through ribosome assembly on mRNA. (a) In *E. coli*, an initiation complex forms between mRNA, the 30 S subunit and initiation factors IF1 and IF3 (i). This is driven by base pairing between the SD sequence and a complementary stretch of bases within the 16 S rRNA chain (ii). This positions the small subunit such that IF2(GTP)–fMet–tRNA$_i^{fMet}$ can pair with the initiator AUG codon within the mRNA (iii). Release of IF1 and IF3 allows binding of the 50 S large subunit to form the A, P and E sites. This results in GTP hydrolysis of the IF2(GTP)–fMet–tRNA$_i^{fMet}$, which positions the tRNA into the P site, and releases IF2(GDP) (iv). This initiation complex is now ready for peptide synthesis to commence. (b) In eukaryotic cells, initiation takes place by the interaction of a 40 S eIF2(GTP)–Met–tRNA$_i^{Met}$ complex (i) with the m^{7}G cap of the mRNA chain, aided by an initiation factor, IF4 (ii). This pre-initiation complex translocates along the mRNA in a 3′ direction (iii) until an initiation AUG site is detected (iv). At this position, the 60 S large subunit binds, codon–anticodon pairing is completed, which drives GTP hydrolysis, releases eIF2(GDP), and positions the Met–tRNA$_i^{Met}$ into the P site (v).

○ How will these polypeptides differ?

● They will differ in the amino acid content of their N-terminal regions.

The importance of this will become apparent later in this chapter when we discuss how the N-terminal region influences protein localization within the more compartmentalized eukaryotic cell.

11.4.2 Elongation on the ribosome

Once the tRNA$_i$ is located in the P site, the methionine it carries is positioned within the ribosomal catalytic site, the A site is formed and the next stage – elongation – can commence.

○ What reaction occurs during peptide bond formation?

● A condensation reaction between the amino (–NH$_2$) and carboxyl (–COOH) groups of two amino acids with elimination of water (Figure 2.18).

Thus, for the first peptide bond to form after initiation, an EF(GTP)–tRNA$^{amino\ acid}$ locates in the A site, and pairs with the mRNA. If the pairing is correct (as detected by the sensor in the small subunit), GTP hydrolysis occurs in the EF, exposing the amino acid attached to the tRNA. This amino acid swings into location, placing its terminal –NH$_2$ group adjacent to the terminal –COOH group of the initiator methionine. Peptide bond formation occurs, the overall energy for the condensation reaction being provided by breakage of the high-energy bond linking the methionine to its tRNA$_i^{Met}$. Thus, a dipeptide is formed, attached to the tRNA in the A site. For the next amino acid to be joined, the recipient –COOH group must now be shifted into the P site. This is achieved with the assistance of an elongation factor, which translocates the discharged tRNA$_i^{Met}$ into the E site, from where it exits the ribosome. The incoming tRNA–dipeptide now moves into the P site. Elongation continues through this repetitive cycle, with all subsequent AUG codons within the ORF being recognized by EF(GTP)–tRNA^{Met}, until a stop codon is reached, whereupon termination of translation occurs.

Figure 11.10 shows a closer view of the respective N- and C-termini of two amino acids attached to the tRNAs located in the A and P sites, highlighting the proximity of the –NH$_2$ and –COOH groups that will form a new peptide bond. The ribosome functions as a peptidyl transferase. Whether the ribosome's contribution to the catalysis of peptide bond formation is limited to the proper positioning of these residues, or whether evolutionarily conserved ribosomal rRNA residues contribute chemically to the catalysis, is still uncertain.

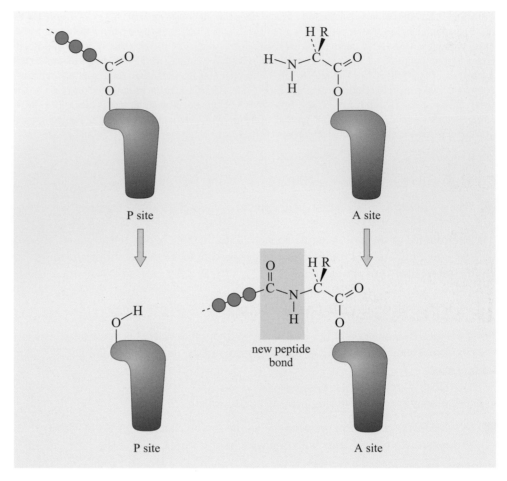

Figure 11.10   Peptide bond formation at the ribosome active site. The location of tRNA molecules (within the A and P sites of the ribosome) positions the −NH$_2$ and −COOH groups of the attached amino acids immediately adjacent to each other to allow for peptide bond formation. Note that following bond formation the growing peptide chain is attached to the tRNA in the A site.

11.4.3 Termination by shape mimicry

When a ribosome translocating along the mRNA encounters a stop codon, no tRNA–EF complex exists with the appropriate anticodon. So how does the presence of a stop codon in the mRNA lead to termination of peptide synthesis? The answer lies in specialized proteins termed **termination factors (TFs)** (also called release factors), which mimic the shape of a portion of tRNA–EF(GTP). Termination factors have a three-dimensional structure that mimics the three-dimensional shape of the tRNA–EF complex, as can be seen by comparing their structures (Figure 11.11).

This shape mimicry allows termination factors to interact with the ribosome in the same way that EF(GTP)–tRNA does (Figure 11.12). In the equivalent location of the anticodon, TFs contain short stretches of amino acid residues which recognize the stop codons (UAG, UGA and UAA). Their binding leads to cleavage of the last tRNA from the peptide chain at the ribosomal catalytic site, and ultimately leads to ribosome disassembly into separate large and small subunits.

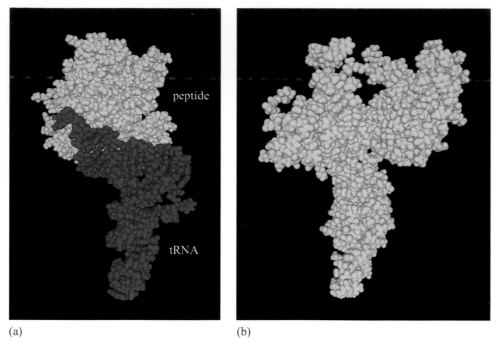

(a)   (b)

Figure 11.11   Shape mimicry by termination factors. (a) The three-dimensional shape of a
portion of the EF(GTP)–tRNA complex that enters the ribosomal A site (EF protein cyan, tRNA
blue) is mimicked by (b) translation termination factors such as human TF (pdb file 1dt9, space-
filling format). In the case of the termination factors, this is a single polypeptide.

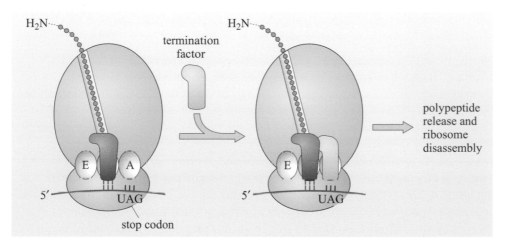

Figure 11.12
Termination factors bind ribosomes
stalled at stop codons. When a stop
codon is reached, no tRNA anticodon
is available to match the codon.
Termination factors use shape mimicry
to bind to the A site, contacting
mRNA while doing so. This leads to
the release of the peptide chain and
disassembly of the ribosome.

Given the highly conserved structure of the ribosome and the universality of the
stop codons, it is not surprising to see a high level of evolutionary conservation
in the amino acid sequence composition of termination factors. This can be seen
in Figure 11.13, where the three-dimensional structure of an *E. coli* TF is shown
after an evolutionary comparison with known translation termination factors found
in databases of all organisms for which the complete sequence is known. Areas of
high evolutionary conservation are shown in red. Two areas show high degrees of
conservation – the sites that interact with the A site of the ribosome, and the region
corresponding to the tRNA anticodon stem–loop structure.

Figure 11.13
Amino acid conservation in translation termination factors. (a) A space-filling view of the *E. coli* termination factor (pdb file 1gqe). (b) Representation of the amino acid evolutionary conservation is shown projected onto this space-filling view. The degree of conservation is visualized in colour, with white indicating no conservation, pink and purple an intermediate level and cherry red a very high level of conservation. The program used to generate this image is Consurf, in which the *E. coli* TF was compared with all other TF in the genomic databases (Glaser *et al.*, 2003).

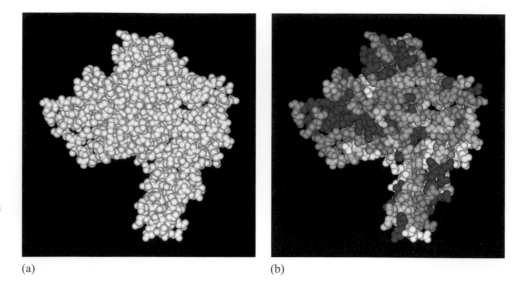

(a)   (b)

11.4.4 Multiple ribosomes can translate a single mRNA

As mentioned earlier, translation is a highly dynamic process. In prokaryotes, translation on the ribosome occurs in conjunction with mRNA synthesis, with up to 30 ribosomes positioned on an mRNA chain as it emerges from the transcription machinery. Each ribosome catalyses peptide bond formation at an average rate of 15 amino acids per second, meaning that each can synthesize an average-sized bacterial protein in less than 2 minutes. As the Shine–Dalgarno sequence drives initiator complex assembly, polycistronic mRNAs carrying several SD sequences can be simultaneously translated (Figure 11.14a).

In eukaryotes, on the other hand, mRNA is processed as described in Chapter 10 (Section 10.6), which can take up to 30 minutes, but nuclear export, ribosome formation and protein synthesis can occur up to 24 hours later. Ribosome assembly at internal sites (IRES) allows simultaneous translation of a mRNA from several AUG initiator codons. One feature that allows multiple ribosomes to work on a single mRNA chain is found at what are termed **polysomes**. In these cases, mRNAs form looped structures via interactions between proteins bound to the poly A tail at the 3′ end, such as poly A binding protein (PABP) and the IF4 protein bound to the 5′ end (Figure 11.14b (ii)). This provides a means of maximizing the use of ribosomes. As translation termination occurs close to the m^{7}G end of looped mRNA, newly disassembled 40 S ribosomal subunits, assisted by IF1, IF3 and other components of the initiation machinery, can be immediately re-engaged on another round of translation.

11.4.5 The regulation of mRNA translation

The regulation of translation is one way in which a cell can regulate how much of any particular protein is available within the cell. There are many ways in which the whole process of translation can be regulated – for example, by limiting the availability of any of the key components we have described so far.

◯ What effect would this have on the translation of an individual mRNA?

● Limiting the availability of a component of the translation machinery would have a generalized effect, decreasing translation of all mRNAs in the cell.

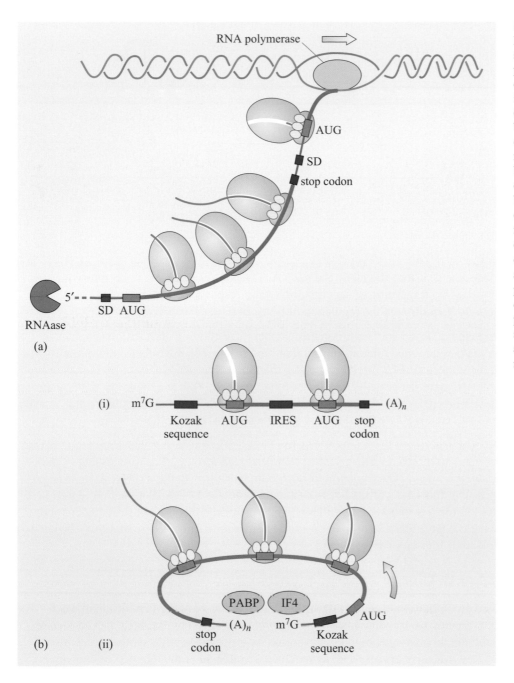

Figure 11.14
Multiple ribosomes can translate a single mRNA chain. (a) A typical prokaryotic polycistronic mRNA, carrying multiple AUG initiator codons in which each open reading frame (ORF, denoted by thickened line) can be translated by multiple ribosomes, each independently assembled. Often mRNAs are simultaneously degraded by RNAse proteins. (b) In eukaryotes, complex processing of mRNAs occurs before the translation machinery is engaged. Once exported to the cytosol, ribosome assembly occurs at the 5′ end of the mRNA. (i) If the mRNA contains an IRES, initiation can occur at an internal AUG site, generating proteins with differing N-termini as described in Section 11.4.1. (ii) At polysomes, mRNAs often form looped structures via interactions between IF4 and PABP, increasing the cycling of ribosomes on the mRNA.

This may be desirable at certain stages of a cell's life, such as when growth stops or when a cell becomes senescent. However, in many cases, the rate of synthesis of specific proteins must be altered. As outlined in Chapter 10, cells frequently achieve this through alterations in transcriptional regulation and mRNA stability. In prokaryotes simultaneous RNAase degradation occurs (Figure 11.14a). However, there are times when a cell requires regulation of specific mRNAs at the translational level.

One way in which regulation is achieved is through the formation of secondary structures within an mRNA (Figure 11.15). These can shield key sequences – such as the prokaryotic Shine–Dalgarno sequence, or the m⁷G cap of eukaryotic mRNAs – from the translation machinery. Secondary structures can also interrupt or block

Figure 11.15
The regulation of translation by mRNA secondary structure. Secondary structure in mRNA is commonly used to regulate access to mRNA for translation. In prokaryotes (a), translation is commonly regulated through removing ribosome access to (i) the Shine–Dalgarno sequence and (ii) AUG initiator codons. In eukaryotes (b), secondary structure (i) or binding of translation regulatory factors (ii) in the 5′ UTR prevents ribosomes assembled at the 5′ end from translocating to the AUG initiator codon.

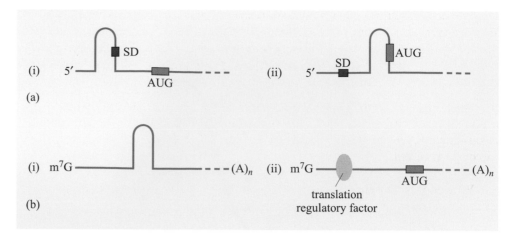

ribosome translocation along the mRNA. This allows a cell the opportunity to regulate the translation of specific mRNAs in response to environmental cues more rapidly than through the regulation of transcription.

In many cells, another common mechanism through which regulation is achieved is via translation regulatory factors that bind to specific mRNAs to inhibit their translation, either by directly blocking the translation machinery or by sequestering mRNAs until the proteins they encode are required. This is a common strategy during development in many eukaryotes and, as we shall discuss later in this chapter, is used to target and regulate translation at specific sites in mammalian neurons.

Recent analysis of the micro-RNAs (miRNAs; Section 10.6.4) has shown that many of these small RNA chains, such as that produced through dicer processing of the *C. elegans lin-4* gene, function through base pairing with the 3′ UTR of their target genes, in this case a critical developmental gene, *lin*-14. This interaction results in a stall to the translation of the mRNA (by mechanisms that are not fully understood), which extends the role of miRNAs from that seen in mRNA degradation (Chapter 10) to one of translational regulators.

11.4.6 Quality control in translation

The incorporation of the wrong amino acid into the growing peptide chain, such that it could destroy the function of the protein or, even worse, create an unwanted function, is obviously highly undesirable for any cell. Peptide synthesis is a highly energy-intensive process and, as we shall see later, so is the removal of damaged or non-functional proteins. Cellular systems are in place to prevent synthesis of defective proteins.

⬜ What systems (not just translational) have you studied so far that are directed toward preventing the incorporation of the wrong amino acid into a protein?

⬛ These include DNA replication and repair processes (Chapter 9), which serve to prevent errors appearing as mutations in protein-coding DNA regions; transcription-coupled repair, which prevents damaged DNA from being used as a transcriptional template (Chapter 9) and therefore being incorporated into mRNA codons; aminoacyl synthases, which charge tRNAs specifically with the amino acid matching its anticodon (Section 11.2); and EF–tRNA anticodon–mRNA codon pairing, as detected by the small ribosomal subunit (Section 11.3).

Despite these checks, there are situations when damage or errors arise in mRNAs. We shall now briefly consider the quality-control processes that operate to manage them. The first involves the detection of broken mRNA chains. These are effectively prevented from accumulating in prokaryotes, as translation occurs simultaneously with transcription and mRNA is degraded rapidly (see Figure 11.14a).

In eukaryotes, the situation is different, as mRNAs are exported from the nucleus and undergo extensive processing before reaching the translation machinery. Broken eukaryotic mRNAs are usually degraded because of the absence of either the m^{7}G cap or the (A)$_n$ tail.

◯ Why does the absence of the m^{7}G cap or the (A)$_n$ tail lead to degradation?

● The m^{7}G cap and the (A)$_n$ tail protect mRNA from nucleases (Section 10.6.4 and Figure 10.43).

Two specialized translation-associated pathways have been described in eukaryotic cells, which add further to these quality-control processes; most is known about these pathways in the yeast *S. cerevisiae* (Figure 11.16).

The first of these occur in budding yeast, which recognizes the presence of aberrant or premature stop codons within a protein-coding region. This is called **nonsense-mediated decay (NMD)**. The exact process by which this occurs, and how a premature stop codon is distinguished from the genuine one, is currently rather poorly understood, but it is thought to involve a translation-like process. When such a stop codon is detected within an mRNA, it is prevented from exiting the nucleus, and is degraded, thus precluding its translation (see Figure 11.16a). Nonsense-mediated decay is also found in mammalian cells, although the exact components and pathway are unclear. It does, however, play a central role in the removal of mRNAs carrying premature stop codons. In one gene that is commonly mutated in human breast cancer, called BRCA1, over 90% of the mutations that cause disease are premature stop codons, caused by insertion or deletion mutations in the DNA, which result in frame-shifting in the protein. In these cases, the gene is transcribed, but the mutant mRNA is detected by the NMD machinery and specifically degraded.

Figure 11.16
Non-stop and nonsense-mediated decay pathways in budding yeast. The absence of stop codons or occurrence of unusual stop codons in mRNA is managed by two systems in yeast. (a) A normal mRNA is exported into the cytosol. (b) mRNAs are screened for the presence of premature stop codons by the nonsense-mediated decay (NMD) machinery. When premature stops are encountered, mRNAs are degraded, preventing their translation. (c) mRNAs that do not contain a stop codon are exported as usual, but result in a stalled ribosome complex. These are rescued through the action of the Ski7–exosome complex, which releases the stalled polypeptide and targets the mRNA for degradation. This is called 'non-stop decay'.

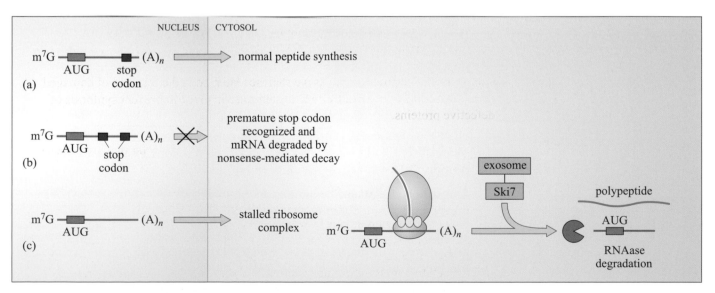

A second system involves mRNA with no stop codon, such as can occur when mutations arise, either by altering the codon in the DNA, or by premature mRNA polyadenylation.

○ What will happen to translation if a mRNA with no stop codon at the end of the protein coding region is encountered?

■ If the mRNA had both m^7G and $(A)_n$ ends intact, it would not be recognized as being broken. As no stop codon is present for termination factor binding, then peptide cleavage and ribosome disassembly cannot occur. Translation would continue until the end of the mRNA chain was reached, whereupon the translation complex would stall.

Eukaryotic cells have specific systems to cope with this situation. Such a stalled ribosome–mRNA complex is recognized in the budding yeast by what is called the **'non-stop' decay** machinery (see Figure 11.16c). A protein called Ski7, which is a component of the exosome (Section 10.6.4), binds to the stalled ribosome. This leads to the tRNA–peptide link being broken, and the ribosome being disassembled. The peptide is targeted for degradation, and the exosome proceeds to degrade the faulty mRNA from its 3′ end.

From the preceding sections, you should now have a good understanding of how translation of an mRNA takes place on a ribosome. However, this is only part of the process of producing a mature functional protein. In the next section, we shall turn our attention to how the translation machinery and the peptide itself influence protein structure. In particular, we shall examine how eukaryotic cells initiate the subcellular targeting of proteins as they are being actively translated.

Summary of Section 11.4

1   Ribosomal initiation complexes form through interactions between the small ribosomal subunits and mRNA. These assemble at the SD sequences through direct pairing in prokaryotes, forming an initiator complex, which is inserted into the P site after AUG pairing. In eukaryotes, assembly is at the 5′ m^7G cap of the mRNA, followed by scanning to detect the AUG initiator site, assisted by the Kozak sequence.

2   Peptide bond formation occurs between an incoming amino group and the terminal carboxyl group of the peptide chain and is catalysed by a peptidyl transferase activity.

3   Many ribosomes can translate the same message simultaneously as a polycistronic mRNA complex (prokaryotes) or polysomes (eukaryotes).

4   Highly evolutionarily conserved translation termination factors mimic the shape of the EF–tRNA complex to pair with stop codons, release the completed peptide, and lead to ribosome disassembly.

5   Translation is regulated by limiting access to mRNA sites (prokaryotes) or by preventing ribosome scanning (eukaryotes).

6   In eukaryotic cells, damaged mRNAs with premature stop codons are degraded, and mRNAs with no stop codons, which lead to stalled ribosomes, are recovered and broken down by specific pathways.

11.5 Protein processing and sorting

Figure 11.8 shows how the nascent peptide chain extends from the catalytic site of the ribosome, through a groove or tunnel, which can accommodate 20 or so amino acids, and within it the polypeptide chain remains unstructured. Its surface is formed by RNA residues, is uncharged and allows unhindered progress through it. As the polypeptide emerges from the ribosome, the N-terminus is released first and, in most cases, folding into secondary and higher-order structures can begin immediately.

○ What are the key stages in protein structure formation?

● The burying of hydrophobic regions and other non-covalent interactions drive the formation of the loosely folded molten globule. The structures formed are limited by the geometry of the peptide bond, and consist of both α helix and β sheets (see Section 3.2).

The loose structure of the molten globule will start to form within seconds of synthesis, unless specific proteins are present to prevent it. This adoption of higher-order structure, associated with active peptide synthesis, called **co-translational folding**, is a highly dynamic process, with further covalent linkages, secondary modifications and tertiary-structure formation occurring as a continuum. Thus, even as new amino acids are being added catalytically within the ribosome, the extruded portion of the polypeptide is being actively processed.

○ Give examples of types of proteins and their locations within the eukaryotic cell.

● Microtubule components, signalling factors (cytosolic proteins), receptors, adhesion molecules, ion channels, porins, lipid-linked proteins (membrane proteins), DNA and RNA polymerases, histones, transcription factors (nuclear proteins), components of the electron transport chain, ATP synthase (mitochondrial proteins).

In this section, we shall examine various processes associated with translation in the eukaryotic cell and see how peptide-encoded signals determine the processing pathway used. An overview is given in Figure 11.17. The amino acid content of the signals will be discussed in more detail in Chapter 12, when compartmentalization is described in more detail.

The eventual destination of a protein directly affects its translation. Cytosolic proteins and proteins destined for organelles within the cell are synthesized on free ribosomes within the ER. For other proteins, recognition of a signal sequence within the nascent peptide directs the ribosomes, with their associated growing polypeptides to the ER membrane, to which they attach. These attached ribosomes give the ER membrane a rough appearance under the microscope – hence the term **rough ER**. The proteins made at these attached ribosomes extend into the ER lumen as they continue to be synthesized, and are destined for processing through the Golgi complex in what is termed the **secretory pathway**, with many being localized to the cell membrane and lysosome. We shall introduce these pathways in Section 11.5.2, and the downstream pathways will be further discussed in Chapter 12. Many other proteins continue to be made on non-attached ribosomes in the ER, and will be localized within various intracellular regions. We shall start by describing these proteins, and discuss their localization within the cell.

Figure 11.17
An overview of protein localization associated with translation. (a) During translation, the nascent polypeptide emerges from the ribosome. (b) The presence of an ER-specific peptide signal sequence directs the binding of the ribosome–mRNA complex to the ER membrane, where synthesis continues. In this case, the protein is synthesized across the ER membrane into the ER lumen, a process called 'co-translational localization'.
(c) In the absence of an ER localization sequence, translation continues on free ribosomes without attachment to the ER membrane, and polypeptides are further processed or localized post-translationally to various organelles or cellular structures.

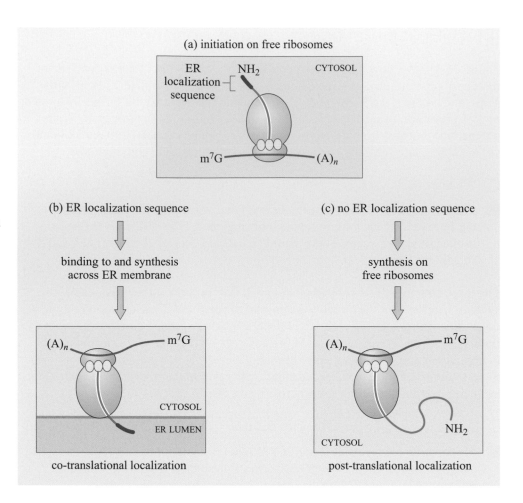

11.5.1 Post-translational localization signals

(a) Mitochondrial and chloroplast uptake

Despite the fact that mitochondria and chloroplasts carry their own genetic material, the great majority of proteins in these cellular organelles are encoded by nuclear genes. The cell therefore needs to be able to target these proteins to the appropriate organelles. As their synthesis proceeds, a short signal sequence within the N-terminal region of the nascent peptide is recognized by the cell (see Figure 11.18). In the case of proteins destined for the mitochondrion, this signal sequence usually consists of a stretch of lysine or arginine residues present within the 20 amino acids at the N-terminus.

The exact amino acid sequence varies depending on the eventual localization within the mitochondrion, but all these peptide signals form amphipathic α helices as the polypeptide is being formed. This is recognized as a signal early in the synthesis process, and directs the binding of chaperone proteins such as Hsp70 (Section 3.3.1) to the extending nascent peptide chain. These chaperones serve to maintain the polypeptide in an unfolded state, which is essential, as only unfolded proteins can be transported across the mitochondrial double membrane.

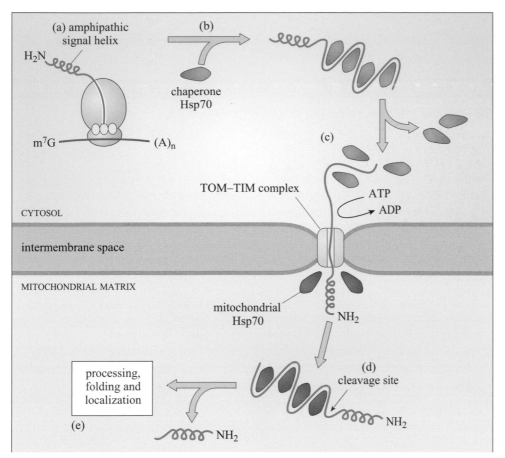

Figure 11.18
Post-translational localization of proteins to the mitochondrion. (a) During synthesis, a short amphipathic peptide helical sequence within the N-terminal region of the nascent peptide is recognized. (b) After binding to chaperone Hsp70 proteins, the polypeptide is targeted to the mitochondrial surface. (c) The polypeptide is bound and transported through the TOM–TIM receptor–pore complex with release of the cytosolic chaperones, and binding of mitochondrial Hsp70. The signal sequence is cleaved (d), processed, folded and localized (e), directed by secondary signal elements in the N-terminal region.

When the polypeptide reaches the mitochondrial membrane, it is captured by receptor proteins on the mitochondrial surface (Figure 11.18). Polypeptide translocation occurs through a receptor–pore complex, called the **TOM–TIM complex**, which spans both the inner and outer mitochondrial membranes. In this way, proteins are imported across the mitochondrial double membrane into the mitochondrial matrix, where mitochondrial Hsp70 chaperones bind and assist in their folding. The signal sequence is cleaved from the incoming protein, and in some cases this reveals a second signal sequence, which directs the newly imported peptide into one of the two mitochondrial membranes.

Translocation into the mitochondrion requires ATP hydrolysis during the initial binding and transfer stages. In addition, the proton motive force that exists across the membrane due to oxidative phosphorylation (Section 4.5) also appears to contribute to the energy requirements of import, since in the presence of agents such as cyanide (which bind to complex IV of the electron transport chain), transport is inhibited, even though ATP is present.

For plants, a very similar process occurs in chloroplasts, with the polypeptide translocation signal consisting of a short stretch of hydrophobic amino acid residues, together with serine and threonine. Transport from the ribosome into the chloroplast stroma again requires chaperone-mediated maintenance of the unfolded state. As in mitochondria, transport of the polypeptide across the membrane requires ATP. However, this process is not dependent on any proton motive force. Once inside the chloroplast stroma, cleavage of the signal peptide reveals secondary signals, which direct localization, for example, to the thylakoid.

(b) Peroxisome uptake

The only signal required to direct peroxisomal localization of a protein such as catalase is found in the C-terminal end of the protein.

▢ Where do you expect synthesis and folding of such a polypeptide to occur?

◼ With no N-terminal signal to direct ER membrane localization, ribosomes carrying catalase mRNA would not become attached to the ER for translation. Folding would therefore occur in the cytosol.

As the signal sequence is found at the C-terminal end of the polypeptide (the last section to be synthesized), the protein will already have become folded by the time this signal emerges from the ribosome. In these cases, therefore, the tertiary structure will already be formed. A C-terminal Ser–Lys–Leu element is sufficient to direct the localization and internalization of fully folded protein into the peroxisome and the signal sequence remains uncleaved.

(c) Nuclear uptake

Maintenance of the nuclear compartment requires many proteins, involved in the processes of DNA storage, replication and transcription. These proteins are all synthesized on free ribosomes, their transport into the nucleus being directed by a short signal peptide consisting of one or two short stretches of five basic amino acids, which are collectively known as a **nuclear localization signal** or **NLS**.

The pathway through which uptake of NLS-containing proteins occurs is shown in Figure 11.19, and involves various transporter proteins and a protein called Ran(GAP).

▢ With which other process is Ran(GAP) involved?

◼ mRNA transport out of the nucleus (Section 10.6.2).

All import to, and export from, the nucleus occurs through specific structures on the surface of the nuclear membrane called nuclear pores, which consist of proteins called 'porins'. After release from the ribosome, processing and maturation, NLS-containing polypeptides form a complex with the **importin A** and **importin B** proteins, the NLS region binding specifically to the importin A. Importin B has a highly flexible structure, allowing it to interact with a range of cargo proteins. The importin–cargo complex is then transported through the nuclear pore in a process mediated by ATP, and involves interactions with the nuclear pore complex component proteins. Once inside the nucleus, the complex dissociates when it interacts with a G protein called Ran. In its GTP-bound form, Ran interacts with the importin B subunit, displacing importin A and releasing the cargo polypeptide into the nucleus. Both the importin A and the importin B–Ran(GTP) complex are cycled back to the cytosol, where importin B is released for further transport by GTP hydrolysis on Ran stimulated by Ran(GAP).

These different mechanisms of transport and localization of newly synthesized polypeptides highlight the importance of peptide-encoded signals for determining the localization of newly synthesized proteins. In the cases outlined so far, these signals have directed how proteins are processed for further post-translational localization. As we shall now see in the case of proteins targeted to the ER, some signals serve to direct the positioning of ribosomes in what is called **co-translational localization**.

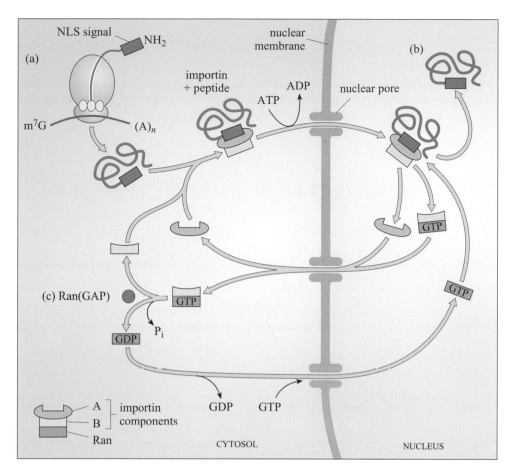

Figure 11.19
A nuclear localization signal directs uptake through nuclear pore complexes. (a) Proteins containing NLS are targeted into the nucleus by the importin A/B complex, which binds to the NLS. ATP-driven transport occurs though the nuclear pore. (b) Once in the nucleus, interaction between Ran(GTP) and importin B triggers release of the peptide. (c) Importin A and the Ran(GTP)-importin B are transported back to the cytosol. Here Ran(GAP) activity triggers GTP hydrolysis on Ran, releasing importin B.

11.5.2 Co-translational localization and processing in the ER

As outlined earlier and presented in the Figure 11.17 overview, many proteins destined for certain location or export routes are targeted to the ER membrane via the recognition of a short sequence of amino acids in the nascent peptide chain, which serve as recognition signals. In addition to this signal sequence, other signals present within the growing peptide chain determine how it is processed. These signals trigger processing events such as cleavage and the threading of the polypeptide across the membrane.

(a) The ER localization sequence directs binding to the ER membrane

As the nascent peptide emerges from the ribosome, those molecules containing an ER localization sequence are immediately bound by a protein called ER-SRF (signal recognition factor; Figure 11.20), which induces a temporary halt in peptide bond formation at the ribosomal catalytic site. The stalled ribosome is then bound by an SRF receptor on the ER membrane surface, after which it is docked onto a transmembrane transport channel. At this point, the nascent polypeptide chain containing the ER localization sequence is translocated into the transport channel. Once this has occurred, the recognition factor and receptor are released, and peptide synthesis on the ribosome is resumed. In this example of a secreted protein, the peptide chain is retained within the channel, and the growing polypeptide is cleaved. The extending polypeptide chain extrudes into the ER lumen, being driven by continued peptide bond formation at the active site.

Figure 11.20
ER signal peptide recognition drives membrane binding and translocation of the polypeptide chain. (a) An ER localization signal in the nascent peptide chain is recognized by a signal recognition factor, SRF. (b) This stalls translation until the SRF–ribosome complex has bound to the SRF receptor on the ER membrane surface, and (c) the complex has engaged with the transport channel. (d) The signal peptide sequence is transferred to the channel and, as the SRF is released, translation recommences at the ribosome. (e) In this protein, the signal peptide sequence is cleaved, and the new polypeptide is synthesized directly into the ER lumen, (f) whereupon it is released for processing.

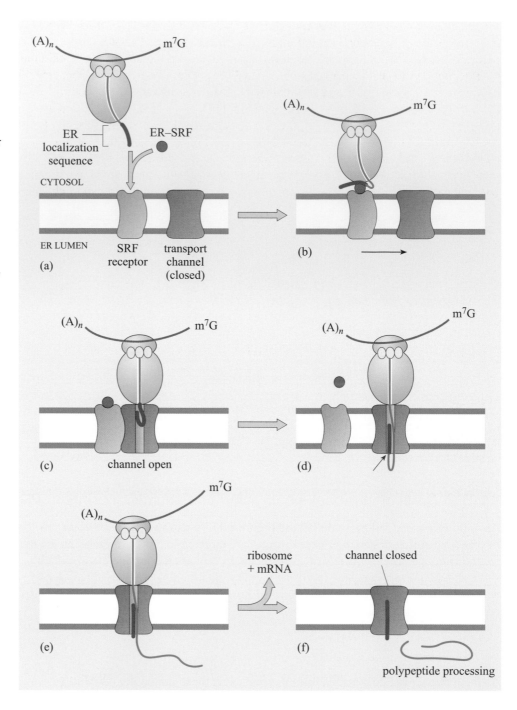

If many ribosomes engage due to looping of the mRNA (as shown in Figure 11.14), this can establish a continual production of protein into the ER lumen from a single mRNA molecule. When the ribosome completes synthesis on reaching a termination codon, it is released from the mRNA and the completed polypeptide is released into the ER lumen for further processing.

For secreted proteins that exist as free structures, the process as outlined above is straightforward. Many proteins within the eukaryotic cell, however, are attached to or span the membrane, in some cases crossing the membrane many times. An ER localization sequence triggers attachment of the ribosome to the ER membrane as in

Figure 11.20. In this case, the signal sequence is not retained in the channel, and the N-terminus extrudes into the ER lumen. The localized protein has to adopt a particular conformation, which is achieved through another signal element within the peptide, which directs the channel to halt translocation and to release the ribosome back into the cytosol (Figure 11.21). This **halt signal sequence** remains within the transport channel, and, depending on where it is located within any particular polypeptide, varying proportions of the final protein will become translocated into the ER lumen. As the ribosome becomes detached from the ER membrane, synthesis continues, but now the nascent peptide remains on the cytosolic side of the ER membrane. Termination of translation results in a single-pass transmembrane protein, with the halt signal remaining in the membrane on release from the transport channel.

⬭ Considering the eventual localization of the portion of the polypeptide containing the halt signal, what properties do you think the amino acids in this signal might possess?

⬤ As the halt signal sequence eventually forms the transmembrane spanning domain, this portion of the polypeptide will be an α helix with hydrophobic amino acids.

An important point to note from this example is that if the protein depicted in Figure 11.21 was destined eventually for the external surface of the cell, the part of the protein that extends into the ER lumen (the N-terminal end in this case) will eventually be on the outside of the cell. (An example of this orientation is seen with glycophorin monomer discussed in Section 6.4.3, and seen in Figure 6.21.)

In many cases, however, proteins are orientated within membranes in the opposite configuration – that is, with the C-terminal end of the peptide on the outer surface.

⬭ Considering what you have learnt about the machinery and signals involved, can you predict how a single-pass protein is synthesized with its N-terminus on the cytosolic side of the ER? (*Hint* Consider the location of the signal that initially targets the ribosome to the ER membrane.)

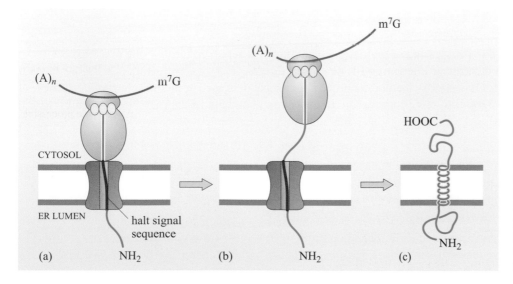

(a)   NH₂   (b)   NH₂   (c)

Figure 11.21
A single internal translocation halt signal sequence directs the formation of a transmembrane protein.
(a) Proteins that will eventually span the membrane contain a signal sequence (red) that halts peptide translocation through the transport channel, (b) leading to detachment of the ribosome from the transport channel while synthesis continues. (c) On completion of synthesis, the polypeptide is released from the transport channel. The C-terminal portion of the polypeptide remains on the cytosolic side of the ER membrane, and the N-terminal portion remains within the ER lumen.

■ If the ER localization sequence is not *at* the N-terminal end of the peptide, but rather is further along the chain, the N-terminal regions will have begun folding before the signal is detected. On recognition and subsequent binding to the ER membrane, synthesis would then continue, and the nascent chain would pass through the channel into the ER lumen, leaving the folded N-terminal end on the cytosolic side.

This is how single-pass membrane-spanning proteins with a C-terminus on the outside of the cell are synthesized (Figure 11.22). In this case, the ER signal sequence is not cleaved from the extending polypeptide, and remains as the transmembrane domain.

Figure 11.22
(a) During peptide synthesis, an ER localization signal within the growing peptide chain is bound by the SRF (not shown), which translocates the ribosome to the ER membrane as shown in Figure 11.20a and b. (b) As synthesis continues, the newly synthesized portion of the polypeptide chain is synthesized through the transport channel, and the N-terminal portion of the polypeptide remains on the cytosolic side of the ER; the portion of the polypeptide containing the signal sequence remains in the transporter complex. (c) On completion of synthesis, the N-terminal portion of the polypeptide remains on the cytosolic side of the ER membrane, the C-terminal portion remains within the ER lumen and the signal sequence forms the transmembrane domain.

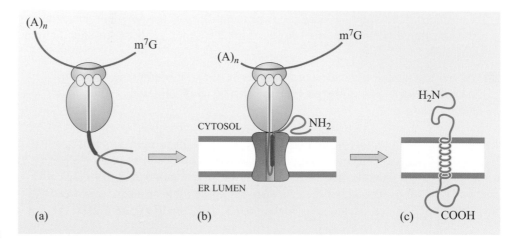

There are many cases where proteins pass through the membrane a number of times, such as is seen with many receptors and channel proteins.

☐ Which examples have you already encountered?

■ Examples discussed so far include bacteriorhodopsin, with seven membrane-spanning α helices (Section 6.4.3), and connexins, with four α helices (Section 6.4.5).

The localization of multipass polypeptides is achieved through the presence of consecutive alternating ER binding and halt signals, as is illustrated in Figure 11.23 for a four-pass membrane protein such as connexin. These multiple signals allow a growing polypeptide chain to be woven in and out of the membrane, each of the signal sequence regions remaining in the membrane.

We have given you a very general overview of how the different configurations of proteins found in the eukaryotic cell arise during co-translational localization paths, directed by signals within the growing polypeptide chain itself. The presence of these signals in peptides can be exploited experimentally to specifically localize recombinant proteins, as described in Box 11.3.

As mentioned earlier, and hopefully what is clear from your studies of the previous sections, the processes described here are highly dynamic, with synthesis, folding and, in some cases, localization occurring sequentially. In the next section, we shall

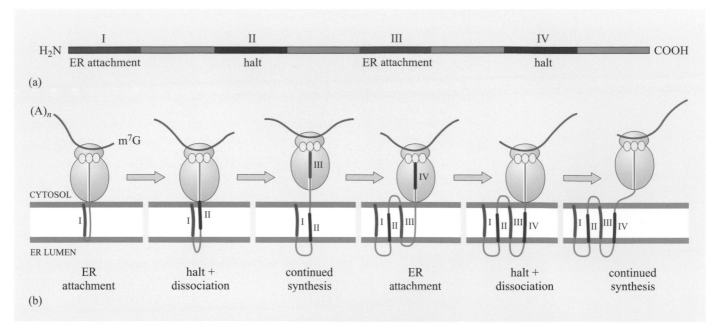

(a)

(b)

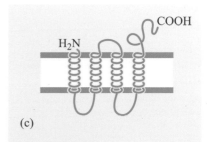

Figure 11.23 Multipass proteins result from multiple signals in the growing polypeptide.
(a) A polypeptide that will span the membrane four times is shown as a linear structure with four
alternating ER localization and halt signals (I–IV) numbered from the N-terminal end. (b) During
synthesis, signal I directs attachment to the ER membrane and synthesis through the transporter
until signal II is reached, when the ribosome is released from the ER membrane. As signal III is
synthesized, the ribosome again attaches to the ER membrane until signal IV is reached. (c) The
result is a four-pass membrane protein.

(c)

Box 11.3   The use of signal peptides for investigation of cellular dynamics

Recombinant DNA techniques allow ready exploitation of
the various peptide signals described in this chapter for the
study of eukaryotic cells. For example, it is possible to drive
the localization of a protein to a cellular compartment where
it is not normally found. A common use of this approach
is to utilize transgenes. An example of fluorescent proteins
is the green fluorescent protein (GFP) from the jellyfish.
Variants in the emission spectrum for these proteins have
been created using site-directed mutagenesis, producing
GFPs, which appear blue or yellow. Fusing to subcellular
localization signals allows simultaneous multicolour
detection of compartments. An example of this is shown in
Figure 11.24. You have an opportunity to examine several
examples of fluorescent proteins and the use of localization
signals within the *Movie gallery* (see Study Skills file).

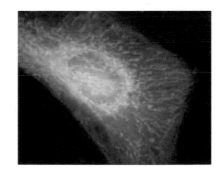

Figure 11.24   Fluorescent proteins
used to examine subcellular structure. A
human cell in which fluorescent proteins
are expressed: GFP-blue fused to a nuclear
localization signal, and GFP-yellow fused
to tubulin to localize microtubules.

follow the process of protein production further by examining peptide processing and folding within the ER lumen. Although we shall be focusing on the ER lumen, it is important to realize that proteins synthesized within the cytosolic portion of the ER undergo similar processes.

Summary of Section 11.5

1   Post-translational localization signals for cytosolic proteins determine transport to, and uptake into, the nucleus, mitochondria, chloroplasts and peroxisomes.

2   Nuclear uptake utilizes importin proteins, and is regulated through binding of the Ran(GTP) protein.

3   Co-translational protein localization uses signal peptides within the nascent peptide chain to signal ribosome attachment to the ER membrane or a halt to attachment.

4   Membrane-spanning polypeptides are synthesized via alternating ER translocation and halt signals, which lead to a protein being woven in and out of the membrane through a cycle of ribosome attachment and detachment.

5   Signalling peptides can be used to drive localization of proteins to specific cellular compartments.

11.6 Post-translational modification

The assembly of proteins into secondary, tertiary and quaternary structures (as discussed in Chapter 3) is usually accompanied by other modifications to and between amino acid residues. In this section, we shall discuss where and how some of these modifications occur within eukaryotic cells, and how some have active roles in the folding process whereas others have structural roles.

☐ Which post-translational modifications are found in proteins, and which are formed exclusively in the ER lumen? (These were discussed in Section 3.3.3.)

■ Some examples include disulfide bridge formation, methylation, acetylation, phosphorylation, lipidation (prenylation, fatty acylation and GPI-linkage) and glycosylation. The modifications that only occur within the ER lumen are glycosylation and disulfide bridge formation. In the case of lipidation, only GPI linkage occurs in the ER lumen.

The specific details of these modifications have already been discussed in Chapter 3; in this section, we shall be focusing on their role in protein structure formation and regulation.

11.6.1 Attachment to lipid anchors in the ER lumen

Many polypeptides on the outer surface of the plasma membrane are attached to the membrane by GPI linkages as described in Section 3.3.3. Such polypeptides are first co-translationally transported across the ER membrane as explained earlier, utilizing an ER localization signal and a translocation halt signal. The resultant transmembrane protein, which is positioned with its N-terminal end in the ER lumen, has one additional GPI-attachment signal sequence (Figure 11.25).

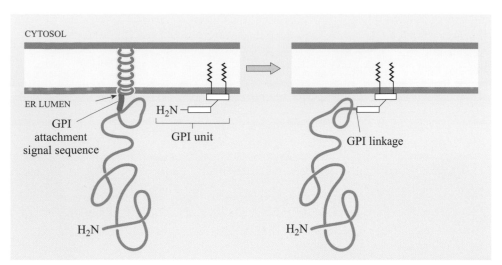

Figure 11.25
Attachment of a polypeptide to a GPI anchor is signalled by a specific peptide signal sequence. After ER membrane translocation, a GPI attachment signal lying adjacent to the ER lumen surface is cleaved by a protease, and the C-terminus of the polypeptide is linked to the amino end of a pre-assembled GPI unit. GPI-linked proteins such as this will eventually lie on the cell membrane surface.

On completion of synthesis, this lies just to the N-terminal side of the translocation stop signal, such that it ends up lying immediately next to the ER membrane on the lumenal side.

After release of the polypeptide from the transport channel, the peptide signal is recognized by a protease within the membrane, which cleaves the polypeptide chain and links it to a pre-assembled GPI unit located in the membrane. The resultant GPI-linked polypeptide now lies attached to the lumenal face of the ER membrane, and will eventually lie on the extracellular surface of the cell membrane after processing through the Golgi apparatus. The short polypeptide remaining in the ER membrane after cleavage is then targeted for degradation.

11.6.2 Glycosylation of proteins in the ER lumen

Glycosylation of proteins in the ER occurs though N-linked bonds that form between the sugar residue and the NH_2 groups of asparagine residues within the protein. The N-linked sugar chain added typically contains 10–14 internal sugar residues, whereas the O-linked chains are shorter. N-glycosylation is performed by membrane-bound glycosylases whereas O-glycosylation is performed by lumenal enzymes. The chains are also initially modified to carry 4–6 glucose units at their end. You will see later how this glycosylation step, and the glucose units in particular, play key roles in protein folding.

11.6.3 Cofactor-assisted folding: chaperone molecules

We described earlier how chaperone proteins such as Hsp70 play crucial roles in maintaining the unfolded state of mitochondrion- and chloroplast-targeted proteins. Before we discuss how such chaperones function in folding, it is important to emphasize how correct folding is essential to the cell. Translation is energetically costly, and the cell has mechanisms in place that ensure only functional proteins are produced. As we have seen, many different cellular pathways ensure that only non-mutant and undamaged mRNAs are translated. It is perhaps not surprising, therefore, to learn that only correctly folded proteins are allowed to exit from the ER for further processing and localization. This involves many different cofactors. A general overview of how this is achieved is shown in Figure 11.26.

Figure 11.26
Overview of protein-folding pathways in the ER lumen. The lumenal sections of newly synthesized polypeptides undergo glycosylation as they are extruded into the ER lumen. Chaperone proteins serve to assist the correct folding. Cycles of folding and refolding occur in the lumen until a sensor system determines that the protein is correctly folded, such that the polypeptides can form correct quaternary structures. Irreversibly misfolded proteins are transported across the ER membrane for degradation.

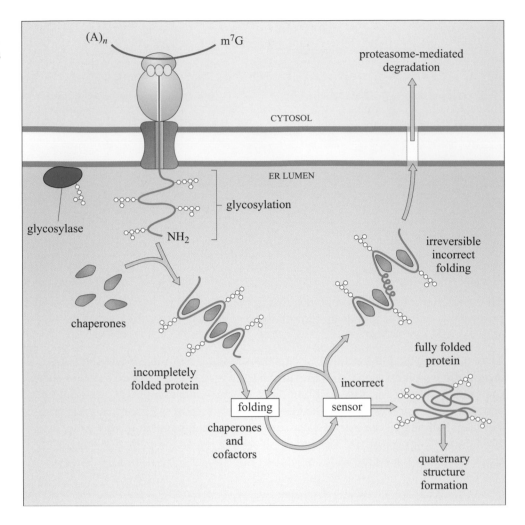

The first role for folding cofactors is to prevent proteins from forming aberrant structures. This role is played by chaperone proteins like Hsp70, as we saw with the mitochondrial-targeted proteins. By preventing misfolding, chaperones enhance the formation of the energetically more favourable structures. Hsp70 acts by detecting and binding to stretches of hydrophobic residues within the polypeptide chain, a process that requires ATP hydrolysis.

○ How does binding of stretches of hydrophobic residues allow chaperones such as Hsp70 to detect unfolded peptide chains?

● Stretches of hydrophobic residues are normally buried within the protein structure. If they are exposed such that Hsp70 can then bind, this is an indication that the protein is either incompletely or incorrectly folded.

If left undetected, proteins with exposed areas that are very hydrophobic tend to undergo a process called **aggregation**, whereby the polypeptides coalesce, eventually reaching a concentration at which precipitation occurs. We shall see later how this can have serious consequences for both individual cells and for whole organisms.

Advances in genomic sequence collection have allowed extensive comparisons of many thousands of proteins to be made, and as more X-ray diffraction and NMR data is obtained, we have a much greater knowledge of the portions of proteins that are folded into separate domains. Almost all separately folding protein domains are between 100 and 300 amino acids in length. In the case of proteins, where many domains are present, these are usually joined by flexible regions. In this case, it is most likely that chaperones such as Hsp70 stabilize the unfolded state until a whole domain has been synthesized on the ribosome, before allowing the domain to form as a single unit. Thus, maturation of a multidomain protein would proceed through a sequential folding of individual domains.

Two other types of cofactor play key roles in the formation of tertiary structure in the ER lumen by enhancing the formation and stability of the correct structure. The first are proteins called **lectins**, of which the membrane-bound **calreticulin** is a good example. Lectins bind to other proteins through interactions with the terminal glucose units on the sugar side-chains. This interaction enhances the activity of the second cofactor enzymes that act on the polypeptide chain. Such enzymes include those that catalyse the formation of disulfide bonds between suitably positioned cysteine residues, and enzymes that catalyse alterations in the *cis–trans* isomerization of the peptide bond (see Section 3.2.1) to allow for accommodation of more stable structures if required.

11.6.4 Polypeptide glycosylation: a sensor for folding

Glycosylation of newly synthesized polypeptides occurs as the growing polypeptide chain enters the ER lumen, such that as the fully synthesized polypeptide is released into the lumen it is fully glycosylated. The length of the glucose chain at the end of the glycosyl chain serves as an indicator of protein folding (Figure 11.27). This is achieved through the cyclical action of two enzyme activities within the ER lumen, which add or remove glucose residues to the end of the glycosyl chain. The presence of glucose on these side-chains allows membrane-bound calreticulin to retain the protein within the ER until it is fully folded, allowing disulfide bridge

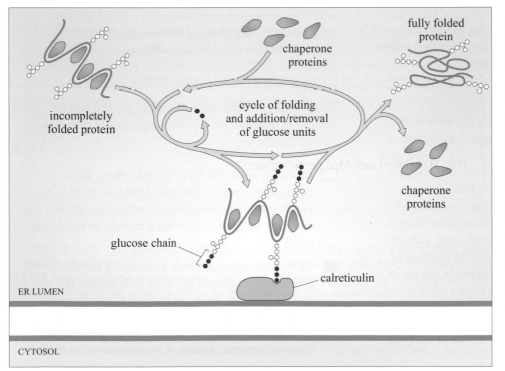

Figure 11.27
Removal of the terminal glucose units on glycosyl chains acts as a sensor for correct protein folding. Polypeptides that are incompletely folded carry glycosyl chains with terminal glucose units. The glycosyl chains allow the peptide chain to be retained in the ER lumen via binding to calreticulin, facilitating the action of enzymes that assist folding or stabilize tertiary structure. As folding continues, glucose units are gradually removed from the maturing polypeptide. When folding is complete, all the glucose units (red) are removed and the polypeptide is no longer held within the ER by calreticulin. These mature proteins are then allowed to exit the ER for transport into other compartments, or to the cell surface.

By exploiting these requirements, it is possible to obtain high quantities of proteins in eukaryotic cells (see Figure 11.28b).

One particular transgenic animal system in sheep has been developed to obtain high expression of proteins for therapeutic use in humans. Protein expression has been engineered through the introduction of DNA sequences into a vector to drive appropriate expression in mammary cells, and processing to ensure secretion of the required protein in milk. Sheep genetically modified to secrete human clotting factor (factor IX) for the treatment of haemophilia have been produced; these animals are a source of large amounts of protein easily extracted from their milk.

In many cases, as we saw in the case of experiments used to determine the genetic code (Section 11.1), proteins can be synthesized using extracts of cells that contain the necessary components and catalytic activities for translation to occur. Such extracts are prepared under conditions that preserve the enzyme activity of the cells. Cell extracts from eukaryotic cells include those made from wheatgerm and rabbit reticulocytes. These can be incubated with synthetic mRNAs to produce full-length proteins, a technique that has been exploited as a means of screening for human genes carrying premature stop codons associated with human disease.

○ Can you think of such a gene?

● The BRCA1 gene discussed in Section 11.4. Over 90% of mutations in this gene are premature stop codons, which lead to nonsense-mediated decay of the mRNA.

In a commonly used laboratory diagnostic test, it is possible to amplify the BCRA1 exons by PCR from genomic DNA, and produce a synthetic mRNA from them (Box 10.1) which includes an initiation AUG codon (Figure 11.28c). These can then be mixed with whole cell extract, and the products examined by SDS–PAGE.

○ What result would you predict for *in vitro* translation of an mRNA with a premature stop codon?

● The polypeptide produced would be shorter than the full-length version.

Figure 11.28c shows an example of this test, called the **protein truncation assay**. Such tests are commonly used for several human genetic diseases.

Summary of Section 11.6

1   Appropriate signal peptides within polypeptide chains lead to cleavage, and ligation to membrane-bound GPI units.

2   Newly synthesized polypeptides are glycosylated as they are synthesized into the ER lumen.

3   Protein folding is assisted by chaperone proteins, which stabilize structures, and enzymes that form disulfide bridges and isomerize peptide bonds.

4   Maturing proteins are held in the ER lumen by lectins, and through glucose units on glycosyl chains. Cycles of removal and addition of glucose accompany folding.

5   Proteins can be synthesized in various systems by exploiting recombinant DNA techniques to create expression vectors for prokaryotic and eukaryotic cells.

11.7 Protein degradation

Proteins are a substantial component of any cell, and many enzymes exist to degrade them. For the most part, extracellular proteins are degraded by enzymes termed 'endoproteases', examples of which include trypsin and chymotrypsin. These cleave all peptide chains internally to leave smaller fragments, and various other proteases (exoproteases) then degrade these fragments through sequential digestion, removing one residue at a time.

☐ Why are such non-specific degradation pathways unsuitable for intracellular degradation?

◼ These types of non-specific degradation enzymes could obviously prove potentially hazardous to the cell in which controlled and specific degradation is required.

11.7.1 Intracellular protein degradation

The cell has a constant turnover of all its proteins. Some of this turnover is related to the replacement of components that have become damaged in some way, by oxidation, denaturation or misfolding, for example. In other cases, it is part of the regulatory machinery, as is the case with many regulatory proteins involved in the cell cycle (described in Chapter 8) and in transcriptional control (described in Chapter 10). In the case of infection with viral agents, incoming proteins must also be removed.

For degradation of proteins within the cell, two main pathways exist. The first uses the lysosome, a small membrane-bound organelle carrying many degradation enzymes, not only for proteins, but also for nucleic acids, lipids and other intracellular components.

The second pathway for protein degradation is the **ubiquitin-mediated pathway**. This pathway has two major components – ubiquitin ligase, which actively identifies target proteins, and the degradation machinery, called the **proteasome** (see Chapter 3). Figure 11.29 is an overview of how this system functions. The key components in the process are the ubiquitin ligases, which, by virtue of a recognition domain, are responsible for targeting proteins for degradation. Obviously, in any single cell there will be a wide variety of proteins that need degrading.

☐ Can you recall examples of the specific targeting of proteins for degradation being used as a means of regulation?

◼ Cyclins and cyclin kinase inhibitors (Section 8.3.3).

So how is this specificity achieved? The answer to this question lies in the presence of many different types of ubiquitin ligase; typically a mammalian cell will have up to 300 versions, some capable of recognizing different types of damage to a protein (such as oxidative damage, damaged amino acids or misfolding), others recognizing classes of proteins, and, in other cases, highly specific recognition of individual targets.

Once a target protein is recognized for degradation, it is tagged by the ligase with ubiquitin, a small protein of 76 amino acids. The ubiquitin is attached to a lysine residue in the target protein, and many rounds of this ubiquitin addition step result in targeted proteins carrying a chain of ubiquitin molecules (Figure 11.29).

Figure 11.29
Pathways of protein ubiquitin addition, and degradation in the proteasome. (a) Damaged or misfolded proteins, or those targeted for degradation, are recognized by ubiquitin ligases through specific interactions. (b) Binding results in transfer of a single ubiquitin molecule to a lysine residue in the protein; (c) this is repeated to generate a protein carrying a long chain of ubiquitin molecules. (d) This protein, with its multiple ubiquitin attachments, is transported to a cylindrical structure called a proteasome, within which ATP-driven unfolding and peptide cleavage occur (e) to generate short peptide fragments, and (f) free ubiquitin which is reattached to the ligase utilizing ATP.

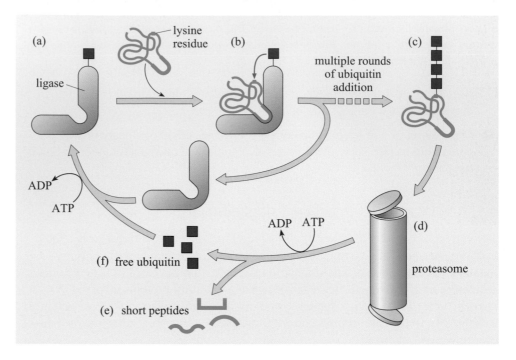

The protein with multiple ubiquitin molecules bound is now transported to a proteasome, a complex of proteins that functions as an ATP-dependent protease. The components of the proteasome form a closed chamber, into which the targeted protein is placed, as shown schematically in Figure 11.29. Essentially, the proteasome can be considered as a digestive barrel, with a main body and caps at each end. The structure of the mammalian proteasome, which consists of 28 different proteins, is shown in Figure 11.30. Proteins targeted to the proteasome are degraded to short peptides, usually 15–20 amino acids in length, which, on release, are degraded by other cellular proteases. Released ubiquitin is recycled back onto ligase, utilizing 1ATP.

The proteasome pathway plays a crucial role in the mammalian immune system. The **class I major histocompatability complex (MHC)** proteins serve to transport a sample of peptides from within the cell to the cell surface, where they can be monitored by the immune system. On the cell surface, the peptides carried by MHC proteins are displayed to passing T lymphocytes, which will respond to 'foreign' antigens.

A proportion of all the short peptide chains released from the proteasome (representing a sampling of all internal proteins within the cell) is transported back into the ER via a specialized transporter called the TAP-1/2 transport channel (Figure 11.31). Within the ER lumen, they are degraded from their termini into shorter peptides, when they become associated with newly

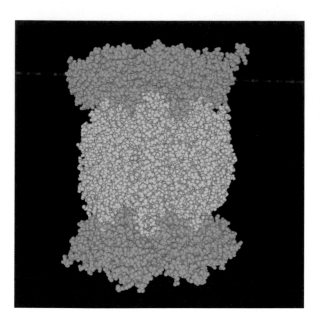

Figure 11.30
Space-filling representation of the mammalian proteasome, which contains 28 different proteins, highlighting the barrel-shaped body (cyan) and the cap structures at each end (green) (based on pdb file 1iru).

synthesized class I MHC proteins lying attached to the inner surface of the ER lumen. MHC proteins carry a peptide-binding pocket within which the peptide sits. After subsequent processing, the peptide–MHC protein complexes will eventually be located on the outer surface of the cell.

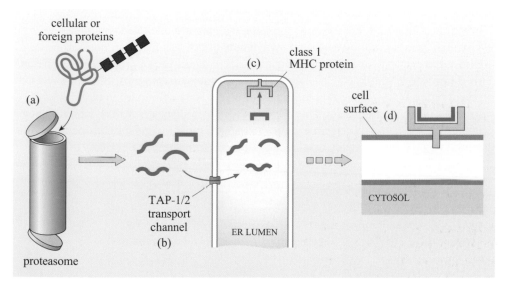

Figure 11.31   The proteasome generates short peptides, which are eventually displayed on the cell surface by class I MHC proteins. In mammals, all cellular proteins, including foreign proteins, are eventually degraded via the proteasome pathway. (a) This includes any proteins from invading pathogens. (b) A sample of the short peptides is transported to the ER via the TAP-1/2 transport channel, where they are sequentially digested. (c) class I MHC proteins that are assembled in the ER lumen have antigen binding domains, which bind to many short peptides of 8–9 amino acids (one peptide per MHC molecule). (d) These class I MHC proteins eventually end up on the cell surface, where the bound peptides are recognized by the immune system.

○ Why is it advantageous for cells to present peptides in this manner?

■ It allows the body's immune system to screen the internal contents of every cell. As any cell can become infected with a virus, this pathway ensures that cells are constantly monitored.

Cells that are identified as containing 'foreign' antigens, indicative of infection, are targeted for destruction by apoptosis (Chapter 14).

11.7.2 Ubiquitin ligases as switches in regulatory pathways

Once a target protein has been tagged for degradation by ubiquitin, its removal from the cell is extremely rapid. It is perhaps not surprising, therefore, that this process has been widely exploited by regulatory networks within the eukaryotic cell to regulate pathways by targeted elimination of critical components within those pathways. Central to this activity is the utilization of the specific recognition stage between the target protein and its specific ubiquitin ligase. In general, this recognition stage has been exploited as a switch in two ways. In some cases, the visibility of the target protein site is regulated; in others, it is the binding site on the ligase that is regulated (Figure 11.32). Target site exposure can arise in many ways including phosphorylation, chain cleavage, conformational shifts in structure, or allosteric effects through binding or dissociation of other proteins or ligands. The ligase, of course, can be similarly regulated.

Another example of the exploitation of this system is in determining the differential stability of proteins. In yeast cells, the stability of a protein is determined by the N-terminal amino acid. For example, proteins with an arginine residue at their N-terminal are very rapidly degraded, with a half-life of less than 4 minutes. In contrast, the presence of a glycine residue results in a half-life of greater than 30 hours. This difference in stability is driven by differential rates of ubiquitin attachment, based on recognition of the different N-terminal amino acids by a ubiquitin ligase. Similar rules exist in mammalian cells. This is exploited by regulatory enzymes, which cleave proteins to expose new N-terminal amino acids with rapid degradation properties. Thus, a central degradation pathway is utilized to determine the half-life of many proteins.

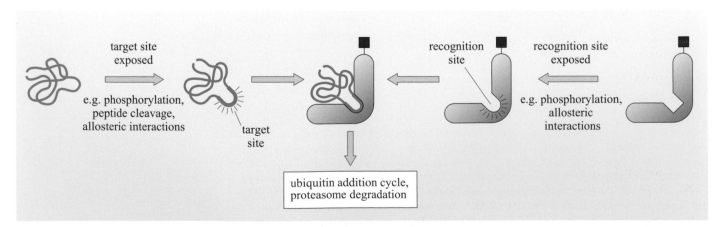

Figure 11.32   The regulation of protein degradation through ubiquitin ligase recognition. Once a target protein is bound to the recognition site, ubiquitin is attached, and it is targeted for degradation via the proteasome. This process is regulated by preventing the specific interaction between target and ligase molecules. The target site on the protein can be masked in various ways, and a protein's stability can therefore be regulated according to whether the target site is exposed or not. Similarly, the recognition site in the ligase can be masked, allowing its regulation by various means as shown. The ligase–protein complex then undergoes further processing as in Figure 11.29.

11.7.3 The accumulation of degradation-resistant proteins

As mentioned earlier, if hydrophobic regions of peptides, which are normally found buried within the tertiary structure of proteins, are exposed and not refolded by chaperone molecules, it can lead to unwanted protein–protein interactions and aggregation. Aggregation is often in the form of fibrils, called plaques or tangles. These contain high densities of peptide fragments, and can be found both within and outside the cell (Figure 11.33). If the aggregates are resistant to cellular proteases and pathways such as the proteasome, their accumulation can be toxic to the cell. In many cases, aggregates contain fragments of a target protein that have multiple ubiquitin attachments, and contain components of the proteasome. This is an indication of the cell's attempts to degrade them, and is seen in many different human neurodegenerative diseases. Cells in the mammalian brain appear to be especially vulnerable to such aggregation.

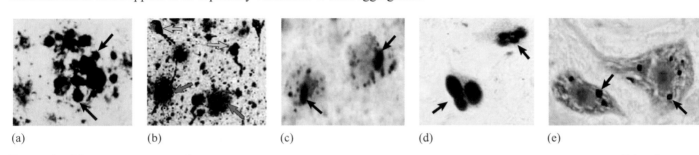

(a)   (b)   (c)   (d)   (e)

Figure 11.33   Protein aggregates in brain cells associated with human neurodegenerative disease. Arrows highlight (a) extracellular plaques in prion disease, (b) extracellular plaques (blue) and cytosolic tangles (yellow) in Alzheimer's disease, (c) nuclear aggregates in Huntington's disease, (d) cytosolic aggregates (known as Lewy bodies) in Parkinson's disease, and (e) nuclear aggregates in amyotrophic lateral sclerosis.

Summary of Section 11.7

1   Endoproteases are responsible for most extracellular protein degradation.

2   Intracellular degradation can occur through lysosomes or through ubiquitin attachment of proteins by specific ligases, which recognize target sites on proteins.

3   Degradation takes place in the proteasome, requires ATP, and generates short peptides of 15–20 amino acids.

4   The cell uses both protein target site exposure and ubiquitin ligase activity as regulatory control points.

5   Misfolded proteins may become aggregated and lead to human neurodegenerative diseases.

11.8 Regulating translation

Before we finish our discussion of translation, we shall briefly examine one other aspect of the regulation of translation – how some cells exploit the cellular location of the translation machinery for a specific purpose. You have already seen examples of how the eukaryotic cell regulates levels of RNA and protein through the various pathways discussed in Chapter 10 and in this chapter involving transcription, translation and protein degradation. You will also recall that mRNA can become partitioned within the cell (Section 10.6.4) and be translated locally. Thus, it will perhaps not come as a surprise to you to discover that in some cells, the translation machinery, or specialized versions of it, are also found localized to certain areas.

An example of this is the localized protein synthesis that occurs in dendrites in neurons of the mammalian brain. Neuronal cells contain many synapses, and these differ in the quantities and types of proteins present. This contributes both to their individual functionality and to regional specializations within the nervous system. The majority of proteins are made conventionally in the cell body and exported to the dendrites. Heterogeneity, however, is generated in part by selective localization of mRNAs to sites of translation located immediately adjacent to a synapse. In response to signalling across the synapse, local protein synthesis is modified, so altering the level of proteins at that specific synapse.

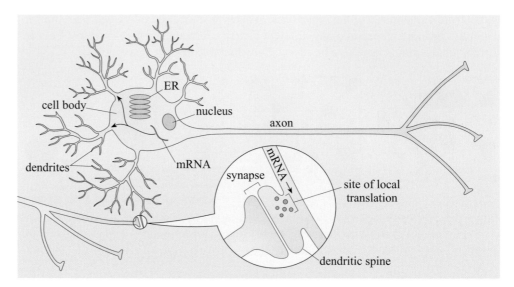

Figure 11.34   Local protein synthesis in dendrites of the mammalian brain. Protein synthesis in neurons occurs both in the cell body and at sites of local ribosome activity adjacent to a synapse. In the latter case, some mRNAs are transported to these sites along dendrites to sites of synaptic interaction (dendritic spines). Translation at such sites is often in response to synaptic activity.

Summary of Section 11.8

Protein expression can be regulated temporally through local sites of protein production.

Learning outcomes for Chapter 11

When you have studied this chapter, you should be able to:

11.1 Define and use each of the terms printed in **bold** in the text.

11.2 Describe the use of the techniques used for the study of intercellular processes.

11.3 Discuss the role of molecular shape mimicry in translation.

11.4 Relate the structure of the ribosome and its role in the translation process.

11.5 Discuss, with relevant examples, how cellular protein levels are regulated at key points during the translation process.

11.6 Describe, with relevant examples, how protein signal sequences direct localization to various cell compartments.

11.7 Describe how translation is utilized to form variously orientated membrane-spanning proteins.

11.8 Discuss the pathways of protein degradation, its role in normal cellular metabolism, and where it goes wrong in human disease.

Questions for Chapter 11

Question 11.1

Outline the roles that the large and small ribosomal subunits play in translation.

Question 11.2

How does the translation process differ between the prokaryote cell and the eukaryote cell?

Question 11.3

What stages or processes associated with translation help to maintain the expression of the genetic code?

Question 11.4

How is shape mimicry used by components of the translation machinery?

Question 11.5

Which is the most suitable protein expression system in which to produce large quantities of a bacterial catalase and human insulin? Explain your reasoning.

References

Glaser, F., Pupko, T., Paz, I., Bell, R. E., Bechor-Shental, D., Martz, E. and Ben-Tal, N. (2003) ConSurf: identification of functional regions in proteins by surface-mapping of phylogenetic information, *Bioinformatics*, **19**, pp. 163–164.

Nissen, T., Hansen, J., Ban, N., Moore, P. B. and Steitz, T. A. (2000) The structural basis of ribosome activity in peptide bond synthesis, *Science*, **289**, pp. 920–930.

Sachs, M. I. and Geballe, A. P. (2002) Sense and sensitivity-controlling the ribosome, *Science*, **297**, pp. 1820–1821.

Further sources

Li, F., Xiong, Y., Wang, J., Cho, H. D., Tomita, K., Weiner, A. M. and Steitz, T. A. (2002) Crystal structures of the *Bacillus stearothermophilus* CCA-adding enzyme and its complexes with ATP or CTP, *Cell*, **111**, 815–824.

Olsen, P. H. and Ambos, V. (2003) The *Lin-4* regulatory RNA controls developmental timing in *C. elegans* by blocking Lin-14 protein synthesis after the initiation of translation, *Developmental Biology*, **216**, pp. 671–680.

Varshavsky, A. (2003) The N-end rule and regulation of apoptosis, *Nature Cell Biology*, **5**, pp. 373–376.

ANSWERS TO QUESTIONS

Question 8.1

The mitotic spindle, composed of microtubules. The spindle microtubules are established by the microtubule organizing centre (MTOC).

Question 8.2

Checkpoints are points in the cell cycle at which the state of the cell is monitored to ensure that progression to the next stage of the cycle is appropriate. An example would be the check for genome integrity before entering mitosis. Checkpoints are important because if a cell proceed through the cell cycle inappropriately, severe consequences may ensue. These consequences include failure to complete mitosis and daughter cells receiving incomplete or damaged DNA.

Question 8.3

The two components are cyclin and Cdk (cyclin-dependent kinase). There are many cyclins and Cdks in vertebrate cells and fewer in yeast cells. Each cyclin–Cdk complex has kinase activity by which the activity of specific components of the cell cycle machinery are controlled.

Question 8.4

Because colchicine prevents the assembly of microtubules, the mitotic spindle will fail to form, so the kinetochore–microtubule attachment cannot occur, resulting in cell cycle arrest at the spindle checkpoint, i.e. a metaphase block.

Question 8.5

The MTOC in animal cells is the centrosome, while the corresponding structure in yeast cells is the spindle pole body (SPB).

Question 8.6

START is a checkpoint past which yeast cells can only proceed, committing to mitosis, if environmental conditions such as adequate nutritional resources or absence of mating pheromone are met. Its counterpart in mammalian cells is the restriction point. Both are G1 checkpoints, acting to control the G2/M transition.

Question 8.7

Astral microtubules radiate from the spindle pole to the cell cortex. Kinetochore microtubules extend from the spindle pole to the kinetochore. Interpolar microtubules extend from the spindle pole to the spindle equator, where they overlap microtubules extending from the other pole.

Question 8.8

Anaphase A begins with the sudden loss of cohesion between chromosomes. The chromosomes are pulled toward the poles by kinetochore microtubules. During anaphase B, the spindle lengthens by the sliding of microtubules that overlap in the equatorial region of the spindle, further moving the chromosomes apart.

Question 8.9

Cytokinesis in animal cells involves the contractile ring, a complex structure containing actin and myosin II filaments, among other components. In contrast, plant cells assemble vesicles carrying cell wall components at the phragmoplast – the remains of the overlapping microtubules at the spindle equator.

Question 8.10

DNA replication is triggered by increase in cell mass.

Question 9.1

Pulsed labelling allows the labelling of the newly synthesized DNA chains at sites of active DNA synthesis. A commonly used nucleoside analogue is bromodeoxyuridine (BrdU). Newly synthesized DNA is then detected directly or isolated using an antibody directed toward BrdU. Examples include the direct visualization of origins on extended DNA strands after pulsed labelling (Box 9.1, Figure 9.3) and the direct isolation of BrdU-labelled DNA using antibodies and quantitative PCR detection (Box 9.2, Figure 9.10).

Question 9.2

Newly replicated DNA is hemi-methylated and not yet subjected to DNA twisting into supercoils. DNA in a metaphase chromosome has undergone methylation at 5′-CG sites; it has been packaging into nucleosomes through the assembly of new histone octamers, which introduces supercoiling into the helix; nucleosomes have been modified by histone modifying enzymes and chromatin modifying proteins; scaffolds have been assembled and condensed through interaction with histones H1 and other proteins.

Question 9.3

Replication fidelity depends primarily upon the appropriate pairing between the incoming nucleotide and the template DNA strand. This pairing occurs within the nascent base-pair pocket of the DNA polymerase. Mispaired bases are transferred into the 3′–5′ exonuclease site where they are removed. A second stage in maintaining the fidelity of replication occurs at the level of post-replicative DNA repair, which involves both the DNA mismatch repair and copy repair systems.

Question 9.4

DNA damage or base mispairings are detected either through the binding of specialized proteins that recognize specific forms of damage (e.g. O^6-methylguanosine), scanning for damage by 'base flipping' (e.g. DNA glycolyases), or through more generalized proteins that recognize the distortion of the DNA helix caused by the damage.

Question 9.5

Together, ORC components and the Cdc6 protein regulate the initiation of DNA synthesis at the replication origins of yeast. When the cell cycle progresses to S phase, these become phosphorylated, which triggers DNA synthesis. Both the ATM and ATR proteins interact through checkpoint controls with cell cycle components through the detection of double-strand breaks and of regions of unreplicated DNA which are indicative of unreplicated regions.

Question 10.1

Initial RNA synthesis is limited by steric hindrance. Multiple failed initiations often occur before the polymerase can enter the elongation phase of transcription. This is facilitated by the polymerase adopting a conformation involving a tunnel, through which the nascent RNA chain can emerge as it is synthesized.

Question 10.2

DNA binding proteins make contact with specific nucleotide sequences in the DNA double helix by specific amino acid–nucleotide contacts; these are related to the sequence of amino acid residues in the DNA binding domain. Heterodimerization permits the recognition of a greater range of specific DNA sequences than would be afforded if only homodimers could form.

Question 10.3

The *trp* operon encodes five enzymes required for the synthesis of the amino acid tryptophan. Transcription of the single polycistronic transcript is controlled in two ways. In the presence of tryptophan (when biosynthesis of tryptophan is inappropriate), a repressor protein binds the operator, preventing transcription of the operon. In the absence of tryptophan, the repressor is unable to bind the operator, and transcription can begin. The second system of transcriptional control is known as attenuation. This utilizes a short open reading frame, *trpL*, containing two adjacent Trp codons. Because translation begins very soon after transcriptional initiation, the progression of a ribosome along the first ORF of the mRNA influences the formation of secondary structure in the mRNA. When tryptophan levels are low, the ribosome stalls at the Trp codons, and an RNA secondary structure that permits continued transcription is adopted. Otherwise the RNA forms a secondary structure that suppresses further transcription.

Question 10.4

There are three eukaryotic RNA polymerases, in comparison to the single RNA polymerase found in a typical prokaryote. Each eukaryotic polymerase shares certain core subunits, but possesses several unique subunits. In comparison to prokaryotic RNA polymerases, the eukaryotic polymerases are more complex in terms of the number of constituent subunits, although several subunits correspond to subunits of prokaryotic RNA polymerase.

Question 10.5

Enhancer elements are DNA sequences that function to stimulate the transcription of specific genes in a position- and orientation-independent manner. In other words, an enhancer normally located upstream of a gene will still exert its enhancer activity if experimentally relocated downstream of its target gene. Silencer elements function in a similar manner, but reduce transcription. Both silencer and enhancer elements can function at distances of many kilobases from their target gene. Insulator elements serve as 'boundaries', across which enhancer or silencer effects cannot act, and thereby prevent enhancers or silencers from influencing the expression of inappropriate genes.

Question 10.6

Female mammals have two X chromosomes as opposed to the single X chromosome of male mammals. In order to ensure that the overall transcriptional activity of X chromosomal genes is the same in both sexes, one of the X chromosomes in females is inactivated by chromatin modification. Specific forms of histones are found to be enriched or depleted in an inactive X chromosome compared with the active homologue. The process of X inactivation is regulated in two distinct steps: establishment and maintenance. During establishment, an RNA species known as *Xist*, transcribed from the X inactivation centre (XIC), directs the association of HDACs and HMTs to one of the X chromosomes. These enzymes modify the histones, and repress transcription. Later, during the maintenance phase, these alterations are brought about by DNA methylation.

Question 10.7

A microarray is a dense array of spots of DNA on a glass chip, corresponding to a large number of genes, often in the tens of thousands. These spots of DNA may be cDNA clones or specifically synthesized oligonucleotides. Microarrays can be used to monitor the changes in expression levels of large numbers of genes in response to experimental intervention – for example, the transcriptional response to treatment with a toxic substance, as shown in Figure 10.33. These experiments are carried out by synthesizing fluorescently labelled cDNA molecules from RNA isolated from experimental samples, and hybridizing them to the DNA immobilized on the microarray. The level of each mRNA in the original sample is reflected by the intensity of the fluorescence of hybridized cDNA at its corresponding DNA spot on the microarray chip.

Question 10.8

The four main modifications are the addition of an m^7G cap at the 5′ end, the addition of a poly(A) tail at the 3′ end, splicing and in some cases, editing.

Question 10.9

miRNA molecules are transcribed as palindromic sequences, which can form stem–loop structures by self-annealing. These molecules are exported to the cytoplasm, where they are processed into ~21 bp double-stranded molecules by the dicer complex. From these duplex RNAs, single-stranded molecules associate with a complex known as RISC, and target RISC to specific mRNAs by virtue of sequence complementarity. RISC then degrades the target mRNAs.

Question 10.10

Synthesis of rRNA molecules in eukaryotes occurs in the nucleolus, and is catalysed by RNA polymerase I. The three major rRNA molecules, 5.8 S, 18 S and 28 S, are transcribed as a single primary transcript, the 45 S transcript. The 45 S transcript is initially chemically modified by 2′-OH methylation at about a hundred sites, and then processed by cleavage to release the mature rRNA molecules.

Question 11.1

The small ribosomal subunit has its major role in the interactions with mRNA. It is involved in the formation of the initiation complex, which in prokaryotes involves direct base-pairing. It also provides a structure on which tRNA anticodons pair with codons within the mRNA, acting as a sensor for appropriate pairing. The A, P and E sites lie at the interface of the two ribosomal subunits. The large subunit provides the catalytic site within which peptide bond formation occurs. It also carries the tunnel through which the newly synthesized peptide passes. In eukaryotes, the large ribosomal subunit acts as the interface with the ER membrane, allowing docking and synthesis into the ER lumen.

Question 11.2

Differences include: initiation, which in prokaryotes occurs directly at the AUG site directed by Shine–Dalgarno pairing with the small ribosomal unit, but occurs through interactions either at the 5′ end or at an IRES in eukaryotic cells. Specific initiator tRNAs carry formylmethionine in prokaryotes and methionine in eukaryotes. Translation is continuous with transcription in prokaryotes, whereas it occurs after nuclear export of mRNA to the ER or cytosol in eukaryotes. Components of the ribosomal RNA, which make up the small and large ribosome subunits, also differ in their S value and number of associated proteins.

Question 11.3

You may have thought of the sensor detecting the stringency of the tRNA–mRNA pairing, the stringency of the tRNA charging by the aminoacyl synthase, nonsense-mediated decay and non-stop decay, which prevents protein synthesis from damaged mRNAs, and processes that ensure appropriate folding, which will prevent malformed proteins from being produced.

Question 11.4

Shape mimicry is used by termination factors, which are proteins that have a similar three-dimensional structure to the EF–tRNA complex, and allow them to interact with the stop codon in the mRNA and also to interact with the ribosomal catalytic region.

Question 11.5

Bacterial catalase could easily be produced through over-expression, using a plasmid vector carrying bacterial transcription signals within bacteria such as *E. coli*. Human insulin will require synthesis in a eukaryotic system and will therefore require an expression vector that carries suitable transcriptional signals. To ensure appropriate processing of the protein, the most suitable system would be a mammalian cell line.

ACKNOWLEDGEMENTS

Every effort has been made to contact copyright holders. If any have been inadvertently overlooked, the publishers will be pleased to make the necessary arrangements at the first opportunity. Grateful acknowledgement is made to the following sources for permission to reproduce material within this book.

Chapter 8

Figure 8.1 Stein, G. S., Wijnen, A. J., van Stein, J. L., Lian, J. B. and Owen, T. A. (August 2001) 'Cell cycle', in *Encyclopedia of Life Sciences*, London: Nature Publishing Group, http://www.els.net/; *Figure 8.5a* Copyright © Hiro Ohkura, University of Edinburgh; *Figure 8.5b* Dr Rong Li, Harvard University; *Figure 8.6*: Dr Jordan Raff, Wellcome Senior Research Fellow; *Figure 8.7* Copyright © Dr Andreas Merdes, University of Edinburgh; *Figure 8.8a* Copyright © Jones and Sgouros, licensee BioMed Central Ltd; *Figures 8.8b, 8.17* Copyright © The Institute of Cancer Research; *Figure 8.9a* Burke, B. (August 2000) 'Nuclear envelope: organization and dynamics', in *Encyclopedia of Life Sciences*, London: Nature Publishing Group, http://www.els.net/; *Figures 8.12, 8.13* Fukasawa, K. (University of Cincinnati College of Medicine) Introduction, *Oncogene*, 2002, vol. **21**, copyright © Nature Publishing Group; *Figure 8.14* Taken from www.teaching-biomed.man.ac.uk; *Figures 8.15a, b, 8.16a, b* Redrawn from Alberts, B. *et al.* (2002) *Molecular Biology of the Cell*, 4th edn, Garland Science, Taylor and Francis Group; *Figure 8.18* Copyright © Western Kentucky University; *Figure 8.22a, b (part)* Kitazono, A. A., Fitz Gerald, J. N. and Kron, S. J. (December 1999) 'Cell cycle: regulation by cyclins', in *Encyclopedia of Life Sciences*, London: Nature Publishing Group, http://www.els.net/; *Figures 8.22b (part), 8.27, 8.30* Novak, B., Sible, J. C. and Tyson, J. J. (September 2002) 'Checkpoints in the cell cycle', in *Encyclopedia of Life Sciences*, London: Nature Publishing Group, http://www.els.net/; *Figure 8.31* Reprinted from *Journal of Molecular Biology*, **31**, 1968, Cooper, S. and Helmsletter, C. E., p. 3, copyright © 1968, with permission from Elsevier.

Chapter 9

Figure 9.3b(i) Lengronne, A., Pasero, P., Bensimon, A. and Schwob, E. (2001) 'Monitoring S phase progression globally and locally using BrdU incorporation in TK yeast strains', *Nucleic Acids Research*, **29**(7), Oxford University Press; *Figure 9.5* Gilbert, D. M. 'Making sense of eukaryotic DNA replication origins', *Science*, **294**, 5 October 2001, American Association for the Advancement of Science; *Figure 9.7* Reprinted from *Cell*, **54**, McCarroll, R. M. and Fangman, W. L., p. 505, copyright © 1988, with permission of Elsevier; *Figure 9.8* Raghuraman, M. K. *et al.*, 'Replication dynamics of the yeast genome', Science, **294**, 5 October 2001, American Association for the Advancement of Science; *Figure 9.9* Schubeler, D. *et al.*, 'Genome-wide DNA replication profile for *Drosophilia melanogaster* ...', *Nature Genetics*, **32**, November 2002, copyright © Nature Publishing Group; *Figure 9.10b* Hansen, R. *et al.*, 'Role of late replication timing in the silencing of X-linked genes', *Human Molecular Genetics*, **5**, p. 1348, copyright © 1996 Oxford University Press; *Figure 9.10c* Scott Hansen, R. (1997) 'A variable domain of delayed replication in FRAXA fragile X chromosomes: X inactivation-like spread of late replication', *Proceedings of the National Academy of Sciences, USA*, **94**,

Chapter 10

Chapter 11

INDEX

Note: Entries in **bold** are key terms. Page numbers referring to information that is given only in a figure or caption or a table are printed in *italics*.

cyclin D *37*
>role in restriction point 40

cyclin-dependent kinases (Cdks) 35, *37*

cyclin kinase inhibitors (CKIs) *37*, **38**

cytokinesis 10
>in animal cells 27–9
>in plant cells 29, *30*

cytosine methylation 80, 137–8

D

dam methylase 69, *70*

deamination of DNA 90

degradation-resistant proteins 207

depurination of DNA 90

Dictyostelium discoideum (a slime mould), telomere sequence *83*

differential splicing 149–52

dimerization 115

diseases *see* human diseases

DNA
>cloning 200–2
>in eukaryotes 123
>radiation damage 94, 95
>recombinant techniques 86, 195
>recombination 98–103
>synthesis of mRNA from 107–10, *125*
>*in vitro* synthesis of RNA from 111–12

DNA bases
>mispaired 92–3
>removal of damaged 90, *91*

DNA binding proteins
>classes of 113–15
>methylation-specific 138
>target site recognition 115–17
>transcriptional regulators 118–21, *128, 129*

DNA damage
>repair 89–98
>response to 41–2

DNA glycolyases 90, *91*

DNA helicase 54, *55, 75, 76*

DNA methylation 69, *70*, 78
>in eukaryotes 80, 137–40

DNA polymerases 71–6
>in coordinated strand synthesis 77–8
>DNA polymerase I *70*, 71, 72, *73*
>DNA polymerase III *70*, 71, 72, *74*
>elongation of DNA chains 70–6
>in eukaryotes 78
>mitochondrial replication 88
>synthesis errors 92

DNA primase 68, *69, 74, 77*
>in eukaryotes 78

DNA replication
>in bacterial chromosomes 48–9
>chromatin structure 80–2
>copy repair 93–4, 95
>in eukaryotes 78–9
>initiation of 42–3, 54–67
>mechanics of 67–80
>mitochondrial 88
>origins 54 5
>in S phase 8–9
>telomeres 82–7

DNA topoisomerase 75 6

dnaA protein 54, *55, 69, 70*

dnaB protein 54, *55, 69*, 75, *76*

dNTP, polymerization 71, 72, *73*

double-strand breaks
>recombination 99–100
>repair of 94–5, *97*

Drosophila melanogaster (fruit-fly)
>cell cycle 8
>chromatin remodelling 140
>cytokinesis 29, 30
>embryonic cell *12,* 14, 21, 155–6
>homologous chromosomes 142
>homologous recombination 85–7
>mRNA *143,* 155–6
>polytene chromosomes 134–5
>replication origins 58, *59*
>sex determination 150–2
>telomeres 87
>temporal replication 64, *65*

Drosophila white gene 136

dyneins 23

microtubules 20

mRNA degradation *157*

nonsense-mediated decay 185

replication origins 56–60

RNA polymerases 124

telomere sequence *83,* 85

temporal replication 61–4

scaffold attachment regions (SARs) 133

scanning of mRNA **177,** *178*

Scc proteins 16, *17*

SCF complex 36, *37,* 38

Schizosaccharomyces pombe (fission yeast)

cell cycle research 13–14

replication origin 58, *59*

telomere sequence *83*

secretory pathway 187

securin 26, *27*

sense strand **123**

separase 25, *27*

activation 45

sequence analysis, in replication origins 58

serine, 166,*167*

sex determination pathway 150–2

shape mimicry by termination factors 180–1

Shine–Dalgarno (SD) sequence 176, *178, 184*

sigma (σ) factor *108,* 109

signal recognition factor (SRF) 191, *192, 194*

silencers 129

'silencer' elements 136–7, 141

single-stranded binding protein (SSBP) 77, 78

sister chromatids 16, *17*

in anaphase 25, *27*

in the mitotic spindle 23, *24*

site-specific recombination 101–2

Ski7 protein *185,* 186

slime mould *see Dictyostelium discoideum*

small nuclear RNAs (snRNAs) 148, *149*

Smc1/Smc3 dimer 16, *17*

somatic pairing 142

SP6 RNA polymerase *112*

spacer regions 161

spindle checkpoint 44–5

spindle pole *see* mitotic spindle

spindle pole body *13,* 20

splice site consensus sequences 148, *149*

spliceosome 147–9

splicing 123

of mRNA 147–52

START 39, 41

starvation, effect on G1 checkpoint 39

stop codon, in mRNA 180–1, 185–6

strands, DNA

antisense 123

cleavage 100

invasion 99–100

recombination 98–103

synthesis 76–8

see also double-strand breaks; lagging strand

Svedberg (S) units 173

SXL protein 150, *151,* 152

synchronization of cells 10, 14

syncytium 14

T

T7 RNA polymerase 109–10, 112

TAP-1/2 transport channel 205

TATA binding protein (TBP) 126–7, 161

TATA box 124, *126*

telomerase 83–7

telomeres 82–7

telophase *9,* **10,** 27–30

template strand 123

termination factors (TFs) 180–1, *182*

Tetrahymena thermophila (a protoctist), telomere sequence *83*

TOM/TIM complex 189

topoisomerases 75–6

TRA protein 150, *151*

transcription *36*

in chromatin 134–44

in DNA damage 41

in eukaryotes 122–34

in prokaryotes 106–13

see also post-transcriptional events

transcription-coupled repair 94, *97*

transcription factors 126–30